exploring

ENVIRONMENTAL SCIENCE

with children and teens

EILEEN G. HARRINGTON

D1211947

ala
editions

An imprint of the American Library Association
Chicago | 2014

EILEEN G. HARRINGTON is the health and life sciences librarian at the Universities at Shady Grove in Rockville, MD. Previously, she oversaw the Naturalist Center at the California Academy of Sciences, a natural history museum, aquarium, and planetarium. She has served as a reviewer for various manuscripts submitted to *Children & Libraries*. Eileen has been a formal and informal educator both in the United States and in Latin America and has developed curriculum materials in both English and Spanish. She has a bachelor of arts in environmental studies and biology from Macalester College, St. Paul, MN, a master's degree in environmental studies from York University, Toronto, and a master's degree in library and information studies from the University of Wisconsin–Madison.

Printed in the United States of America
18 17 16 15 14   5 4 3 2 1

Extensive effort has gone into ensuring the reliability of the information in this book; however, the publisher makes no warranty, express or implied, with respect to the material contained herein.

ISBN: 978–0-8389–1198–3 (paper).

Library of Congress Cataloging-in-Publication Data

Harrington, Eileen G.
    Exploring environmental science with children and teens / Eileen G. Harrington.
pages   cm
Includes bibliographical references and index.
    ISBN 978-0-8389-1198-3 (alk. paper)
    1. Children's libraries—Activity programs—United States. 2. Environmental
  sciences—Study and teaching—Activity programs—United States. 3. Young adults'
  libraries—Activity programs—United States. 4. School libraries—Activity programs—
  United States. I. Title.
  Z718.3.H37 2014
  027.62′5—dc23

                                                                    2013039149

Book design by Kim Thornton. Cover images © Marish/Shutterstock, Inc.

⊗ This paper meets the requirements of ANSI/NISO Z39.48–1992 (Permanence of Paper).

CONTENTS

FIGURES

ACKNOWLEDGMENTS

There are several people I would like to thank who have supported me throughout this project. I am extremely grateful to my editor, Stephanie Zvirin, for her guidance and thoughtful advice to a first-time book author.

Many thanks to my colleagues at the California Academy of Sciences, particularly the staff in the Naturalist Center and the Early Explorer's Cove who helped develop and implement many of the activities found in this book. I also appreciate their support during the process of writing this book and all that I have learned from them to help become a better educator and librarian.

Thanks to Anne Lundin and Madge Klais for fostering my interest in and knowledge of children's literature. The passion both of you have for teaching and children's books is contagious, and I hope I can pass that passion on to others through this book.

Finally, I am forever grateful for the never-ending love and support of my family.

NURTURING FUTURE ENVIRONMENTAL LEADERS IN LIBRARIES AND MUSEUMS

All summer we went on safari to Africa—an imaginary foray into the sights, sounds, and smells of this fascinating continent through books, specimens, and crafts. One week during the Science Story Adventures program I led at the museum where I worked, we learned about elephants. After reading an engaging story about a young elephant growing up in her herd, we donned our own construction-paper elephant ears and placed socks over our arms to represent trunks and began to communicate as elephants would. Just as all mothers like to keep their young safe, we flapped our ears and made soft rumbling noises to call back our young elephants that had wandered away from the herd. When we noticed a lion hiding in the grass, we held our ears straight out to make ourselves look bigger and raised our trunks, giving off a large, trumpeting blast. After reading another story about elephants and their behaviors, we created our own elephant puppets, complete with a movable trunk and ears so we could continue our elephant-communication explorations at home.

Informal environmental education programs such as this one are becoming increasingly important given some of the realities we face today.

Several reports and articles written over the past decade have stressed the shortcomings of science education in US schools.[1] With the implementation of No Child Left Behind, science education in our K–12 schools has often taken a backseat, with greater emphasis placed on math and reading. A large-scale study on third-grade classrooms across the country found that on average 48 percent of instructional time is spent on literacy and language arts activities, 24 percent on math, and 5 percent on science.[2] The lack of science instruction students receive in the formal education system has had effects on student performance on standardized tests measured both nationally and internationally. The 2009 results of the National Assessment of Educational Progress, which measures students' achievement in different subjects in fourth, eighth, and twelfth grades, found that 34 percent of fourth graders, 30 percent of eighth graders, and 21 percent of twelfth graders scored at the "proficient" level or higher, meaning they have "competency over challenging subject matter."[3] Student performance on international assessments, which compare US students with those from other G-8 or Organization for Economic Cooperation and Development member countries, has either remained flat or shown decline in science literacy. The 2006 Program for International Student Assessment results in science ranked US students below fifteen of twenty-four other countries.[4]

Other studies have shown some positive changes in science and math. A report published by the American Association of University Women found that between 1990 and 2005, the number of credits in math and science that high school students were taking increased, along with a steady increase in grade point averages in science and math classes.[5] This same report pointed out, however, that those from traditionally underrepresented groups in the sciences, such as Latinos and African Americans, are less likely to have access to advanced courses in science and math in high school. Libraries and museums can play a role in helping to fill in some of the gaps in science education for all students.

These deficiencies in science education and literacy become even more troubling given the complex and myriad environmental problems we face in the world today. Issues such as climate change, genetically modified foods, dwindling natural resources, habitat loss, and the contamination of our oceans do not have simple solutions or answers and require an understanding of and respect for multiple viewpoints. Science is one of various tools that we will need to help solve the environmental problems we are facing now and will face in the future. Studies have shown that when introduced to science at an early age, children are more likely to go into science as a career.[6] We will need future scientists to help tackle these environmental problems, or even if students do not go into science, a scientifically literate citizenship is imperative to help direct policy decisions. As Ursula Franklin, a renowned physicist, author, and educator, has urged: "The task of the future is to build knowledge and understanding among and between citizens and scientists, so that the distinction between the two groups disappears—so that both become citizen scientists, potentially able to solve our problems together."[7]

Another reason to encourage environmental programming in libraries and museums is that children (and adults) are increasingly facing a disconnection with nature. As science education experts Camino, Dodman, and Benessia point out, "We are witnessing a massive increase in the knowledge of our planet, but this has come with an increasing separation of most of humanity from the natural systems that support us and of which we are a part."[8] As our understanding of the workings of our planet increases, our connection to what is natural decreases. More and more humans live in an urban environment. Many children have never swum in a lake or seen a bald eagle, our national symbol, in the wild. Most don't know what part of the plant many of the vegetables they eat come from. Richard Louv has termed this condition "nature-deficit disorder," which is also linked to many other ills, from childhood obesity to social isolation and depression.[9] It can also lead to a lack of empathy for wildlife, and some might argue that you cannot protect what you do not know or care about, thus making environmental education all the more important.

Given this landscape, libraries and museums can play an important role in increasing young people's exposure to environmental issues and in developing science literacy. In many ways, both of these types of institutions possess characteristics that make them ideally situated to engage young people in science and the natural world. The audience that comes to museums or libraries come there of their own free will. They visit because they want to be there, so in some ways, they are more invested in their learning than those in a traditional classroom. Programs can build on and nurture environmental interests that children already possess, possibly leading them to a desire to go into this field as a career in the future. Also, informal educational programs do not have as many restrictions as the formal school system, such as curriculum guidelines, so they can respond more quickly and innovatively to the changing needs and interests of the communities they serve. Finally, libraries and museums provide learning opportunities that children might not experience in their schools, such as intergenerational learning and increased opportunities for underrepresented groups in the sciences. A study that looked at the impact of a science center on its community found that "adults strongly agreed that the Science Center created opportunities for them to talk with their children about science and technology, and that it gave their child opportunities in life not supported by other organizations or institutions in the community."[10] Museums and libraries create spaces for the sharing of knowledge among family members and increase exposure to science for groups of people from a variety of backgrounds.

Often libraries do not jump to mind when people think about environmental programming, and many librarians do not come from a science background. Literature on environmental or science programming is largely absent from the library field, and most curriculum or activity books on the subject are geared toward classroom teachers or informal environmental educators. This book will help give confidence to librarians that environmental programming is something they can and should do in their libraries.

At the same time, many programs that are second nature to librarians are not those that one immediately associates with a science center or natural history museum. Museum educators might not have a background in literacy development or children's literature, both of which can be utilized to foster scientific literacy. These things are also the purview of children's librarians and the library literature. In this way, this book will help introduce museum educators to some of these types of programs and resources that they can incorporate into their programs. Although library-museum partnerships do exist, in many ways they are not as common as one would think. Another goal of this book is to foster these partnerships by highlighting ways to create linkages and to draw on each other's strengths.

The overall approach to the programs and activities outlined in this book follows a desire to engage the whole child. Programs that foster a sense of wonder for the natural world and help children to see the connections between them and their environment call upon the use of their heart. These types of programs are connected to the emotional or empathetic aspects of their personality and can help children see the intrinsic value of the natural world. Other activities may focus more on intellectual pursuits in which children can develop their critical-thinking skills rather than just partaking in the accumulation of facts or new knowledge of certain issues. Programs that engage the physical aspects of learning allow children to do real science and/or environmental projects. Children need to be able to apply what they are learning in real-life situations in order to truly develop their skills and values. Often these types of programs also draw on children's own personal experiences, which can make them more meaningful to them and lead to lasting change. The different programs in the book emphasize some or all of these different aspects of learning. They also are meant to be guidelines, but they are by no means a one-size-fits-all solution. You can and should adapt and alter them to meet the needs and desires of your own communities.

The following is an overview of the various chapters in this book. Chapters 2–4 focus on what many will recognize as more traditional library programs. Chapter 2 outlines recommendations for creating environmental-themed family storytimes and includes ten ready-made programs. Chapter 3 provides the ins and outs of developing environmental book clubs for tweens and teens, as well as sample discussion guides for ten books. Chapter 4 explores preschool programming, specifically a simple lab-based program that allows preschoolers to begin to think and act like scientists.

Self-directed programs abound in chapter 5. These include kits that visitors can borrow to undertake their own nature explorations after visiting a museum or participating in a library program. The chapter also includes an overview on creating discovery centers in libraries and museums, along with some sample themes.

Chapter 6 focuses on citizen science, an area of science education that is gaining popularity in museums and schools. It examines the various approaches to citizen science; possible partnerships between libraries, schools, and museums for implementing citizen science projects; and ways that libraries and museums can act as hubs for disseminating citizen science information.

It's all in the family in chapter 7 with family science workshops. Recommendations for developing and delivering this type of program are included, along with sample workshops.

For those young people that want to get out and make a difference, chapter 8 focuses on environmental action clubs. Tips and tricks on how to organize a club at your museum or library are included, as well as ways that librarians can help with the background research that might be necessary to implement a project.

It is my hope that by providing concrete ways to implement environmental programming in libraries and museums, as well as a variety of options, will inspire educators and librarians to do just that. Given the many challenges we face, it is imperative that we support one another in working for a sustainable future. We can also encourage the young people with whom we work to do the same.

NOTES

1. Philip Bell, Bruce Lewenstein, Andrew W. Shouse, and Michael A. Feder, eds., *Learning Science in Informal Environments: People, Places, and Pursuits* (Washington, DC: National Academies Press, 2009); Richard A. Duschl, Heidi A. Shweingruber, and Andrew W. Shouse, eds., *Taking Science to School: Learning and Teaching Science in Grades K–8* (Washington, DC: National Academies Press, 2007); George Griffith and Lawrence Scharmann, "Initial Impacts of No Child Left Behind on Elementary Science Education," *Journal of Elementary Science Education* 20 (2008): 35–48; National Center for Education Statistics, *The Nation's Report Card: Science* (Washington, DC: US Department of Education, 2011); National Science Board, *Science and Engineering Indicators 2010* (Arlington, VA: National Science Foundation, 2010); Ronald W. Marx and Christopher J. Harris, "No Child Left Behind and Science Education: Opportunities, Challenges, and Risks," *Elementary School Journal* 106, no. 5 (2006): 467–447.

2. National Institute of Child Health and Human Development Early Child Care Research Network, "A Day in Third Grade: A Large-Scale Study of Classroom Quality and Teacher and Student Behavior," *Elementary School Journal* 105, no. 3 (January 2005): 305–323.

3. National Center for Education Statistics, *The Nation's Report Card: Science* (Washington, DC: US Department of Education, 2011).

4. National Science Board, *Science and Engineering Indicators 2010* (Arlington, VA: National Science Foundation, 2010).

5. Catherine Hill, Christianne Corbett, and Andresse St. Rose, *Why So Few? Women in Science, Technology, Engineering and Mathematics* (Washington, DC: American Association of University Women, 2010).

6. Robert H. Tai, Christine Qi Liu, Adam V. Maltese, and Xitao Fan, "Planning Early for Careers in Science," *Science* 312 (2006): 1143–1144.

7. Ursula M. Franklin, *The Ursula Franklin Reader: Pacifism as a Map* (Toronto: Between the Lines, 2006), 317.

8. Elena Camino, Martin Dodman, and Alice Benessia, "Language and Science," in *Science Society and Sustainability: Education and Empowerment for an Uncertain World*, ed. Donald Gray, Laura Colucci-Gray, and Elena Camino (New York: Routledge, 2009), 71.

9. Richard Louv, *Last Child in the Woods: Saving Our Children from Nature-Deficit Disorder* (Chapel Hill, NC: Algonquin Books of Chapel Hill, 2005).

10. John H. Falk and Mark D. Needham, "Measuring the Impact of a Science Center on Its Community," *Journal of Research in Science Teaching* 48, no. 1 (2011): 1–12

READING ROOTS: SCIENCE STORYTIME

Kindergarten through Third Grade

S torytimes have long been a staple of library programming for children. One of the main reasons they remain a core focus of libraries is the many benefits they provide. Storytimes help encourage a love of reading and regular library use by children. With the current trend of actively including parents or caregivers in the programs, they provide a space for children and their accompanying adults to spend quality time together. They also foster early literacy skills, and librarians can model many techniques that caregivers can employ at home to assist in their children's development.

The use of science-related books in storytimes can tap into and expand these benefits. Regularly reading to children helps them develop new vocabulary. Science has a vocabulary of its own, and the use of informational books in storytimes can help children become familiar with and feel more comfortable using this type of language. Studies have shown that using picture books to teach about science can help children build background knowledge about scientific concepts, and picture books can help make complex or abstract concepts easier to understand.[1] Also, picture books often will have better graphics or photos than science textbooks to help explain scientific concepts. Picture books can make science more human and easier to relate to for children, particularly fiction books that depict children like them exploring nature and/or making discoveries. The stories found in trade books tend to be more relevant to children's everyday lives, as well.

In addition to the various benefits already outlined, using informational books on science in storytimes can help increase the circulation of these types of books. In many libraries, children and their caregivers often overlook or bypass informational books in favor of fiction books. They are seen as something to go to only for reports or other schoolwork, not for recreational reading. At the same time, children are innately curious and want to make sense of the world around them. Informational texts can help answer questions they have about the natural world. Using nonfiction books in storytimes opens children's eyes to the wonders and wealth of information found between books' covers. An experiment by a third-grade teacher in a school in the Los Angeles area to bolster her classroom library with more science books clearly demonstrates this.[2] At the beginning of the year, her students almost never looked at the science-related books, particularly the nonfiction ones. The teacher began reading informational books about science, and she immediately observed them visiting the science section more frequently and choosing books to read during free-choice reading time, particularly ones she had read out loud to them. She also allowed her students to take books home, and one student expressed that he liked to take science informational books home to share with his brother. This exposure to science-related books tapped into the students' interests and spread to their families, as well.

STRUCTURE OF SCIENCE-BASED STORYTIMES AND PROGRAMMING TIPS

Following this section are examples of science-based storytimes that my former staff and I have delivered at the California Academy of Sciences, a natural history museum, aquarium, and planetarium. They are designed for school-age children from kindergarten through third grade, but many of them can be adapted for younger children. They all follow the same basic structure: make an introduction, read a story, do an activity, read another story, and a do a craft. The program generally lasts about thirty to forty-five minutes. All of the programs are based on a theme and relate to exhibits in a museum or museum-wide programmatic themes. In school libraries, these themes could relate to what students are studying in their science classes. In public libraries, the themes might relate to a summer reading program, or they could relate to various holidays or special events such as Earth Day (April 22), Arbor Day (April 29), International Migratory Bird Day (second Saturday in May), or World Oceans Day (June 8).

The introductory activity helps set the stage for the entire program. Some librarians like to have a set welcoming song they use at every storytime, but you could also start with a song that relates to the theme. Introducing the topic and asking questions that derive from what the children already know about it or relating it to their own experiences can be a great way to immediately draw them into the topic. For example, when doing a storytime on birds, you can ask children if they saw any birds on their way to the library or museum today, or when doing one on gardens, you can ask if anyone has a garden at home or at school, and if so, what they grow in it.

Following the introduction, you read the first book. There are various things to keep in mind when selecting books for storytimes. Both fiction and nonfiction books work. Books that tell a good story and have simple texts and graphics that complement the text work well. With some books, however, it might be necessary to abbreviate or edit the text while reading because of length or inaccuracies. Some books might be excellent overall but have one or two slightly scientifically inaccurate or misleading statements. You can either edit these out or use them as a teaching moment. It is also important to make apparent what is real in the story and what is idealized or not quite true, since sometimes children might not realize that certain parts of the story are in fact fiction. One way to do this is to introduce the story by letting the children know that some of it is not quite true and then having them see if they can pick out the fact from the fiction.

The following authors have written several science-related books that work well in storytimes:

Jim Arnosky	Lois Ehlert
Bob Barner	Steve Jenkins
Nic Bishop	Sandra Markle
Jan Brett	Wendy Pfeffer
Jannell Cannon	Robin Page
Eric Carle	April Pulley Sayre
Joy Cowley	

The following are good sources for reviews or recommendations of science-related children's books:

Outstanding Science Trade Books for Students K–12 (www.nsta.org/publications/ostb/)—An annual annotated list of recommended science trade books, which is compiled by a panel of reviewers from the National Science Teachers Association in cooperation with the Children's Book Council

Science Books & Films (www.sbfonline.com/Pages/welcomesplash.aspx)—A review journal of science resources for all ages published by the American Association for the Advancement of Science

Science & Children (http://learningcenter.nsta.org/browse_journals.aspx?journal=sc)—A journal published by the National Science Teachers Association that includes reviews of science books for children

Teachers' Choices Reading List (www.reading.org/Resources/Booklists/TeachersChoices.aspx)—An annual annotated list of books that will "encourage young people to read . . . and that contribute to learning across the curriculum."

Once you have the books selected, make the reading as interactive as possible while also encouraging the children to begin acting like scientists. The following are skills that scientists employ in their work:

- asking questions
- observing
- estimating, predicting, and formulating hypotheses

- measuring
- recording observations
- experimenting
- recognizing patterns
- sorting and classifying
- communicating predictions, results, and conclusions

These skills can be incorporated into the reading of books during storytime. Ask questions that are open-ended while reading, such as, "What if . . . ? What do you see? How many?" Have the children make predictions about what is going to happen next on the basis of the illustrations, what has already happened in the story, or their own personal knowledge. Assign them a task before beginning the story, such as counting how many mammals they see in the story or sharing what they think is real and what is not. In making the reading more interactive, you are also developing the children's communication skills.

The activity portion of the storytime can also foster many of these same skills. The activities can include an exploration of natural history specimens, simple experiments, or a game. A list of resources with simple experiments and environmental games can be found at the end of this chapter. The use of natural history specimens, in particular, provides an opportunity for children to interact with animals up close and in a way that they might not otherwise have an opportunity to do so. People tend to want to protect what they know and care about. Having experiences with natural history specimens from an early age helps foster a respect for and love of the natural world. Many museums have educational collections of natural history specimens that they can use for this type of programming. For school or public libraries, there are online sources for purchasing natural history specimens or teaching resources, including replicas of animal skulls. A list of resources can be found at the end of this chapter.

The crafts should be simple since they are just one part of a larger program. Also, in a museum setting, it is best to avoid crafts that involve painting or that need to sit to dry for a while since they will likely need to be transported throughout the museum for the rest of the visit. As much as possible, the craft should have some scientific accuracy to it or tie into some aspect of what the children learned about the topic that day. Leaving the craft for the end of the activity also allows for those children that do not enjoy doing crafts to leave without disrupting the flow of the program. A list of resources for simple crafts can be found at the end of this section.

Include a display of books and media related to the theme. This can also include curricula or activity books for parents and caregivers. Having the display allows for further exploration and can be a way to keep people who come early to the storytime occupied while they wait for it to start.

Another way to extend the experience is through a related handout. This should include the learning outcomes of the activity, which are tied to state school content standards, the titles of the books read, an overview of the activities, instructions for the craft, and a list of further resources about the topic to explore. To be more ecologically minded, post these handouts on your library's website or a blog rather than printing them out. You could offer to print them out, however, for those who do not have access to a computer or the Internet at home.

For the sample storytimes that follow, I have used the state content standards for California, since that is where the museum I worked at is located.[3] Most state standards are listed online, however, and you could incorporate those standards that align with the activities for your own state. Using the state standards helps guide the choice of books and activities. It also reinforces for parents and caregivers the importance of storytimes in the educational development of their children. In addition, it provides an easy way for school librarians to connect with what the students are doing in their regular classes. For the most part, the storytimes align with science content standards, but sometimes they also cover other standards, such as social studies, since as humans we are a part of our environments. Humans can gain resources from the environment while also having an impact on it. The environment can also influence the culture of people in a certain region or country.

Museums that implement storytimes can also extend the program by connecting it to their exhibits. One way we did this at the California Academy of Sciences was by focusing on Africa for an entire summer in our storytimes and connecting it to our African Hall exhibits. We developed African Safari Cards, which are trading cards that highlight the dioramas and live animals in this exhibit. Each card has a photo of an animal or plant found in the African Hall on one side. The other side includes an interesting fact about the animal or plant; a Fact Quest challenge in which children need to look at the diorama or exhibit and read the labels to find the answer to the question; and an I Spy activity in which the children look in the diorama or exhibit to find something else related to the animal or plant. At the end of each storytime, we gave the children one of the African Safari Cards that related to the theme of the storytime. By the end of the summer, the children could collect all of the cards. The cards can also be found on our blog, the *Naturalist Notebook*, at www.calacademy.org/academy/exhibits/naturalist _center/nnotebook/?p=899. Other museums could develop similar cards for their exhibits.

SAMPLE STORYTIMES

African Primates

Learning Outcomes
- Plants and animals have predictable life cycles. (Grade 2— Life Sciences)
- Adaptations in physical structure or behavior may improve an organism's chance for survival. (Grade 3—Life Sciences)

Read-Aloud Books
- *Gorilla's Story*, by Harriet Blackford and illustrated by Manja Stojic (Boxer Books)
  - Young readers can journey with a gorilla from birth to adult-hood as he learns how to survive in his habitat. This narrative nonfiction book provides a wealth of information about gorillas, accompanied by lush paintings that transport the reader to Africa.

- *Baboon*, by Kate Banks and illustrated by Georg Hallensleben (Farrar, Straus, and Giroux)
  - A young baboon sets out with his mother and encounters a variety of animals, each one expanding his view of the world around him. When they return at the end of the day, he realizes that the world is a large and wondrous place.

Materials
- pictures of primates
- replica of a gorilla skull (see resource list at end of this chapter)
- model or picture of a life-size gorilla hand

PROCEDURE

Introduce that today's theme is African primates. Ask the group if they know what a primate is. If they don't, give them some examples (monkeys, apes, and humans). Then ask them what makes a primate a primate. Go over the four main groups of primates, showing pictures of them as you introduce each group. Ask, "What are some examples of primates from Africa?"

Let the group know that the first story is about the life of a gorilla. Have the children look for ways that gorillas are like us and different from us while listening to the story.

Read *Gorilla's Story*

Ask the group, "How are gorillas like us?" and "How are they different from us?" You can use the facts in the "Science behind the Topic" section to help guide your discussion.

Have the group examine the replica of a gorilla skull. Ask, "By looking at its teeth, what do you think gorillas eat?"

Have the group examine the gorilla hand replica or look at a picture of a life-size gorilla hand. Have them compare it to their own hand. Ask them, "How is it the same? How is it different?" Talk about the different ways a gorilla hand is designed to help it survive.

Introduce the next story by letting the group know that it is about a baby baboon that is discovering things about the world around him.

SCIENCE BEHIND THE TOPIC

Primates are a group of mammals that include monkeys, apes, and us—*Homo sapiens*. There are four main groups of primates: New World monkeys, Old World monkeys, apes (includes humans), and prosimians (includes lorises, tarsiers, bushbabies, and lemurs). One way to distinguish monkeys from apes is that all monkeys have tails, but apes do not have tails. Also, monkeys tend to be smaller than apes.

One of the best-known primates from Africa is the gorilla. Gorillas are the largest apes alive today. Males weigh 300–500 pounds (136–227 kilograms); females weigh 150–200 pounds (68–91 kilograms). Males grow a band of white fur on their back as they grow older, which is why they are called silverbacks. Gorillas live in groups, called troops, led by a silverback, with some females and their young. The silverback protects its troop by standing up on his hind legs, roaring and barking, and beating its chest when danger is near. There are two species of gorillas: western gorilla (*Gorilla gorilla*) and eastern gorilla (*Gorilla berengei*) (both have sub-species). The western gorilla lives in lowland tropical rainforests, and eastern gorillas live in mountain forests, bamboo forests, and higher tropical rainforests. Gorillas have no natural predators but are endangered. This is a result of the loss of their habitat, which is cleared for agriculture, and people hunting them for bush meat.

Gorillas eat mainly plants—fruits, shoots, leaves, and stems. They eat more than one hundred types of plants, including bananas, wild celery, ginger, and cassava. Occasionally, they eat small insects or birds' eggs. Most of the plants they eat are tough, so they need sharp teeth and strong jaws to grind them up.

A gorilla's hand helps it survive in various ways. Since gorillas are mainly herbivores, having large hands helps them to climb trees and wrap their hands around branches to get their food. Like all primates, they have fingers with nails. They also have a thumb, which most primates have. They can use their thumb to grab things. They can also use their fingernails to pick up small objects and remove small plant material and bugs from their fur. They also use their hands to walk. Gorillas are knuckle walkers. They curl their fingers under, which makes their hand like a foot. This puts a lot of pressure on their fingers, so gorillas need to have very large and strong hands to be able to do this. The only primates that knuckle walk are gorillas, chimpanzees, and bonobos.

Read *Baboon*

Ask, "Is a baboon a monkey or an ape? How do you know?" (Baboons are monkeys because they have tails).

Craft: Primate Hands

Craft Materials
- gorilla hand (actual size) sheet (from "Primate Hands" template, at www.calacademy.org/academy/exhibits/naturalist_center/ nnotebook/wp-content/uploads/2010/08/primate_hands _template.pdf)
- pencils
- crayons, colored pencils, or markers

Directions
1. Print the gorilla hand sheet.
2. Trace your hand inside the gorilla hand.
3. On each finger and the thumb of the gorilla hand, write or draw how you and gorillas are alike.
4. Color in the hands or decorate them with pictures of primates or other animals and plants you might find in Africa.

FURTHER READING FOR KIDS

Hadithi, Mweyne. *Baby Baboon*. Boston: Little Brown, 1993.

Hatkoff, Juliana, Isabella Hatkoff, Craig Hatkoff, and Paula Kahumbu. *Looking for Miza: The True Story of the Mountain Gorilla Family Who Rescued One of Their Own*. New York: Scholastic Press, 2008.

Redmond, Ian. *Gorilla, Monkey & Ape*. New York: DK Publishing, 2000.

Turner, Pamela S. *Gorilla Doctors: Saving Endangered Great Apes*. Boston: Houghton Mifflin, 2005.

RESOURCES

San Diego Zoo. "Gorilla." www.sandiegozoo.org/animalbytes/t-gorilla.html.

Sjoner, Rebecca, and Bobbie Kalman. *Monkeys and Other Primates*. New York: Crabtree Publishing, 2006.

Wexo, John Bonnet. *Gorillas*. Mankato, MN: Creative Education, 1991.

Animal Parents

Learning Outcomes
- Plants and animals have predictable life cycles. (Grade 2—Life Sciences)
- Organisms reproduce offspring of their own kind, and the offspring resemble their parents and one another. (Grade 2—Life Sciences)
- Adaptations in physical structure or behavior may improve an organism's chance for survival. (Grade 3—Life Sciences)

Read-Aloud Books
- *Safe, Warm, and Snug,* by Stephen R. Swinburne, and illustrated by Jose Aruego and Ariane Dewey (Harcourt Brace)
    - Rhyming text introduces readers to the many ingenious ways that animal parents, from kangaroos to killdeers, protect their young. More detailed information about each animal is included at the back of the book.

- *Mister Seahorse,* written and illustrated by Eric Carle (Philomel Books)
    - After receiving some eggs from Mrs. Seahorse to keep safe in his pouch, Mr. Seahorse sets out to explore the watery depths and encounters other fishy daddies who care for their young along the way.

SCIENCE BEHIND THE TOPIC

Many animal parents, like human parents, play an important role in the development of their offspring. They provide food, shelter, and protection from predators. They often teach their young the skills they need to survive on their own. In many cases, it is the female animal that cares for her young, but in some species, the male also plays a role. For example, emperor and king penguin fathers spend several months incubating a single egg by holding it on the top of their feet while the mother goes off to the ocean to feed. The male has a loose fold of skin that goes over the egg on top of their feet to help keep it warm. All the male emperor or king penguins huddle close together and shuffle along very slowly to keep themselves and their eggs warm.

Materials
- construction-paper elephant ears
- paper clips
- Hacky Sacks or round beanbags

PROCEDURE

Introduce the storytime by asking, "Why do you think we have families? What does the family do for a baby?"

Introduce the first story and tell the participants that while you are reading it, they should think about the different ways that each mother is looking after her young.

Read *Safe, Warm, and Snug*

Ask the participants in what ways they saw the mothers looking after their young. Let the participants know that one way that animal parents help take care of their young is through different ways of communicating with them. Do the elephant communication activity from *Elephants and Their Young*, by Jean C. Echols, Jaine Kopp, Ellen Blinderman, and Kimi Hosoume.

Talk about how in many cases it is the animal mother that takes care of the young, but that there are also times when the father does. Give the example of male emperor or king penguins, and then have the children pretend they are daddy penguins with eggs by placing a Hacky Sack or a round beanbag on their feet and slowly moving across a designated space.

Introduce the next story, which is about animal fathers that live in the ocean and take care of their young.

Read *Mister Seahorse*

Ask the children, "How did the fish fathers take care of their young?" "Did any of them seem unusual to you?" Let them know that they will have an opportunity to make their own Mr. Seahorse.

Craft: Father Seahorse Puppet

Craft Materials
- Father seahorse and babies template (from "Animal Parents" Science Story Adventures online handout, at www.calacademy .org/academy/exhibits/naturalist_center/nnotebook/wp-content/ uploads/2011/05/animal-parents.pdf)
- crayons or colored pencils
- scissors
- craft sticks
- Scotch tape

Directions
1. Color in the father seahorse, babies, and pouch. Draw eyes on the father and babies.
2. Cut out the father seahorse, pouch, and babies. For the babies, you do not need to be exact when cutting them out since they are so tiny. You can just cut a circle around them.
3. Tape the pouch on the front of the father seahorse and a craft stick to the back of him. Stick the baby seahorses in their father's pouch.

FURTHER READING FOR KIDS

Bauer, Marion Dane. *The Very Best Daddy of All*. New York: Simon and Schuster Books for Young Readers, 2004.

Carle, Eric. *Does a Kangaroo Have a Mother, Too?* New York: HarperCollins, 2000.

Kroll, Virginia. *Motherlove*. Nevada City, CA: Dawn Publications, 1998.

Stein, David Ezra. *Pouch!* New York: G. P. Putnam's Sons, 2009.

RESOURCES

Echols, Jean C., Jaine Kopp, Ellen Blinderman, and Kimi Hosoume. *Elephants and Their Young*. Great Explorations in Math and Science. Berkeley, CA: Lawrence Hall of Science, 2001.

Markle, Sandra. *A Mother's Journey*. Watertown, MA: Charlesbridge, 2005.
PBS. "Animal Super-Dads." www.pbs.org/wgbh/nova/seahorse/superdads
.html.

Coral Reefs

Learning Outcomes

- Students know examples of diverse life forms in different environments, such as oceans, deserts, tundra, forests, grasslands, and wetlands. (Grade 3—Life Sciences)
- Living organisms depend on one another and on their environment for survival. (Grade 4—Life Sciences)

Read-Aloud Books

- *Life in a Coral Reef*, by Wendy Pfeffer and illustrated by Steve Jenkins (HarperCollins)
  - Dive into the wonder and beauty of a coral reef. Narrative text introduces readers to the different types of corals and the many unusual denizens of a coral reef. Brightly colored collage illustrations make it seem like the animals are popping right off the pages.

- *Fish Wish*, written and illustrated by Bob Barner (Holiday House)
  - A young boy imagines what it would be like to be a fish living in a coral reef. Simple yet active text and brilliant illustrations make this an ideal read-aloud.

Materials

- map of coral reefs of the world
- coral specimens or photos
- model or diagram of coral polyp anatomy
- paper plates
- bananas
- toothpicks
- sugar sprinkles
- Twizzlers or candy straws (or pretzel sticks) cut into 1-inch pieces
- jam
- round crackers, such as Ritz crackers
- oyster crackers

SCIENCE BEHIND THE TOPIC

Coral reefs are found along a band of Earth on either side of the equator. This area is known as the tropics. This is the same band where you would find rain forests, and like rain forests, coral reefs exhibit high amounts of biodiversity. Coral reefs cover only 1 percent of Earth's surface, but they provide habitat for 25 percent of the world's marine fish species.

People often wonder whether coral is an animal or a plant. Even though its structures can sometimes look plantlike, coral is an animal. It doesn't have leaves or a stem. It doesn't make its own food, like a plant; rather, it eats other organisms to gain energy. Coral does, however, have a mutually symbiotic relationship with a single-celled alga called zooxanthella, which lives inside the tissues of coral. These algae photosynthesize and produce sugars essential for coral's growth and provide nutrition to the host organism. In return, the host coral assists the zooxanthellae by passing on nutrients from its dissolved organic waste. An individual coral animal is called a polyp, but most polyps do not live on their own. Often, many polyps live together in what are known as colonies. These colonies are what people often think are plants.

Coral polyps have a very simple body plan. It is a cylinder with a single opening at one end. This opening is used to take in food and expel waste. The opening is surrounded by tentacles that are used to capture food and to protect against predators. The tentacles have nematocysts, which fire to catch drifting plankton and scare away unwanted visitors.

There are two types of corals: hard and soft. With hard corals, each individual polyp sits in a hard cup that it builds out of calcium carbonate. These cups are often joined together in colonies. The polyps of hard corals have six, or multiples of six, tentacles around their "mouth," or the opening where they take in nutrients. Scientists place these types of coral in the subclass Hexacorallia, which is fitting since *hexa-* means "six." When hard coral polyps die, they leave behind the skeleton of their calcium carbonate cups. These are what you often find on the beach.

Soft corals do not build cups to sit in. Instead, they have an internal skeleton that has bits of calcium carbonate embedded in it. These bits of calcium carbonate are called spicules. Soft corals are in the subclass Octocorallia, and they have eight tentacles around their "mouth," which is also fitting, since *octo-* means "eight." The only part that is left of soft corals when they die is their spicules. These spread out on beaches and can help form sand.

PROCEDURE

Introduce that today's theme is coral reefs. Show the map of coral reefs around the world and explain a little about it. Point out the largest coral reef system in the world, the Great Barrier Reef, which is off the coast of Australia. If the storytime is happening at a museum or aquarium that has a coral reef exhibit, you can talk about that exhibit and any research the staff does on coral reefs. You can also ask the children questions about the exhibit, such as, "Have any of you visited our coral reef exhibit?" "What did you see?" "What were the fish like?" and "What was the coral like?" Alternatively, if the activity is happening in a library, you could also ask if any of the children have been to a museum or aquarium with a coral reef exhibit or to an actual coral reef, and if they have, then ask the same previous questions.

Let the participants know that the first book you're going to read talks about life in a coral reef as its name suggests. Again, if doing the storytime at a museum or aquarium with a coral reef exhibit, you can suggest that while you're reading the book, the children see if they recognize any animals that are in your exhibit.

Read *Life in a Coral Reef*

Ask the participants if they recognized any of the animals in the book. Say, "Let's take a closer look at corals." Show the model or picture of an individual coral polyp and talk about the different parts of its very simple body.

Talk about the characteristics of hard and soft corals, and then show the specimens or photos of each kind of coral.

Have the participants make their own edible hard-coral polyp using the "Build a Coral Polyp" lesson plan from the California Academy of Sciences Teachers website, at www.calacademy.org/teachers/resources/lessons/build-a-coral-polyp. This lesson plan also has a diagram of a coral polyp that you can use.

Bring the kids back together to read the next story, which is about a boy who imagines what he would do if he were a fish living in a coral reef.

Read *Fish Wish*

After reading the story, ask the children what they would like to do if they were a fish living in a coral reef.

Craft: Coral Reef Diorama

Craft Materials
- paper plates
- plastic wrap
- craft knife
- construction paper
- photocopies of marine animals to color (optional)
- colored pencils and crayons
- glue
- Scotch tape
- scissors
- thread
- stapler

Directions
1. Prepare the "windows" of the diorama ahead of time for the kids. To do this, cut out a circle from the bottom of a paper plate using a scissor or craft knife. Tape Saran wrap to the edges of the plate with the face upward.
2. Cut out a circle of blue construction paper and glue it to the bottom of a second paper plate. (You can also precut the circles so kids just have to glue them on.)
3. Have the kids color the marine animals and cut them out, or they can make their own marine creatures and plants using construction paper.
4. Have the kids arrange their items how they want them and then glue down those they want on the blue background.
5. They can also tape lengths of the thread to the backs of some of the marine animals. Tape the other end of the thread to the top

edge of the paper plate so that they hang down as if they were swimming in the diorama.

6. Staple the top plate (the viewing hole) to the bottom plate.

FURTHER READING FOR KIDS

Berkes, Marianne Collins. *Over in the Ocean: In a Coral Reef.* Nevada City, CA: Dawn Publications, 2004.

Boyle, Doe. *Coral Reef Hideaway: The Story of a Clown Anemonefish.* Smithsonian Oceanic Collection. Norwalk, CT: Soundprints, 1995.

Bingham, Caroline. *Coral Reef.* DK 24 Hours. New York: DK Publishing, 2005.

MacAulay, Kelley, and Bobbie Kalman. *Coral Reef Food Chains.* New York: Crabtree Publishing, 2005.

RESOURCES

Ocean World. "Coral Reefs." www.oceanworld.tamu.edu/students/coral/index.html.

University of California Museum of Paleontology. "Introduction to the Anthozoa." www.ucmp.berkeley.edu/cnidaria/anthozoa.html.

World Resources Institute. "Online Global Reefs Map." www.wri.org/publication/reefs-at-risk-revisited/global-reefs-map.

Eggs

Learning Outcomes
- Students know that organisms reproduce offspring of their own kind and that the offspring resemble their parents and one another. (Grade 2—Life Sciences)
- Students know the sequential stages of life cycles are different for different animals, such as butterflies, frogs, and mice. (Grade 2—Life Sciences)

SCIENCE BEHIND THE TOPIC

Spring is a time of new life. In many parts of the world, buds appear on the trees as their leaves return. Animals mate and give birth. Most all reptiles, amphibians, birds, fish, and insects lay eggs rather than giving birth to live young. These eggs come in many different shapes and sizes and are a variety of colors. Some, like birds' eggs, have hard shells, while others, like amphibian eggs, have a soft outer covering. All of them provide nutrients and a safe place for the young animal to grow and develop.

Read-Aloud Books

- *An Egg Is Quiet*, by Dianna Aston and illustrated by Sylvia Long (Chronicle Books)
  - An egg can be many different things: colorful or plain, big or small, rough or smooth. A variety of animals, including birds, fish, and insects, lay eggs. This simple yet informative text and realistic illustrations introduce readers to the world of eggs.

- *A Nest Full of Eggs*, by Priscilla Belz Jenkins and illustrated by Lizzy Rockwell (HarperCollins)
  - A young boy and his friend watch a pair of robins as they prepare a nest, care for their eggs, and tend to their fledglings until they are ready to fly off on their own.

Materials

- Replicas of bird eggs (see resource list at end of this chapter)
- Preserved specimens or photos of other animal's eggs, such as lizards, octopus, and shark egg cases
- Bird's nest specimens or photos

PROCEDURE

This is a good storytime to do in the spring. Ask the participants what they think of when they hear the word *spring*. Ask them, "What is springtime like? What do you see? What happens?" Introduce the first book, which talks about all kinds of eggs. Have the kids look for similarities and differences between the eggs as you read.

Read *An Egg Is Quiet*

Show the participants the replicas of egg specimens if you are able to get some. See if they can guess which kinds of birds they are from. Talk a little about each bird, including how many eggs they lay at a time, how long they care for the eggs, and where they lay their eggs. This can segue into looking at the bird's nest specimens and/or photos. See if the participants can figure out what kinds of bird's nests each one might be.

Remind the participants that in the book you just read, it wasn't only birds that lay eggs. Ask them about what other animals lay eggs. If you have specimens of eggs from other animals, share those and talk about them, or share photos of eggs of different animals.

Talk about how many of these other animals also build nests to lay their eggs like birds do. Ask the participants if any of them have seen nests around their neighborhood or school. Introduce the next story, which is about a robin who builds a nest.

Read *A Nest Full of Eggs*

Remind the participants to keep their eyes out for birds' nests in their neighborhoods. Let them know that they will have the opportunity to create their own "nest full of eggs."

Craft: Robins and Their Nest

Craft Materials
- robins and nest template (from "Eggs" Science Story Adventures online handout, at www.calacademy.org/academy/exhibits/naturalist_center/nnotebook/wp-content/uploads/2011/08/eggs.pdf)
- crayons or colored pencils
- small strips cut from paper bags (about ½ inch × 2 inches)
- glue
- scissors
- light-blue construction paper
- pencils

Directions

1. Color the robins, tree, and inside of the nest on the template.
2. Glue the strips of paper bag around the outside of the nest.
3. Draw and cut out robin eggs using the construction paper. Robins usually lay three to five eggs. Glue these inside the nest.

FURTHER READING FOR KIDS

Baines, Rebecca. *What's in That Egg? A Book about Life Cycles*. Washington, DC: National Geographic, 2009.

Heller, Ruth. *Chickens Aren't the Only Ones*. New York: Grosset and Dunlap, 1981.

Posada, Mia. *Adivina qué está creciendo dentro de este huevo*. Minneapolis, MN: Ediciones Lerner, 2009.

Singer, Marilyn. *Eggs*. New York: Holiday House, 2008.

RESOURCES

Cornell Lab of Ornithology. "All About Birds: American Robin." www.allaboutbirds.org/guide/american_robin/lifehistory.

Frogs and Toads

Learning Outcomes

- Students know that the sequential stages of life cycles are different for different animals, such as butterflies, frogs, and mice. (Grade 2—Life Sciences)
- Students know that organisms reproduce offspring of their own kind and that the offspring resemble their parents and one another. (Grade 2—Life Sciences)
- Students know different plants and animals inhabit different kinds of environments and have external features that help them thrive in different kinds of places. (Grade 1—Life Sciences)

Read-Aloud Books
- *Growing Frogs*, by Vivian French and illustrated by Alison Bartlett (Candlewick Press)
  - A young girl and her mother bring some frog eggs home to watch them develop from tadpoles to frogs, which they then release in a pond.
- *Red-Eyed Tree Frog*, by Joy Cowley, with photographs by Nic Bishop (Scholastic Press)
  - A young red-eyed tree frog wakes up hungry, so he goes out in search of food, trying not to become someone else's meal in the process. Bishop's amazing photographs make for a very up-close and personal view of life in the rain forest.

Materials
- frog and toad specimens or photos of frogs and toads
- chart or photo comparing differences between frogs and toads
- computer or iPad

PROCEDURE

Let the group know that you will be exploring frogs and toads that day. Ask, "Have any of you ever seen a frog or toad in the wild?" Let them know that frogs can be found in a variety of places, as long as there is water. They are found on every continent except Antarctica. Tell the group that frogs are amphibians, and ask them if they know what some of the characteristics of amphibians are. Be sure to mention any characteristics the group doesn't come up with, and let them know that other types of amphibians include newts, toads, and caecilians.

Introduce the first story, which talks about the life cycle of frogs and shows how they spend part of their time on land and part of it in the water.

Read *Growing Frogs*

After reading the book, talk about how in the story they take frog eggs from the pond, but that this is just a story. In real life, many frog species are

SCIENCE BEHIND THE TOPIC

Frogs and toads can be found in a variety of places, as long as there is water. They are found on every continent except Antarctica. They are amphibians, which exhibit the following characteristics:

- Most spend part of their life in the water and part of it on land.
- They are ectothermic (cold blooded).
- They have moist, smooth skin.
- They lay shell-less eggs in the water.
- They shed their skin (we often don't see it because they eat it).

Other types of amphibians include newts and caecilians.

Scientifically, there isn't really a difference between frogs and toads. Scientists refer to all toads as frogs. All frogs and toads are in the order Anura. There are some scientists that refer to "true frogs" and "true toads" as those species in the family Ranidae (true frogs) and Bufonidae (true toads). Other differences between frogs and toads include the following: frogs have teeth in their upper jaw, whereas toads do not have teeth; toads are better adapted to drier conditions; and frogs lay their eggs in clusters, whereas toads lay them in long strips.

endangered, so it isn't a good idea to do this. If a school group or librarian wanted to do this, a teacher or the librarian could probably talk with a scientist or wildlife specialist about finding the eggs or getting ones that were raised in captivity.

Talk about how the story mentions that the mom had heard a lot of noise from the frogs the other night. Often male frogs use different calls to find a mate. Play a few calls of different frogs from Animal Diversity Web (http://animaldiversity.ummz.umich.edu/site/topics/frogCalls.html) using an iPad or a computer. Show the picture of the frog from the book *The Calls of Frogs and Toads*, by Lang Elliot, or photos from the Internet or other books before playing the sounds.

Show the frog and toad specimens or photos. Ask the participants, "How would you describe each one?" Explain the similarities and differences between frogs and toads showing a photo or a chart that points out the differences. If the storytime is being held in a museum or an aquarium that has live toads and frogs on display, you can recommend they look for them and observe them. Suggest they look for any similarities and differences between the two.

The next story is about a frog that is found in the rain forest in Central America who is looking for some food.

Read *Red-Eyed Tree Frog*

Ask the participants, "What other animals did the frog meet when it was looking for food?" "Did it finally find something to eat?"

Craft: Frog Finger Puppet

Craft Materials
- green, yellow, orange, or tan felt
- frog puppet template (from "Frogs & Toads" Science Story Adventures online handout, at www.calacademy.org/academy/exhibits/naturalist_center/nnotebook/wp-content/uploads/2011/08/frogs.pdf)
- scissors
- craft glue
- googly eyes
- black marker

Directions
1. Print out the frog puppet template and cut out the pieces. Use them to trace the parts on the felt and cut them out.
2. Glue the two frog body pieces together along three sides, leaving an opening on one of the shorter ends for your finger.
3. Glue the frog feet to the bottom of the body on the front.
4. Glue the googly eyes to the body toward the top. You can cut a small divot in between the eyes if you want.
5. Draw a mouth and nostrils on the frog using the black marker.

FURTHER READING FOR KIDS

Kalan, Robert. *Jump, Frog, Jump!* New York: Greenwillow Books, 1981.

Lewis, Paul Owen. *Frog Girl*. Hillsboro, OR: Beyond Words Publishing, 1997.

Sayre, April Pulley. *Dig, Wait, Listen: A Desert Toad's Tale*. New York: Greenwillow Books, 2001.

Zollman, Pam. *Cómo crece un renacuajo*. New York: Children's Press, 2008.

RESOURCES

Bishop, Nic. *Frogs*. New York: Scholastic Nonfiction, 2008.

Elliot, Lang. *The Calls of Frogs and Toads*. Mechanicsburg, PA: Stackpole Books, 2004.

Jones, Patricia. "Frog Calls." http://animaldiversity.ummz.umich.edu/collections/frog-calls.

Tesler, Pearl. "The Amazing Adaptable Frog." 1999. www.exploratorium .edu/frogs/mainstory/index.html.

Gardens

Learning Outcomes
- Students know how to identify major structures of common plants. (Kindergarten—Life Sciences)
- Students know that roots are associated with the intake of water and nutrients, and that green leaves are associated with making food from sunlight. (Grade 1—Life Sciences)
- Students know that both plants and animals need water, that animals need food, and that plants need light. (Grade 1—Life Sciences)

Read-Aloud Books
- *The Ugly Vegetables*, written and illustrated by Grace Lin (Charlesbridge)
  - A young girl helps her mother plant their garden, but she wonders why their garden is different from their neighbors'. Instead of lovely flowers, they plant unusual vegetables. The girl soon realizes, though, that the vegetables may look funny, but they sure taste delicious.

- *Whose Garden Is It?* by Mary Ann Hoberman and illustrated by Jane Dyer (Harcourt)
  - Mrs. McGee goes out walking one day and finds a garden. She wonders whom it belongs to and soon finds out that a garden grows and thrives because of many different factors working together.

Materials

- vegetables, fruits, nuts, and herbs that represent the different parts of plants
- Chinese vegetables, such as bitter melon, bok choy, mung beans, or others described in the book *The Ugly Vegetables*
- diagram of the parts of a plant

PROCEDURE

Start out by telling the participants that today you are going to talk about gardens. Ask, "Do any of you have a garden at your house or at your school?" "What do you have in your garden?" "How do you take care of your garden?" "What do plants need to grow?" Introduce the first story by telling the group that it is about a young girl who helps her mother plant a garden, but she isn't too sure about the whole thing.

Read *The Ugly Vegetables*

If you are able to get some Chinese vegetables, you can show those. Then you can show the other vegetables you have brought in. Let the group know that each of these vegetables comes from a certain part of the plant. Ask, "What are some of the different parts of plants?" (Answers are roots, stems, leaves, flowers, fruits, and seeds). If you have a whiteboard or chalkboard in the area, you can draw a diagram of the plant as they tell you the different parts. Alternatively, you could also bring a diagram of the parts of the plant, without the parts identified, and then identify them together. Let the group know that we eat different foods that come from the different parts. Show the kids the different foods and ask them which part of the plant they came from. You can also talk about the function of each part of the plant. For each

SCIENCE BEHIND THE TOPIC

The main parts of a flowering plant include the roots, stem, leaves, flowers, fruit, and seeds. Each of these parts works with the others to help the plant grow, develop, and reproduce. We eat different foods that come from these different parts. The following lists the main functions of these different parts of a plant, as well as examples of foods we eat that come from these parts.

ROOTS

Function: Gather nutrients and water from the soil, and anchor the plant.
Examples: carrot, beet, parsnip

STEM

Function: Contains xylem and phloem. Xylem carries nutrients and water from the roots to the leaves, and the phloem transports food from the leaves to other parts of the plant. The stem also supports the plants' leaves. Some stems are actually underground, like potatoes.
Examples: asparagus, ginger

LEAVES

Function: Absorb sunlight to make food for the plant.
Examples: lettuce, spinach, cabbage

FLOWERS

Function: Help make seeds for new plants. Their colors and pleasant aromas attract pollinators, which help transfer pollen, which helps make new seeds.
Examples: broccoli, nasturtiums, squash blossoms

FRUIT

Function: Helps to spread seeds. Animals eat the fruit and then spread the seeds in their droppings.
Examples: tomatoes, beans, cucumbers, apples

SEEDS

Function: Create new plants.
Examples: sunflower seeds, almonds, peas, corn

Planting a garden can be a great way for children to learn more about the different parts of a plant and their various functions. It can also provide habitat for a variety of animals and be a source of nutritious and delicious food for your family.

type, you can also ask them if they can think of other foods that are also from the same part of the plant.

Talk to the participants about how, as we saw in the first story, not all gardens are vegetable gardens. Some people also plant flower gardens, which can attract pollinators and provide habitat for insects and birds. Let the group know that the next story will look at the many things you might find in a garden while trying to answer the question, whose garden is it?

Read *Whose Garden Is It?*

After reading the story, ask the participants about whose garden they think it is. Talk about the many interconnections in a garden and the benefits of a garden, not just to us but to many other animals, as well.

Introduce the craft by talking about how often gardeners sketch out what their garden will look like before they actually plant it. Using a variety of materials, participants can create their own dream garden that maybe one day they can plant.

Craft: Create Your Own Garden

Craft Materials

- cardstock
- construction paper
- tissue paper
- chenille sticks
- dried beans
- colored pencils
- crayons
- scissors
- glue
- pencils

Directions

On a piece of cardstock, and using the materials provided, create your own garden.

FURTHER READING FOR KIDS

Cole, Henry. *On Meadowview Street*. New York: Greenwillow Books, 2007.

Henkes, Kevin. *My Garden*. New York: Greenwillow Books, 2010.

Pollak, Barbara. *Our Community Garden*. Hillsboro, OR: Beyond Words Publishing, 2004.

Zoehfeld, Kathleen Weidner. *Secrets of the Garden: Food Chains and the Food Web in Our Backyard*. New York: Alfred A. Knopf, 2012.

RESOURCES

Barrett, Katharine D. *Botany on Your Plate: Investigating the Plants We Eat*. Burlington, VT: National Gardening Association, 2008.

Jaffe, Roberta. *The Growing Classroom: Garden-Based Science.* Burlington, VT: National Gardening Association, 2007.

Owls

Learning Outcomes
- Adaptations in physical structure or behavior may improve an organism's chance for survival. (Grade 3—Life Sciences)
- Students know that animals eat plants or other animals for food and may also use plants or even other animals for shelter and nesting. (Grade 1—Life Sciences)
- Students know that organisms reproduce offspring of their own kind and that the offspring resemble their parents and one another. (Grade 2—Life Sciences)

Read-Aloud Books
- *White Owl, Barn Owl*, by Nicola Davies and illustrated by Michael Foreman (Candlewick Press)
  - A young girl and her grandfather put out an owl box hoping to spot the graceful, nocturnal hunter. Their quiet patience pays off, and they, along with the reader, get to observe the many habits of the barn owl. Soft watercolor and pastel illustrations help set the tone of this story of nighttime explorations.

- *Owl Babies*, by Martin Waddell and illustrated by Patrick Benson (Candlewick Press)
  - A trio of owl babies wakes up to find that their mother has gone. They try to reassure one another, hoping that she will come back soon, a situation with which many young children can relate.

Materials
- taxidermy barn owl or barn owl photos
- owl pellets (available for order online from Carolina Biological

Supply Company at www.carolina.com, or Acorn Naturalists, at www.acornnaturalists.com)
- crumpled-up pieces of paper
- iPad or computer

PROCEDURE

Let the participants know that today you are going to talk about owls. Ask, "Have any of you seen or maybe heard an owl?" "If you haven't seen one in the wild, it might be because they are nocturnal. What does nocturnal mean?" "What are owls like?" "What do you know about owls?"

SCIENCE BEHIND THE TOPIC

Owls can be hard to spot in the wild since they are nocturnal. It is more likely that you hear an owl rather than see it while on a nighttime exploration. One of the most widespread species of owl is the barn owl, which is found on every continent except Antarctica. Like other owls, barn owls exhibit many characteristics that help make them excellent hunters. These characteristics include the following:

- **Eyes:** Owls have very large eyes in comparison to other birds, which allow them to let in as much light as possible for night hunting. However, barn owls in particular have smaller eyes as far as owls go. Like humans, they have binocular vision, which means that they use both eyes at the same time to focus on an object. Each eye, however, sees the object at slightly different angles, and the blending of these two allows them to be able to judge how far away an object is or distances between objects, which is known as depth perception. Their eyes are so big, however, that they cannot move them up and down or side to side like we can. This means they have to constantly move their head to follow an animal.

- **Head and ears:** Owls have very large heads—larger in proportion to their body than other types of birds, which allows them to have larger eyes and larger ear openings. The feathers on their face around their eyes form "facial discs," which act like a parabolic dish that draws the sound in and funnels it to their ear openings (they do not have outer ears like we do). Owls have very acute hearing. They can hear a mouse stepping on a twig from seventy-five feet away. Muscles behind the ears also move the facial ruff to aid in hearing, as if the owl were cupping its ears. They have the most accurate ability of any animal tested to locate prey by sound.

Introduce the first story by letting the group know that it is about barn owls, one of the most common owls in the world. Have the participants see if there is one new or interesting thing they notice about barn owls while you read the story with them that they can share with the group when you are done.

Read White Owl, Barn Owl

Ask the kids, "What was something interesting you learned or noticed about barn owls?" Show the taxidermy barn owl or photos of barn owls. Let them know that owls are good predators. Ask, "What is a predator? Looking at this owl specimen and from what we just heard in the story, what about an

- **Feathers:** An owl's flight feathers have soft, fringed edges, unlike the flight feathers of other birds, which are more rigid. This allows them to fly silently. They can better hear prey while they are flying and get closer to the prey without it hearing them.

- **Beak:** Barn owls have a sharp point at the end of their beak to tear flesh, but they never use it as a weapon.

- **Talons:** Barn owls have very strong talons. When an owl is going to capture a mouse or other prey animal, it spreads its talons as far as it can, which gives it a better chance of catching the prey in the dark. Do a demo with a crumpled piece of paper: have kids close their eyes and try to touch a crumpled piece of paper with one finger. Now do the same thing spreading all their fingers as wide as they can. Which was easier?

- **Wings:** Barn owls have longer wings than most owls, which allows them to soar through open fields, where they often hunt. Having larger and longer wings also allows them to fly using a slow wing beat, which is quieter.

Barn owls mainly eat voles, but they also eat other small rodents and bats, as well. When capturing their prey, they tend to swallow it whole. Like all owl species, a barn owl cannot digest everything it swallows, so things such as bones, teeth, and fur are packed into owl pellets, which the owls regurgitate. If you go hiking in a wooded area or grassland near trees, you might find some owl pellets that were left behind. Barn owls average about two pellets per day, and they play an important role in controlling rodent populations, particularly in agricultural areas.

owl makes it a good predator? What characteristics does it have that help it when hunting?" Go over the different characteristics either after one of the participants brings one up or introduce them yourself if no one mentions them.

Ask the participants what they think barn owls like to eat (mainly voles, but they will also eat other small rodents and bats). Talk about how when capturing their prey, barn owls tend to swallow it whole, but like all owl species, a barn owl cannot digest everything it swallows, so things such as bones, teeth and fur are packed into owl pellets, which are regurgitated. Show the owl pellet and explain that it is like what they saw in the book. You can also dissect a pellet before the beginning of storytime to show some of the contents of what's inside. Another option is to have the participants dissect some with you.

Introduce the next book, which is about some baby owls that wake up one night and find that their mother has gone.

Read *Owl Babies*

Ask, "Did their mom come back? Were there times when you were little and your mom or dad went away and you wondered if they would come back? How did you feel?"

Craft: Barn Owl Mask

Craft Materials

- barn owl mask template (from the "Owls" Science Story Adventures online handout, www.calacademy.org/academy/exhibits/naturalist_center/nnotebook/wp-content/uploads/2011/08/owls.pdf)
- card stock
- scissors
- crayons or colored pencils
- crepe-paper streamers
- glue sticks
- craft sticks
- Scotch tape

Directions

1. Print out the owl mask template on card stock.
2. Cut out the mask, including the eye holes.
3. Color the beak and around the eyes.
4. Cut two pieces of crepe-paper streamers that are each about 22 inches long. Scallop the edges of the crepe paper.
5. Glue one of the pieces of crepe paper around the sides and top of the owl head, gluing it on the back of the head and folding it over in places so that it lays on the curves. Trim any excess if necessary.
6. Glue the second piece of the crepe paper in the same way, but off-set it slightly from the first one so that you see the scallops of both pieces.
7. Tape the craft stick on the back of the mask.

FURTHER READING FOR KIDS

Gibbons, Gail. *Owls*. New York: Holiday House, 2005.

Houghton, Gillian. *Búhos, por dentro y por fuera*. Translated by Tomás González. New York: Rosen Publishing, 2004.

Johnston, Tony. *The Barn Owls*. Watertown, MA: Charlesbridge, 2000.

Yolen, Jane. *Owl Moon*. New York: Philomel Books, 1987.

RESOURCES

Biel, Timothy L. *Owls*. Mankato, MN: Creative Education, 1990.

Peeters, Hans J. *Field Guide to Owls of California and the West*. Berkeley: University of California Press, 2007.

Rain Forests

Learning Outcomes

- Students know that different plants and animals inhabit different kinds of environments and have external features that help them thrive in different kinds of places. (Grade 1—Life Sciences)

- Students know examples of diverse life forms in different environments, such as oceans, deserts, tundra, forests, grasslands, and wetlands. (Grade 3–Life Sciences)
- Students know how to identify resources from Earth that are used in everyday life and understand that many resources can be conserved. (Kindergarten—Life Sciences)

Read-Aloud Books
- *The Umbrella,* written and illustrated by Jan Brett (G. P. Putnam's Sons)
  - A young boy goes out for a walk in the cloud forest hoping to see some animals. He leaves his umbrella on the ground while he climbs a tree to get a better view. The young boy can't seem to find any animals, though, since they are more interested in exploring his umbrella.

- *Over in the Jungle: A Rainforest Rhyme,* by Marianne Collins Berkes and illustrated by Jeanette Canyon (Dawn Publications)
  - This playful book can be read or sung, since the melodic text is a variation of the song "Over in the Meadow." Readers travel through the rain forest learning about different rain-forest animals, from boas to parrots. The back of the book includes general information about rain forests and more detailed information about each of the animals.

Materials
- globe or map
- plastic ketchup or mustard bottles (at least 5)
- vanilla extract or vanilla bean
- chocolate bar
- coffee beans
- ginger
- cinnamon sticks
- photos or pictures of a vanilla orchid, cacao tree, coffee plant, ginger plant, and cinnamon tree
- photo of a pygmy marmoset

SCIENCE BEHIND THE TOPIC

Most people think of the Amazon rain forest when they think of rain forests, but rain forests are found throughout the world in a band between the Tropic of Cancer and the Tropic of Capricorn that circles the world. They cover only about 6 percent of Earth's surface, but they are home to more than half of the different types of plants and animals found in the world. Typically, a rain forest is hot and very humid—it rains heavily and frequently. They have very dense foliage and have many unique and often endangered animals and insects.

If you search around your house, you just might be surprised at how many things found there come from the rain forest. For example, rubber bands and other things made out of rubber come from rubber trees that grow in the rain forest. Many medicines we have come from plants found in the rain forest. There are also many foods we eat and drink that come from the rain forest, such as bananas, coffee, chocolate, and coconuts.

PROCEDURE

Before the start of storytime, place each of the products listed above in a ketchup or mustard bottle. For the vanilla, if you are using extract, you might want to pour a little on a cotton ball and place that in the bottle. For the ginger, it works best if you cut it up first. These will be used in an activity after the first story. If you have a larger group (more than ten kids), you might want to make various sets of the bottles and pictures of the plants.

Tell the participants that today you're going to talk about rain-forest habitats. Ask them what comes to mind when they think of a rain forest. Show on the map or globe the band or region where rain forests are found throughout the world, which is in the area between the Tropic of Cancer and the Tropic of Capricorn. Talk about how most people think of the Amazon when they think about rain forests, but that rain forests actually are found in other places in the world, as well. Also mention their high biodiversity.

Introduce the first story, which is about a boy who goes into the rain forest to see some animals. As the participants are listening, ask them to watch out for which animals he sees.

Read *The Umbrella*

After reading the story, ask the kids, "How many animals did the boy see? Were there animals in the rain forest?" Let them know, that just like the boy, they're going to go on a walk through a rain forest. Do the Walk through a Rainforest activity, which is adapted from the traditional call-and-response activity Going on a Bear Hunt. Have the participants repeat each line and do the same actions as you do throughout the activity. To start out, the participants should slap their thighs to symbolize walking.

A Walk through a Rainforest

Look! (*Point*)

Over there! (*Point*)

There are some bushes.

There are some thick bushes.

We can't go this way. (*Lean to one side*)

We can't go that way. (*Lean to the other side*)

We'll have to go through it. (*Make motion with your hands like you are brushing aside branches*).

Look! (*Point*)

Over there! (*Point*)

There's a tree.

There's a tall tree. (*Look up*)

We can't go this way. (*Lean to one side*)

We can't go that way. (*Lean to the other side*)

We'll have to climb it. (*Make a climbing motion, and stand up; stop for a moment to look out when you get to the top, then climb back down and sit down*)

Look! (*Point*)

Over there! (*Point*)

There's a river.

There's a wide river. (*Spread arms out*)

We can't go this way. (*Lean to one side*)

We can't go that way. (*Lean to the other side*)

We'll have to swim across it. (*Make swimming motions*)

Look! (*Point*)

Over there! (*Point*)

There's some mud.

There's some dirty, sticky mud.

We can't go this way. (*Lean to one side*)

We can't go that way. (*Lean to the other side*)

We'll have to go through it. (*Make a sucking sound and hand motions*)

Look! (*Point*)

Over there! (*Point*)

There's a cave.

There's a dark cave.

We can't go this way. (*Lean to one side*)

We can't go that way. (*Lean to the other side*)

We'll have to go in it. (*Look a little scared and nervous*)

Look! (*Point and whisper*)

Over there! (*Point and whisper*)

There are some eyes.

There are some green eyes.

There are some green, mean eyes.

The eyes of . . . the eyes of . . . A JAGUAR!

Do all of the motions in reverse, this time slapping your thighs hard and fast as if you were running until you arrive safely back to storytime.

Now that the participants are back at storytime, you can do a rain-forest products activity. Let them know that there are many things that they might have in their homes that actually come from the rain forest. Show the pictures of the different rain-forest plants that provide products for us (such as vanilla, chocolate, coffee, cinnamon, and ginger). Pass around the bottles with the products in them and have the kids give them a gentle squeeze to smell what is inside. See if they can match the bottles with the picture of the rain-forest plant. If you have a larger group, you might want to make various sets of the bottles and pictures and then divide them into smaller groups to work on matching the products with the pictures.

Introduce the next story, which includes a variety of different animals that live in the rain forest.

Read *Over in the Jungle: A Rainforest Rhyme*

In the book, there are some marmosets. Show the photo of what a marmoset looks like in real life. Let the participants know that a marmoset is a type of monkey, and that there are many different kinds of marmosets. The pygmy marmoset is the smallest monkey in the world, usually only weighing about 119 grams (4.2 ounces). Let the participants know that they will have a chance to make their own pygmy marmoset puppet.

Craft: Pygmy Marmoset Puppet

Craft Materials

- pygmy marmoset puppet template (from the "Rainforests" Science Story Adventures online handout, www.calacademy.org/academy/exhibits/naturalist_center/nnotebook/wp-content/uploads/2011/08/rainforests1.pdf)

- card stock
- crayons or colored pencils
- scissors
- hole punch or push pin
- 5 brass fasteners
- craft stick
- Scotch tape

Directions

1. Print out the pygmy marmoset puppet template on card stock.
2. Color the different parts of the puppet and then cut them out.
3. Make holes with the hole punch or a pin in the places marked on the template with black dots to be able to stick the brass fastener through it. Attach the arms, legs, and tail to the body using the brass fasteners.
4. Tape the craft stick to the back of the puppet.

FURTHER READING FOR KIDS

Carle, Eric. *"Slowly, Slowly, Slowly," Said the Sloth*. New York: Philomel Books, 2002

Cherry, Lynne. *The Great Kapok Tree*. San Diego: Harcourt Brace Jovanovich, 1990.

Forsyth, Adrian. *How Monkeys Make Chocolate: Unlocking the Mysteries of the Rainforest*. Toronto: Maple Tree Press, 2006.

Olaleye, Isaac. *Bitter Bananas*. Honesdale, PA: Caroline House, 1994.

Pratt-Serafini, Kristin Joy, and Rachel Crandell. *The Forever Forest: Kids Save a Tropical Treasure*. Nevada City, CA: Dawn Publications, 2008.

RESOURCES

Lang, Kristina Cawthon. "Pygmy marmoset (*Callithrix pygmaea*)." 2005. http://pin.primate.wisc.edu/factsheets/entry/pygmy_marmoset.

Rainforest Alliance. "Kids' Corner." www.rainforest-alliance.org/kids.

Recycling for Earth Day

Learning Outcomes

- Students understand the importance of individual action and character and explain how heroes from long ago and the recent past have made a difference in others' lives. (Grade 2—History and Social Science)
- Students know how to identify resources from Earth that are used in everyday life and understand that many resources can be conserved. (Kindergarten—Earth Sciences)
- Students know that living things cause changes in the environment in which they live: some of these changes are detrimental to the organism or other organisms, and some are beneficial. (Grade 3—Life Sciences)

Read-Aloud Books

- *We Are Extremely Very Good Recyclers*, by Bridget Hurst and illustrated by Lauren Child (Dial Books for Young Readers)
  - The brother-sister duo Charlie and Lola are back, this time on a campaign for recycling. Soon Lola has all of her classmates on the recycling bandwagon.

- *Recycled!*, by Jillian Powell and illustrated by Amanda Wood (Picture Window Books)
  - Miss Drew's class decides to start a recycling program, but soon, others at school find ways to reuse their recyclables instead.

Materials

- examples or pictures of different types of trash, such as aluminum cans, banana peels, paper, tea bags, plastic containers, and so on.
- recycling, compost, and landfill trash cans or bins

PROCEDURE

Let the participants know that today is Earth Day (or that Earth Day is coming up). Ask them, "What do you know about Earth Day. What kinds of

SCIENCE BEHIND THE TOPIC

The first Earth Day was on April 22, 1970, and it was started by the Wisconsin senator Gaylord Nelson. He noticed the many environmental problems that we were facing and wanted to have a day on which people could do something no matter how big or small to help reverse some of these problems. More than twenty million Americans took part in the first Earth Day. Now there are special events all over the United States and in over a hundred other countries.

One way to celebrate Earth Day every day is by recycling and composting your trash. Recycling saves energy, decreases the need to use more natural resources, and reduces the space needed for landfills. Many cities now have recycling programs, and some even have composting programs. In those places where there isn't a curbside composting program, people can do home composting either with a backyard bin or even using the help of earthworms. Yard trimming and food waste make up about 27 percent of all solid waste in cities in the United States, so composting can help decrease the overall amount of waste while also creating something useful. For more information on composting, see the resources section.

things do people do to celebrate Earth Day?" Share a little about the history of Earth Day if the group isn't aware of it.

Introduce the first story, which is about one thing we all can do to protect the environment.

Read *We Are Extremely Very Good Recyclers*

Ask the children, "What are the items that Lola is collecting? What will happen to them?"

Show the different types of trash cans or bins. Ask the participants, "What kinds of thing do we put into each of these trash cans? Why should we try to reduce the amount we put in the trash can that is for the landfill?" If your city does not have a composting program, you can talk about how you can start a regular compost bin in your own backyard or how you can have a worm compost bin in your house. See the resources section for more information. Show participants the pictures or actual trash items you have brought in and have the children sort them into the right bin.

Let the participants know that another important way to help protect the environment is to reuse things rather than putting them in the landfill or recycling them. The next story is about some people who do just that. Have the kids look for the different ways that things are reused in the story.

Read *Recycled!*

Ask, "What were some ways they reused items? Have you reused any of these items in other ways?" Introduce the craft as another way to recycle something.

Craft: Recycled Earth Ornament

Craft Materials

- old magazines or used greeting cards
- compass or drinking glass
- pencil
- scissors
- glue stick
- piece of yarn about 24 inches long
- bead (optional)

Directions

1. Trace five circles that have about a 3.5-inch diameter on old magazines or used greeting cards. Use a compass or drinking glass as your guide. Trace the circles over the pictures that you want on your ornament.
2. Cut out the circles and fold them in half with the picture you want on the inside. You should now have five semicircles.
3. Glue the semicircle of one picture to the semicircle of another, with the wrong sides facing each other. The picture you want to show should be on the outside. Repeat with four of the circles.
4. Fold the yarn in half. Tie a knot or a bead at the bottom to keep the yarn from falling out of the middle of the ornament. Also, tie a knot a little ways down from the top of the yarn to create a loop to hang it with.
5. Lay the yarn down the center of the ornament and then glue on the last circle. You should now have an orb made out of the five circles.

FURTHER READING FOR KIDS

Barnham, Kay. *Recycle*. New York: Crabtree Publishing, 2008.

Brown, Marc. *Arthur Turns Green*. New York: Little, Brown, 2011.

Gibbons, Gail. *Recycle! A Handbook for Kids*. Boston: Little, Brown, 1992.

Siddals, Mary McKenna. *Compost Stew: An A to Z Recipe for the Earth*.
    Berkeley, CA: Tricycle Press, 2010.

RESOURCES

Environmental Protection Agency. "Composting at Home." www2.epa.gov/
    recycle/composting-home.

Gaylord Nelson and Earth Day: The Making of the Modern Environmental
    Movement. www.nelsonearthday.net/index.htm.

Washington State Department of Ecology. "Waste 2 Resources Kids Page."
    www.ecy.wa.gov/programs/swfa/kidspage/.

Wisconsin Department of Natural Resources. "Composting with Worms."
    http://dnr.wi.gov/org/caer/ce/eek/earth/recycle/compost2.htm.

Seeds

Learning Outcomes
- Students know that both plants and animals need water, that
  animals need food, and that plants need light. (Grade 1—Life Sciences)
- Students know that roots are associated with the intake of water
  and soil nutrients and that green leaves are associated with making food from sunlight. (Grade 1—Life Sciences)
- Students know that flowers and fruits are associated with reproduction in plants. (Grade 2—Life Sciences)

Read-Aloud Books
- *A Seed Is Sleepy*, by Dianna Hutts Aston and illustrated by Sylvia
  Long (Chronicle Books)

- This beautifully illustrated book introduces the reader to a variety of seeds, the many ways they are dispersed, and how they become new plants.

- *This Is the Sunflower*, by Lola M. Shaefer and illustrated by Donald Crews (Greenwillow Books)
  - With bright and bold illustrations, this book follows the life cycle of a sunflower.

Materials
- various types of seeds, such as acorns, maple seeds, coconut, dandelion, berries, and so on (try to get at least one kind of seed that represents different types of dispersal, such as by wind, water, and animal)
- edamame or corn
- humus
- seed germination model or diagram of the different stages of seed germination

SCIENCE BEHIND THE TOPIC

Spring is a time of new life. Animals mate and give birth. In many parts of the world, buds appear on the trees as their leaves return. Sprouts begin to appear from seeds that lay dormant. New growth abounds everywhere.

When most plants want to create new plants of their species, they have to disperse their seeds. But since they wouldn't grow too well all right next to each other, they need to make sure they have enough food, water and space. The movement of seeds is called dispersal. The three main ways seeds disperse are by wind, by water, and by animals. Seeds dispersed by wind, such as maple seeds, tend to be lightweight, so that even a hint of a breeze will carry them away. They also can have special adaptations that help carry them along. The maple seeds have winglike appendages, and often the seeds are high up in the tree, so when a wind comes it twirls them and sends them on their way. Many seeds dispersed by water, such as coconuts, have thick, waterproof shells and enough air inside it to help them float along the water. Coconuts can drift up to 1,250 miles (2,000 kilometers) before they reach land and germinate in new soil. Some seeds that are dispersed by animals have prickles or burrs on them that attach to an animal's fur and get transported elsewhere. Others might be embedded in a tasty fruit, which

PROCEDURE

This can be a good storytime to do in the spring. Ask the participants, "What do you think of when you hear the word *spring*? What is springtime like? What do you see? What happens?" Tell the participants that one thing that is often associated with spring is sprouts or new plants. These often grow from seeds, so tell them that today you are going to talk about seeds. Seeds not only create new plants but also can be food for animals, including humans. Ask the participants if they can think of any seeds that we eat. (Show examples of sunflower seeds, edamame or corn, and humus).

Introduce the first book, which talks about all different kinds of seeds.

Read *A Seed Is Sleepy*

Ask the participants, "Do plants have legs?" When most plants want to create new plants, they have to disperse their seeds. But since they wouldn't grow too well all right next to each other, they need to make sure they have enough food, water, and space. Explain that the movement of seeds is called dispersal. Ask, "What were some of the ways that seeds were dispersed in the book we just read?"

the animal eats and then defecates the seeds elsewhere. Another example, the acorn, is itself a tasty treat to animals. Often squirrels and other animals will store nuts underground in various places. Sometimes the animal will forget about them, and they may sprout.

Once a seed has found a new place to grow, how exactly does it germinate or became a new plant? Seeds have an outer covering known as a seed coat. Like a coat that protects us from the wind and rain, the seed coat (also known as a testa) protects the seed until it is just the right time to start growing. When that time arrives, the seed breaks open its coat, just like we might take off our coat when the weather turns nice. At this point, water enters the seed and causes it to swell, until the seed coat (testa) bursts and the first shoot (plumule) and root (radicle) begin to grow. The plant needs food, which it gets from the first leaves that appear, which are called cotyledons. Cotyledons often look different from the other leaves on a plant, but they are important because they provide the plant with food until its "true leaves" grow. Once the true leaves grow, the cotyledons fall off. The true leaves then make food for the plant through photosynthesis. Besides food, plants also need water to grow, which they get from their roots. Their roots act like straws, sucking up water from the soil. The roots can also get minerals (food) from the soil.

Show three seeds, such as a coconut, a maple seed, and an acorn, or three other seeds that represent the different dispersal methods. Ask the participants how they think each one was dispersed and talk a little about the characteristics of each seed that is dispersed using each of the methods.

Using the seed model or a diagram, go through the different stages of germination with the group. Try to make this as interactive as possible, asking questions throughout the explanation, such as "What do plants need to grow?" "Where do they get water from?" and "Where do they get food from?"

Introduce the next book, which follows the life cycle of a sunflower.

Read *This Is the Sunflower*

Explain that today at storytime, rather than doing a craft, they are going to plant seeds so that they can watch a seed grow at home just like they have been talking about today.

Activity: Planting Sunflowers

Activity Materials
- sunflower seeds
- potting soil
- paper cups or other small containers
- large spoons
- water

Directions
1. Fill a cup or other container about three-quarters full of potting soil using a spoon to scoop it in.
2. Make a few small holes in the dirt and plant 2–3 seeds, depending on the size of the cup.
3. Give your seeds a little water.
4. Recommend that once the plant has lost its cotyledons and has a few true leaves that they transplant it to their yards or a bigger pot since it will need more space to grow.

FURTHER READING FOR KIDS

Carle, Eric. *The Tiny Seed.* Natick, MA: Picture Book Studio, 1987.

Galbraith, Kathryn O. *Planting the Wild Garden.* Atlanta: Peachtree Publishers, 2011.

Macken, JoAnn Early. *Flip, Float, Fly: Seeds on the Move.* New York: Holiday House, 2008.

Pfeffer, Wendy. *From Seed to Pumpkin.* New York: HarperCollins, 2004.

RESOURCES

Benbow, Ann. *Sprouting Seed Science Projects.* Berkeley Heights, NJ: Enslow Publishers, 2009.

Jaffe, Roberta. *The Growing Classroom: Garden-Based Science.* Burlington, VT: National Gardening Association, 2007.

Winter Solstice

Learning Outcomes
- Adaptations in physical structure or behavior may improve an organism's chance for survival. (Grade 3—Life Sciences)
- The position of the sun in the sky changes during the course of the day and from season to season. (Grade 3—Earth Sciences)

Read-Aloud Books
- *Winter Lullaby,* by Barbara Seuling and illustrated by Greg Newbold (Browndeer Press)
  - When winter winds blow, where do the bees go? What do the birds do? How about the snakes? Each page of this book poetically asks these questions and answers them on the following page, allowing for an interactive reading experience in which the kids can try to come up with the answer.

- *The Longest Night,* by Marion Dane Bauer and illustrated by Ted Lewin (Holiday House)
    - On a cold, dark winter's night the animals wonder who will be able to bring the sun back for the dawn. Dramatic and realistic

SCIENCE BEHIND THE TOPIC

Winter in the Northern Hemisphere can be very harsh and cold for many animals. Therefore, animals have adapted in different ways to survive the winter. Some animals, such as wolves, grow a thicker coat of fur to keep them warm throughout the winter. Even with their fur, though, some animals can't find enough food to eat to survive the winter, so they go to sleep, or hibernate.

Only some animals are true hibernators, such as woodchucks, ground squirrels, and bats. They are extremely hard to wake up, their heart rates slow down a lot, and their body temperature goes down dramatically. They periodically wake up to eat or go to the bathroom. For example, while a woodchuck is hibernating, its heart rate goes from its normal eighty beats per minute to four or five beats per minute. In addition, its body temperature drops from 98 degrees Fahrenheit to 38 degrees Fahrenheit.

Other animals are "light sleepers." They take long naps. The light sleepers include bears, raccoons, skunks, and opossums. They easily wake up and often do so to find food. They lower their heart rates, but only by a few beats, and they lower their body temperature, but only by a few degrees.

Reptiles and amphibians don't have fur, and they are ectothermic (coldblooded), so they need to do something special to survive during the winter. Some frogs have special chemicals in their blood so that it doesn't freeze from the cold weather. It acts like an antifreeze. Many frogs also hibernate by burying themselves in the mud. They get oxygen from the surrounding mud. Some snakes will pile on top of each other in burrows to keep warm while hibernating.

Other animals migrate, like birds. There are many birds that come from Canada and the Arctic to California, where it is warmer, over the winter. Birds in other parts of the United States go to Central America for the winter where it is warmer.

The winter solstice is the official first day of winter. It occurs on December 21, and in the Northern Hemisphere it is the shortest day of the year and the longest night. The winter solstice has been celebrated in different ways throughout history and in different parts of the world. Most of the celebrations focus on honoring the sun and all it provides to humans and life on Earth.

watercolor illustrations make readers feel as if they were there in the woods with the animals.

Materials

- raccoon, opossum, or skunk pelt
- taxidermy ground squirrel or woodchuck or pictures of them
- preserved turtle or picture of one
- preserved snake or picture of one
- orange
- two toothpicks
- flashlight

PROCEDURE

Start out by saying that today you are going to talk about winter and the winter solstice. Explain that the winter solstice is the official first day of winter. It occurs on December 21, and in the Northern Hemisphere it is the shortest day of the year and the longest night. Ask the group what comes to mind when they think of winter.

Introduce the first story, which is about what some animals do during winter.

Read *Winter Lullaby*

Ask the participants, "What were some of the things that animals did during the winter? Can you think of some other animals that do something special during the winter?"

Using the specimens or photos, talk about the different things animals do to survive the winter, including growing thicker fur, hibernating, and migrating.

Remind the participants that the start of winter is known as the winter solstice, and it is the longest night of the year in the Northern Hemisphere. Do a demonstration using the orange, toothpicks, and a flashlight to show why this is so. Place one toothpick at either end of the orange. The orange represents Earth and the toothpicks are at the North and South Poles. The flashlight is the sun. As Earth goes around the sun, there are times when the

Northern Hemisphere is closer to the sun and times when it is further away. Turn down the lights and have a volunteer point the flashlight toward the orange. Tilt the top of the orange toward the sun. You will notice that it is getting a lot of light. This represents summer in the Northern Hemisphere. Now, tilt the top of the orange away from the sun. Now the Northern Hemisphere is not getting very much light. This represents winter in the Northern Hemisphere. You can also point out that around the equator there isn't really very much difference in the amount of light they receive. This is why the temperature is pretty much the same all year-round there.

Explain to the group that the winter solstice has been celebrated in different ways throughout history. Select some pages to share from the picture book *The Winter Solstice*, by Ellen Jackson. You can just show the pictures and paraphrase what some of the traditions are. Ask if any of these traditions remind the participants of things we do for certain holidays at this time of year. Tell the group that some people in ancient times would also have special ceremonies to make sure the sun would come back, and that the next story is about some animals in winter that are also missing the sun and wish it would come back soon.

Read *The Longest Night*

Introduce the craft as something that combines different symbols of winter and the winter solstice. It is a snowflake, but it is also meant to be like a stained-glass window, which shows off its colors with the sun.

Craft: Snowflake Stained-Glass Window Decoration

Craft Materials
- snowflake template (from the "Winter Solstice" Science Story Adventures online handout, at www.calacademy.org/academy/exhibits/naturalist_center/nnotebook/wp-content/uploads/2011/08/winter_solstice.pdf)
- black construction paper
- colored tissue paper
- scissors
- glue sticks
- hole punches

- yarn or string
- white colored pencils

Directions

1. Print out the snowflake template and cut it out.
2. Place one piece of construction paper on top of another and fold them in half crosswise. Put the template on the fold and trace the snowflake with the white colored pencil.
3. Cut out two snowflakes by cutting through both pieces of paper.
4. Place the tissue paper in between the two black snowflakes and glue it together. It is all right if some of the tissue paper is outside of the outer rim of the snowflake.
5. Trim the tissue paper so that it is only on the inside of the snowflake.
6. Punch a hole in one side of the snowflake and put a string through it so that you can hang the snowflake in a window.

FURTHER READING FOR KIDS

Bancroft, Henrietta, and Richard G. Van Gelder. *Animals in Winter.* Let's-Read-and-Find-Out Science. New York: HarperCollins, 1997.

Glaser, Linda. *Not a Buzz to Be Found: Insects in Winter.* Minneapolis, MN: Millbrook Press, 2012.

Messner, Kate. *Over and under the Snow.* San Francisco: Chronicle Books, 2011.

Stewart, Melissa. *Under the Snow.* Atlanta: Peachtree Press, 2009.

Van Laan, Nancy. *When Winter Comes.* New York: Atheneum Books for Young Readers, 2000.

RESOURCES

Roach, John. "Antifreeze-Like Blood Lets Frogs Freeze and Thaw with Winter's Whims." *National Geographic.* http://news.national geographic.com/news/2007/02/070220-frog-antifreeze.html.

Wisconsin Department of Natural Resources. "Snug in the Snow." http://dnr.wi.gov/org/caer/ce/eek/nature/snugsnow.htm.

Women Scientists and Naturalists

Learning Outcomes
- Students understand the importance of individual action and character and explain how heroes from long ago and the recent past have made a difference in others' lives. (Grade 2—History and Social Science)
- Students know that the sequential stages of life cycles are different for different animals, such as butterflies, frogs, and mice. (Grade 2—Life Sciences)

Read-Aloud Books
- *Summer Birds: The Butterflies of Maria Merian*, by Margarita Engle and illustrated by Julie Paschkis (Henry Holt)
  - In the 1600s, when Maria Merian was born, people believed that insects were evil and came about spontaneously from mud. Even though she was just a child, Maria didn't believe this was true, and she secretly collected caterpillars and observed their transformation into butterflies. Colorful illustrations, which draw inspiration from Merian's own paintings, complement the story of this amazing female naturalist.

- *Planting the Trees of Kenya: The Story of Wangari Maathai*, written and illustrated by Claire A. Nivola (Farrar, Straus, and Giroux)
  - This inspirational book tells the story of Wangari Maathai, who grew up in the hills of Kenya that were blanketed by trees. She goes away to America to study, and when she returns, she notices that many of the trees have disappeared, that the streams near her house have dried up, and that the soil is no longer good for growing crops. Rather than doing nothing or waiting for the government to do something, Wangari convinces her female neighbors that together they can plant trees and restore the land, thus starting the Green Belt Movement.

SCIENCE BEHIND THE TOPIC

People often ask what the difference is between butterflies and moths. Although there are several differences between moths and butterflies, they also share some common characteristics, since they both belong to the scientific order Lepidoptera. It is also interesting to note that moths make up the majority of this order—about 86 percent of all species. Both moths and butterflies are insects, which means that they have three main body parts—head, thorax, and abdomen. They also have six legs, like all insects. They both have scales on their wings. In fact, Lepidoptera means "scaly winged." Antennae grace the heads of both, and they both have life cycles with several stages.

Although butterflies and moths share many characteristics, they do exhibit some differences. One difference is in their life cycles. Only moths spin cocoons around themselves. Many types of both butterflies and moths spin a thread to attach themselves to a twig or leaf. Then their body becomes covered in a hard outer case called a chrysalis. Moths then spin their cocoon around this hard outer case. Some moths do not form a chrysalis but just spin a cocoon around themselves.

The following table lists the other main differences between butterflies and moths:

BUTTERFLIES	MOTHS
Often brightly colored	Often have drab colors to conceal themselves during the day
Thin body	Stout, furry body
Clubbed antennae—straight at the head and wider at the tip	Straight to feathery antennae; never clubbed
Rest with wings folded upright and above the body	Rest with wings spread open
Fly mostly during the day	Fly mostly at night

Materials

- butterfly specimen or photo of butterfly
- moth specimen or photo of moth
- large plastic insect that is anatomically accurate or diagram of insect with body parts labeled
- close-up picture of butterfly wing that shows its scales

- hand lens (if you have butterfly and moth specimens)
- copies of paintings by Maria Merian, either from the Internet or a book

PROCEDURE

March is Women's History Month, so this storytime could be a good one to do in March, but you really can do it at any time. Start out by asking the children what a scientist is and what scientists do (e.g., make observations, make predictions, test out predictions, describe results). Then ask what a naturalist is and how naturalists are different from scientists. (Usually, naturalists do not have formal training in the sciences, and they tend to be more of a generalist than a specialist—they study many different things rather than just studying one thing.)

Introduce the first story, which is about Maria Merian. Tell the participants that she was a naturalist who lived more than 350 years ago in the 1600s in Germany. This was a time when people often thought that men were smarter than women, and that women couldn't be scientists, let alone naturalists. Let the participants know that as they will see in this story, though, Maria was an amazing naturalist who discovered interesting things about butterflies and moths.

Read *Summer Birds: The Butterflies of Maria Merian*

Let the participants know that Maria Merian had the chance to travel and study animals in other lands. She traveled to South America and wrote books with illustrations of what she saw. You can show examples of her illustrations either from the Internet or books.

Remind the participants that one of the main things that Maria studied was butterflies and moths, and often people wonder what the difference is between the two. Show the children the butterfly and moth specimens or photos. Ask, "What similarities do you notice between the two?" Go over the ways that they are similar, such as the fact that they are both insects and have scaly wings. You can show the insect body diagram or point out the different parts on a plastic insect. Also, highlight their scales on their wings by either bringing hand lenses if you have specimens or by showing a close-up photo of a butterfly or moth wing.

After discussing the similarities, talk about the differences by looking at the specimens or photos. Ask, "What are their bodies like? What colors are they? What about their antennae?"

Introduce the next book, which is about a woman who was a scientist who lived more recently. She played an important role in a movement in Africa to protect the environment there.

Read *Planting the Trees of Kenya: The Story of Wangari Maathai*

Highlight that you have talked about two amazing women today and that there are many more women naturalists and scientists who have lived and are still living today. For the craft, have the participants draw pictures of what they would study if they were scientists. They can either draw themselves doing something or the things they would study.

Craft: If I Were a Scientist

Craft Materials
- worksheets that say, "If I were a scientist, I would study . . ." at the top of them
- crayons or colored pencils

Have the children draw what they would like to study if they were scientists.

FURTHER READING FOR KIDS

Ehrlich, Amy. *Rachel: The Story of Rachel Carson*. San Diego: Harcourt, 2003.

McDonnell, Patrick. *Me . . . Jane*. New York: Little, Brown, 2011.

Napoli, Donna Jo. *Mama Miti: Wangari Maathai and the Trees of Kenya*. New York: Simon and Schuster Books for Young Readers, 2010.

Rooney, Frances. *Exceptional Women Environmentalists*. Toronto: Second Story Press, 2007.

RESOURCES

Brafman, David, and Stephanie Schrader. *Insects & Flowers: The Art of Maria Sybilla Merian.* Los Angeles: J. Paul Getty Museum, 2008.

Greenbelt Movement. "About Wangari Maathai." www.greenbelt movement.org/wangari-maathai.

Resources for Environmental Activities

Garrett, Linda, and Hannah Thomas. *Small Wonders: Nature Education for Young Children.* Woodstock: Vermont Institute of Natural Science, 2005.

Parrella, Deborah. *Project Seasons: Hands-On Activities for Discovering the Wonders of the World.* Rev. ed. Shelburne, VT: Shelburne Farms, 1995.

Sheehan, Kathryn, and Mary Waidner. *Earth Child 2000: Earth Science for Young Children.* Rev. ed. Tulsa, OK: Council Oak Books, 1998.

VanCleave, Janice Pratt. *Janice VanCleave's Big Book of Play and Find Out Science.* New York: Jossey-Bass, 2007.

Resources for Natural History Specimens, Replicas, and Manipulatives

Acorn Naturalists. www.acornnaturalists.com.

Bone Clones. www.boneclones.com.

Carolina Biological. www.carolina.com.

Resources for Crafts

The Best Kids Book Site. www.thebestkidsbooksite.com

Carlson, Laurie M. *EcoArt! Earth-Friendly Art & Craft Experiences for 3- to 9-Year-Olds.* Nashville, TN: Williamson Publications, 1993.

DLTK's Animal Crafts. www.dltk-kids.com/animals/index.html.

Press, Judy. *The Kids' Natural History Book: Making Dinos, Fossils, Mammoths & More!* Charlotte, VT: Williamson Publishing, 2000.

NOTES

1. Carolyn P. Casteel and Bess A. Isom, "Reciprocal Processes in Science and Literacy Learning," *Reading Teacher* 47, no. 7 (1994): 538–545; Dan T. Ouzts et al., "A Learner-Centered Curriculum Based on Award-Winning Literature," *Education* 124, no. 1 (2003): 76–85; Donald J. Richgels, "Informational Texts in Kindergarten," *Reading Teacher* 55, no. 6 (2002): 586–595.

2. Danny Brassell, "Inspiring Young Scientists with Great Books," *Reading Teacher* 60, no. 4 (2006–7): 336–342.

3. California State Board of Education, "Content Standards," www.cde.ca.gov/be/st/ss.

READING FOR A GREENER FUTURE: BOOK CLUBS

Tweens and Teens

ike storytimes, book clubs have a long history with libraries. Over the past two decades they have resurged in popularity, not only in libraries but also in the broader community, partially spurred by Oprah's Book Club and the availability of discussion guides from many publishers and bookstores. The popularity of series for youth, such as Harry Potter and Twilight, increased interest in book discussions among young people as well. In 2000, more than one hundred thousand book clubs existed in the United States.[1]

Counteracting this surge in book clubs is the decline of reading in the United States. A report published by the National Endowment for the Arts found that across demographics fewer Americans spend time reading for pleasure than in the past, and the steepest declines are among young adults. Nearly half of Americans between the ages of eighteen and twenty-four do not read voluntarily at all, and "less than one-third of 13-year-olds are daily readers."[2] In addition, the replication of a 1981 survey given to teachers determined that over the past thirty years, the amount of time devoted to promoting recreational reading in classrooms has not significantly increased and still remains troublingly low.[3] Reading for pleasure helps young people develop literacy skills, which they carry on to adulthood and can influence their success in the workforce and as active citizens in a democracy. With the lack of opportunities to promote recreational reading in classrooms, book clubs in libraries and museums become all the more important.

Book clubs also provide myriad other benefits in addition to developing literacy skills. For avid readers, they offer a place to meet with others who share their passion. Likewise, book clubs welcome those who might be reluctant readers or who struggle with reading and literacy skills in the classroom. A book club can create an environment in which these readers' opinion matters, and they are not judged immediately according to their abilities. This increased confidence can lead to a deeper interest in reading for pleasure.

Book clubs have also been shown to help youth develop socially and emotionally. They allow youth to connect to literature and see themselves in the characters and the experiences they face. As Kunzel and Hardesty point out, "By their nature book clubs encourage teens to think and feel with others, to focus on their inner selves in a meaningful way, and to build shared understanding."[4] In a safe environment, youth can begin to make sense of the world and their place within it, while also developing interpersonal skills that they will use throughout their lives. While discussing and evaluating books, youth foster their communication and critical-thinking skills. Book clubs can also expose them to new ideas and different perspectives.

From a numbers vantage point, book clubs help promote library resources and services and can increase circulation. They can be a good basis for forming partnerships between museums and libraries, which could help both institutions reach new audiences. Museums can tap into the literary expertise and resources of libraries, and libraries can benefit from the expertise of curators or the information found in exhibits to enrich readings of books on certain topics. It might take a little more work in terms of coordination, but there is also the added support and benefits of pooling resources.

PLANNING FOR A BOOK CLUB

The first step to creating a book club is to define clear objectives. There are many different objectives you could include, from increasing circulation to improving specific literacy skills or serving at-risk youth. Turn to your institution's mission statements and goals as a guide to help you determine your objectives. Once you have the objectives clearly established, everything you do and the decisions you make should follow them. On the basis of your objectives, you can then devise measurable goals to ensure that you are on the right track to meeting your objectives.

Surveying your community can assist in the development of your objectives and goals. This might mean doing formal questionnaires or focus groups to get a sense of what the needs and desires of the community are. In a public or school library, you could also do this more informally by talking with your patrons and observing their circulation patterns—which books are most popular, which clubs or programs get the highest number of participants, and so on. Many public libraries have teen advisory boards, which can be a great resource for helping to get a book club started. In museums, you can look at other youth programs you already have to assess what has worked and what hasn't. If you have youth internship programs, use those interns as a focus group to help steer the design of your book club.

Many of the logistical aspects of your planning for a book club will likely emerge as you conduct these community surveys. Deciding how often and when to meet is an important part of the planning process. In a school library, one option is to hold the book club over the lunch period or during a study hall. This provides students who are involved in many other after-school activities or who need to help care for their siblings after school an opportunity to join the club. In public libraries or museums, it might mean having meetings in the evenings, on weekends, or over the summer. Deciding who will lead the book club meetings is also key. In most cases, it will likely be a librarian or a museum educator. Other options, however, include partnering with teachers or adult volunteers. Book clubs for older teens might be led by the teens. The librarian or museum educator might lead the first few meetings to model how it is done, but then slowly turn over the responsibility to the teens. Where the meetings will be located is another factor to take into consideration. Having a space with comfortable seating and a welcoming environment, where you can also have food, is important.

Most book clubs follow the traditional read-and-discuss model, but many different types exist. One obvious type of book club that would easily incorporate environmental themes is a genre- or theme-based book club. Generally, this type of club is a traditional read-and-discuss club, but you would read only environmental or science-based books (both fiction and nonfiction). For some libraries and museums, this will work well. In other cases, this can limit the amount of participation, since it might be hard to find enough of an audience to sustain only reading books from this genre. One way to increase participation might be to promote the club to school-based green teams or other environmental clubs.

Another option is to intersperse titles with environmental or science-based themes in more general book clubs. The following is a sampling of different types of book clubs. Some book clubs pick a model and stick with it, while others mix and match. All of these types of clubs could incorporate environmental books:

- **Intergenerational:** These clubs typically include mother-daughter and father-son members, but they can also refer to teens leading book discussions for elementary school kids. A benefit of these types of clubs is that they can allow groups to interact in ways they might not normally do so, and to see a side of each other that they might not normally see, and so strengthen their relationships.
- **Book-to-Movie:** These tend to be popular among youth, since they bring in another type of media and might draw in youth that are reluctant to read a particular book but are more interested once they have seen the movie. This can lead to discussions that compare the book and movie and why certain things were included in one and not the other.
- **Online Book Clubs:** Similar to face-to-face clubs, there are different versions of online clubs, but most follow a read-and-discuss model. They can be done using a simple blogging software such as Blogger (www.blogger.com) or WordPress (www.wordpress.com). Other libraries have utilized Moodle, an open-source classroom management software. These three types of software can be password protected so that you can control who participates in your book club. Some advantages of online book clubs is that they can

fit more easily in many youths' busy schedules; they can reach an audience that might not be able to physically get to the library or museum easily; and sometimes young people feel more comfortable expressing themselves in an online environment. For more information on establishing an online book club, check out the following resources:

- John, Lauren Zina. *Running Book Discussion Groups.* New York: Neal-Schuman Publishers, 2006, chapter 8.
- Kunzel, Bonnie, and Constance Hardesty. *The Teen-Centered Book Club: Readers into Leaders.* Westport, CT: Libraries Unlimited, 2006, chapter 4.
- Messner, Kate. "Met Any Good Authors Lately?" *School Library Journal* 55 (August 2009): 36–38.
- Scharber, Cassandra. "Online Book Clubs: Bridges between Old and New Literacies and Practices." *Journal of Adolescent and Adult Literacy* 52 (February 2009): 433–37.

- **Book Chat or Booktalk Club:** In this club, everyone reads a different book, perhaps on the same theme, and then at the meeting they introduce their book to the other members in the group. This is an easy book club to plan, and you don't run into the problem of having enough copies of a book for all members. At the same time, however, the discussions tend to be more superficial, and if you have a bigger group, you might have to split into smaller groups to give everyone equal time in presenting their book.
- **Service-Oriented Book Club:** In this club, the participants read a book centered on a particular issue and then develop a service project or volunteer for an organization that tackles that issue. This has the benefit of enriching the book club, but it can involve more planning and staff involvement.

Selecting Titles

Once you have decided on the type of club you want to undertake, the next step is choosing what book to read. Similar to selecting titles for storytime, finding a book that tells a good story is important. Books that include controversy or focus on an issue that is important to young people will also work well. Both fiction and nonfiction can work in book clubs. When using nonfiction, however, books written in a narrative style often work best. In terms of locating science-related books, the following are good sources for finding titles:

- *Outstanding Science Trade Books for Students K-12*
  www.nsta.org/publications/ostb
    - An annual annotated list of recommended science trade books, compiled by a panel of reviewers from the National Science Teachers Association in cooperation with the Children's Book Council

- *Science Books & Films*
  www.sbfonline.com/Pages/welcomesplash.aspx
    - A review journal of science resources for all ages published by the American Association for the Advancement of Science

- *Science & Children*
  http://learningcenter.nsta.org/browse_journals.aspx?journal=sc
    - A journal published by the National Science Teachers Association that includes reviews of science books for children.

- *Teachers' Choices Reading List*
  www.reading.org/Resources/Booklists/TeachersChoices.aspx
    - An annual annotated list of books that will "encourage young people to read . . . and that contribute to learning across the curriculum."

Involving the book club participants in the selection of books, however, will likely ensure greater success. Doing so allows participants to take ownership of the club and feel more invested in the reading. For the first meeting, it is likely that the leader will need to choose the book, but at the end of that first meeting, have three or four other titles available for the participants to look over. You can do a brief booktalk on each one, and then everyone can vote on which one they would like to read next. You could also ask for suggestions from the participants before the meeting for voting on.

Once you have chosen the title for the next book club, give the participants at least a month to read it. Make sure there are plenty of copies of the book available from the library for participants to borrow. The availability of a book (particularly in paperback) might affect the decision to choose it or not. Avoid including the cost of book club books in your regular collection development budget. Include it in your programming budget, and if this is limited, look for small grants or turn to a friends-of-the-library group to help support the book club. For museums, the cost of the books should be included in the programming budget, and likewise, if this is limited, you can look for small grants to help support the club. Museums can also look to create arrangements with their gift stores to carry the books and offer them at a discounted price for book club members who want to purchase the books.

Formulating Discussion Questions

No matter what style of book club you decide to undertake, at some point it will involve discussing the book. Some book clubs have participants prepare questions ahead of time and bring them to the meeting. Others have the participants write down questions at the start of the meeting on note cards. These are then placed in a hat or other receptacle and then picked one by one by the participants and discussed. Often other questions emerge organically as the discussion proceeds.

Whichever way you choose to lead the discussion, however, as the group facilitator, it is a good idea to have some questions prepared ahead of time. While you are reading the book, take notes and mark passages that spark a reaction in you. Look for overall themes and find examples that support that theme. Try to avoid yes-no questions or questions that can be answered in a few words. Include questions that someone could answer even if they have not read the book, given the reality that not everyone will have read the entire book (or any part of it) before coming to the meeting. Usually, there is a larger theme that a book touches on, which people can discuss even without having read it. Having a few fallback questions that you can use with any book is also a good idea. Here are a few possibilities:

- Which character was most like you, and how are you similar?
- What was your favorite section of the book? Why?
- What did you like about this book?
- What did you dislike about this book?
- Did any of the characters surprise you with their actions? In what way?
- What did you think of the illustrations or photos (if applicable)? Did they fit with the text? Did you like them or dislike them?
- What did you think of the ending?
- If you didn't like the ending, how would you change it?
- Why do you think the author chose the title he or she did? If you had to choose the title for this book, what would you call it?

Several resources online provide discussion questions, from book club portals to publishers' websites. Some books now have book club discussion questions in them, as well. The subscription-based readers' advisory database NoveList (www.ebscohost.com/novelist) also includes book discussion questions. In the "Sample Discussion Guides" section, I have included five books for tweens and five books for teens with environmental or science themes and possible discussion questions for each one. The following is a list of additional free online sources of book discussion guides:

- HarperCollins Teaching Resources—www.harpercollinschildrens .com/HarperChildrens/Teachers/TeachingResources.aspx
- Kids' Reads—www.kidsreads.com
- Macmillan Reading Group Guides—http://us.macmillan.com/ teachersandlibrarians/categories/Childrens/Guides/ ReadingGroupGuide
- Random House Reader Resources—www.randomhouse.com/ resources
- Teen Reads—www.teenreads.com

Gathering Background Information

Besides developing discussion questions, having background information prepared before the book club meeting will enrich the discussion. The librarian, museum educator, or adult facilitator could do this legwork, or you could assign it to the book club members. If you have regular members, it might be something that you want to model the first few meetings and then eventually turn over ownership of to the youths. Background information includes a brief biography of the author(s) and critiques of the book. Currently, many authors encourage interaction with their readers through personal websites, blogs, and author talks (both in-person and via digital sources, such as Skype). Mining these resources, including inviting an author to join in your discussion, can enliven the meeting. Depending on the subject matter of the book, you might also want to gather information on the broader historical context, the setting of the book, and current events that relate to the themes of the book. For example, in a discussion of a futuristic novel on the effects of climate change, such as *Exodus,* by Julie Bertagna, gathering basic information on the science behind climate change would prove useful. Having this information not only enriches the discussion but also can help fill in the gaps if a lull in the conversation arises.

Running the Meeting

Everything is prepared and the day has arrived. You have prepared a comfortable space and set out some simple snacks to put everyone at ease and to encourage mingling at the start of the meeting. Generally, it is a good idea to start with an icebreaker, particularly the first time the group is meeting. With intergenerational book clubs, icebreakers can also help encourage an environment of equals, in which everyone, regardless of age, can feel comfortable expressing their opinions. There are many books and online resources for icebreaker ideas. If you can, try to link the icebreaker to a theme from the book. For example, when discussing the book *The Bug Scientists,* by Donna M. Jackson, you can have each participant say his or her name and then the name of an insect that he or she relates to or is most like and why. Even if the same group members meet regularly, having an icebreaker can help set the tone for the upcoming discussion.

After the icebreaker activity, when the participants feel a bit more comfortable, introduce the group's ground rules. These can be established with the participants, or the group facilitator can draw up a list ahead of time and then have the group decide if there is anything they want to add, take away, or change on the list. Often when people write rules, they come at them from a negative perspective—"do not do this," or "you cannot do such and such." Try to accentuate the positive by creating ground rules that emphasize what you will do in the book club rather than what you will not do. The following are examples of positive group norms from the book *The Teen-Centered Book Club*:

> We welcome all ideas for discussion.
> We speak our minds and we listen carefully when others do the same.
> We think—and talk—beyond the book.
> When we disagree, we stick to the point.
> We look at situations in [the] book and topics in discussion from every angle.
> We look for evidence to back up our ideas and opinions.
> When we get angry, we stay quiet or leave the room until we cool off.
> Everyone is welcome, even if they haven't read the book.[5]

Having ground rules that are clearly stated from the beginning helps create a safe environment in which participants are more likely to feel free to share their opinions and experiences. Also, as pitfalls or disagreements arise during the discussion, you can fall back on your ground rules as a guide. Since you might not have the same people coming to each meeting each time, you might want to create the ground rules at the first meeting, and then simply make people aware of them at the beginning of each meeting to save time.

Generally, the adult facilitator will start off the discussion. As mentioned in the section on formulating discussion questions, there are many different ways that the facilitator can do this. Pick the method that works best for your group. It might be the same style each time, or you might switch it from meeting to meeting depending on the mood and makeup of the group.

Once the discussion gets rolling, however, the facilitator should embody his or her title by stepping back and allowing the participants to take the lead and interjecting only if the discussion begins to get off course, if conflicts arise, if a certain few dominate the conversation, or if a lull develops. As the facilitator, it is important to be an active listener so that you can successfully manage the flow of ideas in the group. In many ways, you will want to listen much more than you participate, but at certain points you will need to step in. If the conversation begins to veer into an area very much off topic, acknowledge the participant's comment, and then ask if anyone else has an observation based on the book, or introduce a new question related to the book. When one person seems to be dominating the conversation and another has remained quiet for most of the meeting, you can turn to the quiet participant and ask if he or she agrees or disagrees with what the talkative person has just stated. When conflicts arise, gently remind participants about the group rules. In addition, the facilitator should acknowledge the value of all participants' contributions to the discussion by sprinkling the conversation with comments like "I hadn't thought of that," or "That's an interesting point." For young people who are developing their literacy skills or might not be as successful academically, these types of comments can foster their realization that they do possess these skills and do have something of value to add to the group. The facilitator's tone and demeanor really determine the environment for the book club, so it is important to be self-evaluative and self-aware of your behaviors in this role.

Some book clubs engage in enrichment or additional activities besides a simple discussion. This might include making a craft, doing an experiment, or playing a game related to the book. It might be something that is done on another day, such as taking a field trip related to themes from a book—maybe visiting a museum, a nature preserve, or an organization that works on a related issue. Some groups also bring in guest speakers to do a presentation related to a theme found in the book or to just join in the book group discussion. For example, when reading a book, such as *Hoot,* by Carl Hiaasen, which focuses on kids trying to protect burrowing owls from a building project, you could invite someone who works on raptor rehabilitation to talk to your group.

Whether or not you do an enrichment activity, leave time at the end of the meeting to focus on the next meeting's book selection. Again, as discussed in the "Selecting Titles" section, different book clubs handle book selection in different ways. Choose the method that works best for your group. You might want to get suggestions from the group members ahead of time and then have copies of a few choices at the meeting. After a brief plug for each one, the group can vote on which one they want to read next. Alternatively, you might pick the title ahead of time and do a brief booktalk on it at the end of the meeting.

SAMPLE DISCUSSION GUIDES

The following sections contain sample discussion guides for five books suitable for tween audiences and five books suitable for teen audiences. E ach discussion guide includes a brief description of the book, an icebreaker, author information, background information (for the fiction books), discussion questions, extension activity suggestions, and a further reading section (which includes read-alikes and/or follow-up books that might interest the participants). Most of the books are fiction, but there are a few nonfiction selections. All of the titles would work for an environmental-themed or book-chat book club. If the book suits another particular type of book club, that is noted in the discussion guide. In addition, all these discussion guides could be adapted to create book discussion kits that already-established book clubs, environmental groups, or other youth groups could borrow. This could work well in a library that has limited staff to run its own book club or in a museum setting as a service provided through an education or outreach department.

The Bug Scientists by Donna M. Jackson (Houghton Mifflin)

Type of Book Club: Tween

Book Type: Nonfiction

Book Description: This book introduces readers to the many different careers an entomologist can have, some of which might not immediately come to mind. It highlights four different entomologists, focusing on how they became interested in insects and outlining the nitty-gritty of their work. There is also a section on basic insect biology, as well as a feature on a citizen-science project in which readers can also participate. Photographs of a variety of insects and the scientists who study them are sprinkled throughout the book.

Icebreaker

Tell the participants about Franz Kafka's famous book *The Metamorphosis,* in which a man turns into a cockroach. Ask participants to say their name and then the type of insect they think they would transform into and why.

Author Information

On her website, Donna Jackson states:

> Some people think nonfiction is boring with a capital snooze. But reading nonfiction doesn't have to lull you to sleep. In fact, most of today's nonfiction books use compelling, real-life stories to creatively convey all types of fascinating information. That's one of the reasons I love writing stories about REAL people, places and things.[6]

That's just what Jackson does. She has written many nonfiction books for youth, several of which are part of the Scientists in the Field Series, like *The Bug Scientists.* While growing up in Massachusetts, Jackson showed an interest in telling stories about real people and events from a young age. She wrote for her school newspaper in middle and high school and did graduate work in journalism at the University of Colorado, Boulder. Her books have received various awards. You can find out more about Jackson and her books at her website: www.donnamjackson.net/index.html.

Discussion Questions

- What do you think about Professor Turpin's teaching methods?
- What are some of the benefits of insects to humans?
- What do you think of the photos in the book?
- To a scientist, what's the difference between a bug and an insect?
- How can insects help solve crimes?

- What was one thing that surprised you in this book?
- What was the grossest thing in this book?
- Why do you think most of the entomologists in this book are men?
- What similarities did you notice between the different entomologists in the book?
- How are ants like humans?
- What are the benefits of having a large collection of dead specimens of insects, like the Smithsonian has? Do you agree with scientists collecting animals or plants to study them?

Extension Activities

- As a group, visit an insect zoo or insect exhibit at a local museum or zoo.
- As a group, participate in a citizen-science project such as Monarch Watch (www.monarchwatch.org) or the Great Sunflower Project (www.greatsunflower.org). For more information on citizen science, see chapter 5 in this book.

FURTHER READING

Burns, Loree Griffin. *The Hive Detectives: A Chronicle of a Honey Bee Catastrophe. Scientists in the Field.* Boston: Houghton Mifflin, 2010.

Jackson, Donna. *Extreme Scientists: Exploring Nature's Mysteries from Perilous Places. Scientists in the Field.* Boston: Houghton Mifflin, 2009.

Montgomery, Sy. *The Tarantula Scientist. Scientists in the Field.* Boston: Houghton Mifflin, 2004.

Zollman, Pam. *Don't Bug Me! New York:* Holiday House, 2001.

Hoot by Carl Hiaasen (Alfred A. Knopf)

Type of Book Club: Tween, Book-to-Movie, Intergenerational (Parent-Child)
Type of Book: Fiction
Book Description: Roy's family moves around a lot because of his father's work. Most recently, they have arrived in Florida, where Roy is struggling to fit in at school and misses the mountains and wildlife of Montana, where

they last lived. As in previous schools, Roy has to deal with a notorious bully, but this bully's actions also introduce him to some new friends. With his face shoved up against the school bus window, he spots a mysterious young boy running away from the bus rather than to it. Roy sets out to find out who the boy is, why he was running away, and why he hasn't seen him in school before. His investigations lead him to new friendships and the discovery of some burrowing owls whose homes might be destroyed by the construction of a new pancake restaurant. Can Roy and his newfound friends save the imperiled birds? Quirky characters, adventure, and environmental themes abound in Hiaasen's first novel for young people.

Icebreaker

Print out pictures of different owls found in your area, such as a great horned, barred, barn, western or eastern screech, and burrowing owls. Include the names of the owls with the pictures. Play the different calls of each owl and have the participants work in pairs to try to figure out which owl they think makes that call. For each one, they should write down their guess. Once you have listened to them all, go over the answers. You can find photos and calls of owls at the All About Birds website maintained by the Cornell Lab of Ornithology (www.allaboutbirds.org).

Author Information

Carl Hiaasen was born and raised in Florida and still lives there today with his family. After graduating from the University of Florida, he began working at the *Miami Herald* as a reporter. He still writes a weekly column for the paper. He has written several novels for adults, both on his own and in collaboration with his friend and fellow journalist William D. Montalbano. *Hoot* was the first novel he wrote for young people, but since then he has written three others, *Flush, Scat,* and *Chomp*. His novels all take place in Florida and depict the quirkiness and wilderness of the state. More information can be found on his website: www.carlhiaasen.com/index.shtml.

Background Information

The burrowing owl (*Athene cunicularia*) is one of the smallest owl species. Unlike many other owl species in which one sex is larger than the other, the males and females are about the same size. The average adult is about seven to ten inches tall and weighs between four and six ounces. Their body is brown with white speckles all over. They have very long legs and no ear tufts.

Burrowing owls have a vast range. They are found throughout the United States west of the Mississippi River and in Florida. They are also found in the Prairie Provinces of Canada and in Central and South America. They live mainly in grasslands and deserts, particularly in areas with large populations of burrowing mammals. They can dig their own burrows but tend to take over abandoned burrows made by mammals, such as prairie dogs in North America or viscachas in South America. More recently, they have moved into urbanized areas, such as golf courses, cemeteries, and airports.

Unlike most owls, they are known to be active and to hunt during the day, particularly during the breeding season. They will come out to find nesting material during the day. When it isn't the breeding season, they tend to hunt at dawn and dusk. They hunt more insects during the day and capture more small mammals at night. To hunt insects, they collect animal manure and leave it in front of their burrow. This attracts dung beetles, which they then eat. In addition to insects and mammals, they will also eat small reptiles and birds.

Threats to burrowing owls include habitat destruction due to development, pesticide poisoning, and collisions with cars. The global population of burrowing owls is not considered threatened, but in many states and provinces in North America, their numbers are declining as a result of these threats. Because of this, they are listed as endangered in Canada and Colorado, as threatened in Mexico, and as a species of special concern in Florida and most of the western United States.

For more information on burrowing owls, including photos and videos, check out the following websites:

Arkive. "Burrowing Owl." www.arkive.org/burrowing-owl/athene -cunicularia.
Cheng, Christina. "*Athene cunicularia* Burrowing Owl." 2001. http:// animaldiversity.ummz.umich.edu/site/accounts/information/ Athene_cunicularia.html.
Cornell Lab of Ornithology. "Burrowing Owl." www.allaboutbirds.org/ guide/burrowing_owl/lifehistory.

Defenders of Wildlife. "Burrowing Owl." 2011. www.defenders.org/wildlife_and_habitat/wildlife/burrowing_owl.php.

Discussion Questions

- What do you think about the way that Roy deals with bullies?
- Do you think it was fair that Dana didn't get punished for what he did to Roy? What would you have done if you were the vice principal?
- Roy is the new kid. Have you ever been in a situation where you were the new kid? How did you handle it?
- What things in the story hint at the fact that Roy is interested in nature and wildlife before he even finds out about the owls?
- What are some types of wildlife that live near where you live?
- What are some ways that you can help protect wildlife where you live?
- Roy's mom says that sometimes he will face a problem where his heart will say one thing and his head another. Is it better to go with your heart or your head?
- What do you think of the parents in this book?
- Do you think it is believable that Mullet Fingers could survive on his own and get away with not going to school?

Extension Activities

- Watch the movie version of the book as a group, and compare and contrast the two.
- Invite an ornithologist or a speaker from a raptor rehabilitation organization or habitat restoration organization to come to share with the group about their work.

FURTHER READING

DeFelice, Cynthia C. *Lostman's River*. New York: Macmillan, 1994.

George, Jean Craighead. *The Missing 'Gator of Gumbo Limbo: An Ecological Mystery*. New York: HarperCollins, 1992.

Hiaasen, Carl. *Flush*. New York: Alfred A. Knopf, 2005.

Hiaasen, Carl. *Scat*. New York: Alfred A. Knopf, 2009.

My Life in Pink and Green by Lisa Greenwald (Amulet Books)

Type of Book Club: Tween, Intergenerational (Parent-Child), Service Oriented

Book Type: Fiction

Book Description: Spirited twelve-year-old Lucy knows her family's pharmacy in small-town Connecticut is in trouble. Once a local hangout and booming with business, like many other small stores, it's now struggling to survive. One day the local homecoming queen arrives in the pharmacy with a beauty emergency that Lucy quickly and adeptly solves. The news spreads like wildfire about Lucy's makeover talents and soon others are asking for her help. The new customers might not be enough, but it sparks an idea for a plan to save not only the pharmacy but also to protect the environment. Now Lucy just has to convince the adults in her life that a seventh grader really can make a difference in the world.

Icebreaker

In the book, each chapter starts with a beauty tip, a business tip, or an inspirational quote. Have each member of the group write down one of these three things on a piece of paper, without letting anyone else know what he or she has written. Collect all of the papers and put them in a basket. Have each person draw one (making sure it is not his or her own contribution), and then each person has to figure out who wrote down what. After doing the activity, you can talk about what the participants thought about the author's decision to have quotes and tips at the beginning of each chapter.

Author Information

Lisa Greenwald lived in Fairfield, Connecticut, until the fifth grade. Then she moved to Long Island. Currently, she lives in Brooklyn with her husband and daughter. *My Life in Pink and Green* was her first novel. In addition to writing, she also works in the library at Birch Wathen Lennox School in Manhattan. She has a website with more information about herself, her books, and a blog (www.lisagreenwald.com). In one of her blog postings she says that she is happy to join mother-daughter book discussions via Skype. She also has a section on her website where she talks about her availability for school visits.

Background Information

Shiny, silky hair; vibrant, kissable lips; a flowery smell and no sweat marks—these are some of the promises our personal-care products make, but how do they achieve these promises? Many of the personal-care products we use every day contain any number of toxic and carcinogenic chemicals. These include shampoo, deodorant, cosmetics, and shaving products. The Teens Turning Green website lists thirty chemicals found in common personal-care products that may lead to cancer.[7] Many companies argue that these chemicals are present at only low levels and so are not harmful. People often use these products every day, though, so those low levels begin to add up. Also, we are using a mixture of many different chemicals and still are not clear on what the effects of the interactions between the different chemicals could be.

Shouldn't our government regulate these products to ensure they are safe? They should, but legally they aren't required to do so. The current law, the Food, Drug and Cosmetics Act, was passed in 1938. Under this law, the US Food and Drug Administration (FDA) cannot restrict companies from putting chemicals in their products, nor can it require them to test the safety of those products before they end up on our shelves. The FDA also cannot require labeling of products that might contain harmful chemicals or even the inclusion of all chemicals contained in the product on the label. Under the law, the cosmetics industry is required to have a safety panel, run and funded by the industry's trade association, to assess the safety of their products. In effect, the industry polices itself.

On March 21, 2013, Representative Jan Schakowsky (D-IL), introduced the Safe Cosmetics and Personal Care Act of 2013 (H.R. 1385), which will provide the FDA with the authority to ensure that personal-care products are free from harmful chemicals and the full disclosure of all ingredients contained in a product on its label. The Campaign for Safe Cosmetics highlights these key provisions of the act on its website:

- Phase-out of ingredients linked to cancer, birth defects and developmental harm;
- Creation of a health-based safety standard that includes protections for children, the elderly, workers and other vulnerable populations;

- Elimination of labeling loopholes by requiring full ingredient disclosure on product labels and company websites, including salon products and the constituent ingredients of fragrance;
- Worker access to information about unsafe chemicals in personal care products;
- Required data-sharing to avoid duplicative testing and encourage the development of alternatives to animal testing; and
- Adequate funding to the FDA Office of Cosmetics and Colors so it has the resources it needs to provide effective oversight of the cosmetics industry.[8]

Passage of this bill will help make our personal-care products safer and put US standards in line with those of many European countries, which have already banned the use of many of these chemicals in this type of products. Many companies that sell their products in both the United States and Europe have already reformulated them to meet the standards set in Europe.

There are various things that we can do to help protect ourselves. One is to show support for the passage of the Safe Cosmetics and Personal Care Act. Also, we can look for alternative products that don't contain these harmful chemicals and support green chemistry, which seeks to develop synthetic alternatives that are not harmful to humans or the environment.

The following resources have more information on this issue:

The Campaign for Safe Cosmetics. www.safecosmetics.org/index.
Environmental Working Group. "Skin Deep Cosmetics Database." 2011. www.ewg.org/skindeep/site/about.php.
Grossman, Elizabeth. *Chasing Molecules: Poisonous Products, Human Health and the Promise of Green Chemistry.* Washington, DC: Island Press, 2009.
Malkan, Stacy. *Not Just a Pretty Face:* The Ugly Side of the Beauty Industry. Gabriola Island, BC: New Society Publishers, 2007.
The Story of Cosmetics. http://storyofstuff.org/movies/story-of -cosmetics.
Teens Turning Green: Ethical Lifestyles. www.teensturninggreen.org/ programs/ethical-lifestyle.

Discussion Questions

- What characteristics does Lucy have that helped her solve the challenge of saving her family's pharmacy? Would any of these characteristics also help her solve an environmental problem?
- Have you ever been in a situation that seemed hopeless? What did you do?
- What do you think about wearing makeup?
- Have you ever been in a situation where you felt like adults didn't believe you could achieve something? What did you do?
- Do you have an environmental club at your school? If so, what do you do in your club? If you don't, would you like to start one, and how could you go about doing this?
- What are some environmental problems that you, as a kid, can solve? Are they different from what an adult can do?
- What do you think about Lucy not telling her mother and grandmother about her plan to submit the grant application?
- How would you describe Lucy's relationship with her mother? With her grandmother?
- Lucy and Sunny have a close relationship and really support each other. Who do you have in your life that is like that for you?

Extension Activities

- Have participants do a toxin inventory of personal-care products. Have them look at the different products they use each day to see which ones contain ingredients that might be harmful to their health or the environment. Use the Environmental Working Group's "Skin Deep Cosmetics Database" to help (www.ewg.org/skindeep).
- Similar to Sunny and Lucy, have the participants work on a project with their school environmental club or start a club if they don't already have one. See chapter 8 in this book on environmental action clubs for more information.

FURTHER READING

Friedman, Laurie B. *Mallory Goes Green!* Minneapolis, MN: Carolrhoda
    Books, 2010.
Hirshfield, Lynn. *Girls Gone Green.* New York: Puffin Books, 2010.
Sheldon, Dyan. *The Crazy Things Girls Do for Love.* Somerville, MA:
    Candlewick Press, 2011.

The Omnivore's Dilemma: The Secrets Behind What You Eat (A Young Readers Edition), by Michael Pollan and adapted by Richie Chevat (Dial Books)

Type of Book Club: Tween, Intergenerational (Parent-Child)
Book Type: Fiction
Book Description: Readers join Pollan on his quest to discover exactly where our food comes from and what type of meal is ideal for human health, animal welfare, and environmental protection. In each of the four sections of the book, Pollan explores the food chain for four different types of meals, which he defines as industrial, industrial organic, local sustainable, and do-it-yourself. Pollan argues that as natural omnivores, humans don't have that "built-in instinct that tells us which foods are good for us and which aren't." We eat everything, and in our modern world we are even more separated from where our food comes from that knowing what's good and what isn't becomes even trickier. Some sections are difficult to read and might make you begin to wonder what you can eat without causing harm to someone or something. An afterword titled "Vote with Your Fork" and another section titled "Some Tips for Eating," however, provide concrete and positive steps that young people can take to make their eating habits healthier for them, for the environment, and for society as a whole.

Icebreaker

Before the book club meeting, write different types of foods in the following categories on slips of paper: meat, vegetables, fruit, and dessert. Set up the chairs in a circle. Give each participant a slip of paper that he or she shouldn't show to other people. The leader will start by saying, "I like to eat _____," filling in the blank with one of the categories. Anyone that has something in that category has to stand up and find another seat to sit down in. While the participants are switching seats, the leader also sits down so that one person is left without a seat. That person then repeats the phrase, or he or she can say, "I like to eat everything," and then everyone has to find a new seat. Play a few rounds.

Author Description

Michael Pollan grew up in Long Island, NY. He studied at Bennington College and Oxford University and earned a master's degree in English from Columbia University. He has written numerous books and articles on issues related to food, the environment, and human health. He has received several awards and honors for his books and articles, including that *The Omnivore's Dilemma* was named one of the top ten books of 2006 by both the *New York Times* and the *Washington Post*. In 2009, he was named one of the top-ten "New Thought Leaders" by *Newsweek,* and *Time* included him on its list of the world's one hundred most influential people in 2010. You can learn more about Pollan and his books at the following website: http://michaelpollan.com. The young reader's edition of *The Omnivore's Dilemma* also includes a special Q&A section about Pollan.

Discussion Questions

- What does Pollan mean by the "omnivore's dilemma"?
- Pollan states at the beginning of the book, "But the point of this book is not to scare you or make you afraid of food." Did he succeed, or has he scared you?
- What is a typical supper at your house like?
- What are GMOs? What do you think about them?
- Greg Naylor, the farmer from Iowa in the book, said several times to Pollan, "There's money to be made in food, unless you're trying to grow it." What does he mean by that?
- Do you agree with Pollan that the United States does not have any food traditions?
- Do you think that processed food, like frozen dinners, should be labeled organic?

- How would you define whether something is organic?
- How is the Salatins' farm more like a natural ecosystem?
- What do you think about Pollan's statement, "It's always better to know more rather than less even when that knowledge complicates your life"?
- Are you, personally, truly able to "vote with your fork" at your home and school?

Extension Activities

- Have the participants keep a log of their meals (what they eat and where it comes from) over a period of time and then share their findings with the group to see which category most of their meals and snacks fit into (industrial agriculture, industrial organic, local sustainable, or do-it-yourself).
- Watch and discuss the movie *What's on Your Plate?* The film follows two eleven-year-old girls who live in New York City as they learn about their place in the food chain.

FURTHER READING

Burgan, Michael. *Making Food Choices. Ethics of Food.* Chicago: Heinemann Library, 2012.

D'Aluisio, Faith. *What the World Eats.* Berkeley, CA: Tricycle Press, 2008.

Gund, Catherine, dir. *What's on Your Plate? Kids and Their Families Talk about What They Eat, Where It Comes from, and Why That Matters.* DVD; New York: Aubin Pictures, 2010.

The White Giraffe by Lauren St. John (Dial Books)

Type of Book Club: Tween

Book Type: Fiction

Book Description: "The night Martine Allen turned eleven years old was the night her life changed completely and was never the same again." That night, Martine loses both her parents in a house fire. An only child, she gets sent to live with a grandmother she never knew she had who lives on a game reserve in South Africa. Martine struggles to fit in at her new school and adjust to her new life with a grandmother who doesn't seem to want her there at all. Shortly after she arrives, she hears rumors of a white giraffe living on the reserve. Her grandmother insists it's a legend, but Martine senses that it does really exist and hopes she can protect it from the poachers who have been attacking animals on the reserve recently. The story is one of new beginnings and learning to tap into one's inner strength.

Icebreaker

Have each member of the group write down an animal that you might find in South Africa on a piece of paper, without showing it to anyone else. Collect all of the papers and put them in a bowl. One by one have someone draw a paper and then act out the animal (with sounds) while the rest of the group tries to guess what he or she is.

Author Information

Lauren St. John has worked for many years as a journalist and biographer, but this is her first book for children. She was born in Zimbabwe, and from the age of eleven she lived on a farm that was part game reserve. She drew on many of her childhood experiences in writing this book. She has stated both in an author's note in the book and on her website that in writing the book, she hoped to inspire young people to help wildlife wherever they live and to learn more about or even visit Africa. There are three other books in the White Giraffe series: *Dolphin Song, The Last Leopard,* and *The Elephant's Tale.* For more about Lauren St. John and her books, visit her website: www.laurenstjohn.com/#/home. St. John also includes information about herself and background information about the book in an author's note at the end of *The White Giraffe.*

Background Information

South Africa lies at the tip of Africa, a land of extremes and great beauty. Rugged coastlines hug the country on three sides: the Atlantic Ocean to the west and the Indian Ocean to the south and east. About two-thirds of the country is a plateau covered by the Highveld, or rolling grasslands, and the Bushveld, or grasslands interspersed with trees. The highest point of the plateau is at 8,000 feet (2,440 meters), located in the east near Lesotho, and the lowest point is at 2000 feet (610 meters), located in the west in the Kalahari Desert. Not many people live in the plateau region, so most of it remains wild, but it is also home to many of the vast mineral resources of the country, such as gold, uranium, and diamonds. The Great Escarpment is a chain of mountains that surround the high plateau to the east, south, and west. The eastern region of this chain is called Drakensberg, from the Dutch and Afrikaans for "dragon mountains." The climate in most of the plateau is mild with moderate rain—mainly in the summer as thunderstorms. As the plateau moves toward the south and west, however, it forms the area known as the Karoo, or "land of thirst" in the San language, which, as its name suggests, is extremely arid. The northeastern region of the country is mainly savanna and tends to have a warmer, more tropical climate. Often referred to as the Lowveld, it contains the majority of the wildlife associated with African savannas. South Africa has very few forested areas, and those that exist are found along the southeastern coast. These areas tend to be warmer and more humid.

With its variety of climates and habitats, South Africa possesses one of the highest diversity of plants in Africa, with nearly 20 percent of all plants found on the continent. In addition, about 70 percent of plants in South Africa are endemic, found there and nowhere else in the world. In The White Elephant, the students visit the Kirstenbosch National Botanical Garden, which is an actual botanical garden in the foothills of Cape Town's Table Mountain. The garden features plant communities from around South Africa, but it highlights in particular fynbos, a vegetation type that is part of the Cape Floral kingdom, one of the six floral kingdoms of the world. Fynbos comes from the Afrikaans for "fine bush," and many of the plants in this habitat are small, evergreen shrubs with thin leaves, including ericas (heather) and restios. The other major plant family included in fynbos is the protea, which is the national flower of South Africa. Fynbos plants are adapted to living in the low-nutrient soils of the southwest Cape, and they rely on fire to recycle nutrients back into the soil and for the opening of many of the seedpods of the plants found in this region. It is one of the most diverse vegetation types in the world, made up of about nine thousand species.

The White Giraffe is set in a fictional town, Storm Crossing, which is about two hours outside of Cape Town. The second-largest city in South Africa, Cape Town reflects the history of its country with its multicultural mix and cosmopolitan atmosphere. The Portuguese were the first to round the Cape of Good Hope in the late 1400s looking for a trade route to Asia. They and the Dutch often used the area around Cape Town as a pit stop to trade goods with the local people and to replenish their freshwater supplies. In 1652, the Dutchman Jan van Riebeeck established Cape Town as a permanent settlement, but long before Europeans arrived, the San and Khoikhoi people inhabited the area. As the need for labor grew in the new settlement slaves were brought from Madagascar, India, Ceylon (now Sri Lanka), and Indonesia. In 1814, as a result of wars in Europe, Cape Town fell under British rule. After the Boer War, the British gained control of all of the colonies in South Africa and established the Union of South Africa in 1914, making Cape Town the parliamentary capital of the union and Pretoria the administrative capital. Boer is the Dutch word for farmer and was the name given to early Dutch settlers of Africa. They later came to be known as Afrikaners. In 1948, the Afrikaners' political party, the National Party, came into power and established the system of apartheid. In 1961, Prime Minister Hendrik Verwoerd declared South Africa a republic and withdrew from the British Commonwealth, partly because of international backlash against apartheid. All of these different cultures and ethnic backgrounds can be found in Cape Town today, and Cape Town's history has really shaped what it is today.

As St. John points out in the author's note at the end of The White Giraffe, the savanna described in the book doesn't really exist that close to Cape Town. The Lowveld, or savanna, is further north and to the east, as are the majority of the game reserves, which are home to the large animals mentioned in the book, such as giraffes, elephants, and lions. For example, Kruger National Park, one of the largest game reserves in all of Africa, is located along the country's border with Mozambique and Zimbabwe. Recently, however, many private game reserves have been established outside of Cape Town, similar to the one described in The White Giraffe.

South Africa is home to about forty-nine million people from a variety of backgrounds. The official languages of the country are IsiZulu, IsiXhosa, Afrikaans, Sepedi, English, Setswana, Sesotho, Xitsonga, isiNdebele, Tshivenda, and siSwati. The largest ethnic groups in the country are the Zulu, Xhosa, and Sotho. Although apartheid no longer exists, its legacy lingers, with the majority of the black population still living in poverty while most whites enjoy a comfortable lifestyle. Many neighborhoods still remain segregated, as well, with many blacks still living in townships that were established under apartheid. An influx of people moving from the countryside to large cities like Johannesburg, Durban, and Cape Town has also led to shanty towns springing up in various places.

The following resources provide more information on South Africa:

Blauer, Ettagale, and Jason Lauré. *South Africa*. Rev. ed. New York: Children's Press, 2006.

CIA. "The World Factbook: South Africa." 2014. www.cia.gov/library/publications/the-world-factbook/geos/sf.html.

Gelletly, LeeAnne. *Ecological Issues. Africa: Progress and Problems*. Broomall, PA: Mason Crest Publishers, 2007.

Gleimius, Nita, Evelina Sibanyoni, and Emma Mthimunye. *The Zulu of Africa*. Minneapolis, MN: Lerner Publications, 2003.

Hoberman, Gerald, and John C. Manning. *South Africa's Floral Kingdom*. Cape Town: Gerald and Marc Hoberman Collection, 2008.

Kirstenbosch National Botanical Garden. www.sanbi.org/gardens/kirstenbosch.

Mace, Virginia. *South Africa*. Washington, DC: National Geographic Society, 2008.

South Africa Info. www.southafrica.info.

Discussion Questions

- Do you agree with Martine that bad things usually come in threes? Has this ever happened to you?

- In what ways does Martine find comfort in nature? In what type of environments do you find comfort?
- Did Martine's mother do the right thing in keeping her away from Africa? What would you have done if you were her mother?
- Martine has to adjust to not only a new country but also a new school. Have you ever been the new person in a situation? How did you deal with it?
- What do you think about Martine's gift with animals?
- Martine believes strongly in helping protect animals. In what ways can we protect animals in our own city, state, or country?
- Did your opinion about any of the characters change as the story progressed? In what way?
- What are some ways that traditional healers in Africa have used plants that Martine learns about in the book? Do you know of any plants that grow in your area that have special uses?

Extension Activities

- Have participants research the different plants or animals found in South Africa. On the basis of their research, they can create shoe-box dioramas that depict different plants or animals and then present them to the group. These could also be put on display, along with explanatory signs or notes, in the library or in an area in the museum.
- As a group, visit a natural history museum or a zoo that has an exhibit on Africa.

FURTHER READING

Johnson, Julia. *The Leopard Boy*. London: Frances Lincoln Children's, 2011.
St. John, Lauren. *Dolphin Song*. New York: Dial Books, 2008.
St. John, Lauren. *The Elephant's Tale*. New York: Dial Books, 2010.
St. John, Lauren. *The Last Leopard*. New York: Dial Books, 2009.

The Devil's Teeth: A True Story of Obsession and Survival among America's Great White Sharks
by Susan Casey (Henry Holt)

Type of Book Club: Older Teen, Service Oriented

Book Type: Nonfiction

Book Description: After watching a BBC documentary on great white sharks that make yearly visits to the waters around the Farallon Islands off the coast of California, Casey is hooked. She becomes determined to find a way to tell the story of two shark scientists, Peter Pyle and Scot Anderson, and the mysterious behemoths of the deep they study. Only twenty-seven miles off the coast from San Francisco, the Farallon Islands are a desolate and harsh environment where only a small group of scientists live. To truly dive into her story, however, Casey receives special permission to spend a shark season with the infamous scientists and shadow them in their work. Blood, gore, violent storms, colorful characters, and even a ghost fill the riveting narrative of this book.

Icebreaker
In the book, the scientists give the sharks nicknames to distinguish among them more easily. Many of the nicknames are based on characteristics of each shark. Have each participant say what his or her nickname would be if an anthropologist was studying him or her, and why. When everyone has shared their nickname, the group could discuss whether they think it is a good idea for scientists to give the animals they are studying nicknames. Does this create too much of an emotional connection that prevents them from being good scientists?

Author Information
Susan Casey has had a long career with various magazines. She worked as an editor for Time Inc. and *Sports Illustrated Women*. She also was the creative director for *Outside* magazine, and is currently the editor in chief of *O, The Oprah Magazine*. She has written articles for various magazines and published another book, *The Wave: In Pursuit of the Rogues, Freaks, and*

Giants of the Ocean in 2010. For more information on Casey, you can visit her website: www.susancasey.com. She also has links to many of the organizations mentioned in the book on her website. The publisher of the book also has a website of the book, which includes a brief biography of Casey, a short video of sharks around the Farallones, and links to other organizations (http://us.macmillan.com/thedevilsteeth).

Discussion Questions

- What do you think of Casey's portrayal of great white sharks?
- What does the book show you about being a scientist? What do scientists do? Is this something you would want to do? Why or why not?
- At one point Casey says, "I wondered how a place as primitive as the Farallones could possibly survive sharing a zip code with seven million people. I was afraid that it couldn't." Why do you think it has survived or do you even think it has survived? What do you think the future holds for the Farallones?
- What do you think of the commercial diving operation that operates near the Farallones?
- Do you think some places should be left wild with no human intervention?
- What do you make of the ghost stories on the Farallones?
- How would you describe an obsession? Is Casey obsessed? Are Peter and Scot? If so, in what ways?

Extension Activities

- Invite a shark scientist or marine biologist to talk to the group. If there are not any scientists like this in your area, you could look into having one give a virtual talk via Skype or another teleconferencing system.
- If you live near an ocean, river, or stream, have the group do a beach or watershed cleanup.

FURTHER READING

Benchley, Peter. *Shark Trouble: True Stories about Sharks and the Sea.*
    New York: Random House, 2002.
Eilperin, Juliet. *Demon Fish: Travels Through the Hidden World of Sharks.*
    New York: Pantheon Books, 2011.
Ellis, Richard, and John E. McCosker. *Great White Shark.* New York:
    HarperCollins, in collaboration with Stanford University Press, 1991.
Monninger, Joseph. *Wish.* New York: Delacorte Press, 2010.

Evolution, Me & Other Freaks of Nature
by Robin Brande (Alfred A. Knopf)

Type of Book Club: Teen, Intergenerational (Parent-Child)
Book Type: Fiction
Book Description: Mena was looking forward to starting high school—new friends, new teachers, and new adventures. She had been kicked out of her church right before starting school and has been ostracized by her friends from junior high, so she's looking forward to a fresh start. Instead, she quickly finds herself continuing to be shunned by her old friends and her parents as she becomes embroiled in the debate over evolution versus intelligent design. The only bright spot in her life is her smart, funny, and cute biology lab partner. Will Mena find a way to reconcile her religious beliefs with her blossoming interest in science?

Icebreaker
Evolution has led to the diversity of life we find today. There are different animals that live in the water, some that fly through the air, and others that live on land. Have the members of the group stand in a circle. Give one person a small ball that is not hard (a Hacky Sack will also work). The person should throw the ball to someone else in the circle while saying "land," "air," or "water." Depending on which word the first person says, the second person needs to catch the ball and immediately name an animal that lives there. For example, if the first person says, "Land," then the second person could

say, "Elephant." That person then throws it to someone else, again saying "land," "air," or "water." The person who gets the ball can't repeat an animal that has already been said. If that person does, then he or she is out of the circle. Likewise, if a person takes too long to come up with an answer, he or she has to leave the circle. The last person standing is the winner.

Author Information

Robin Brande worked as an attorney prior to starting her writing career. *Evolution, Me & Other Freaks of Nature* was her first novel for young adults, and she has since written several other books, including *Fat Cat, Doggirl, Replay,* and the Parallelogram series. In several interviews, she has mentioned that she, like Mena, was raised with a fundamentalist Christian background and was kicked out of her church right before high school. She also began to struggle with her faith when she was in high school and began learning things in her science classes that conflicted with the beliefs with which she had grown up. You can find out more about Brande and her books at the following websites:

Becky's Book Reviews—"Interview with Robin Brande," http://
blbooks.blogspot.com/2008/02/interview-with-robin-brande.html.
HipWriterMama—http://hipwritermama.blogspot.com/2008/05/
sbbt-2008-inspiration-evolution-and.html.
Robin Brande's website—http://robinbrande.com.

Background Information:

In 1831, at the age of twenty-two, Charles Darwin boarded the HMS *Beagle* to join a coastal surveying expedition that would take him around the world. Darwin was offered to join the crew as an unpaid naturalist. During the journey, he would make many observations and collect myriad specimens that would inform what would later become one of the most important theories in biology.

At the time that Darwin started his voyage, it was widely believed that all life had arrived on this earth fully formed and had remained unchanged since its creation. What Darwin found on his journey caused him to begin to doubt that this was true. He found fossils of extinct animals, such as a giant sloth, that resembled a modern sloth. At that time, few people were even aware that fossils existed, and the fossils that had been discovered were thought to be animals that had died in the great flood described in the Bible. Darwin saw something different. He was fascinated by the similarities between the fossils and much smaller living animals.

When the *Beagle* visited the Galapagos Islands, Darwin collected many specimens of small birds that had different types of beaks. He assumed that they belonged to different families of birds since they looked so different. It was only later that he would find out that they were all in the same family—they were all finches.

He also made several geological observations that influenced the development of his theory. While on the journey, he read Charles Lyell's *Principles of Geology,* a book that had introduced the idea that Earth is not immutable and has gone through changes due to slow-moving forces. Darwin began to observe different phenomena that seemed to support the arguments Lyell was making. High in the Andes Mountains he discovered fossils of marine organisms, which he concluded could have reached those altitudes only if at one time the mountains had been underwater. He also witnessed volcanic eruptions and experienced an earthquake in Chile, which affected the landscape around where these events took place.

When Darwin returned to England in 1837, he began to analyze all of the specimens he had collected and interpret his many observations from the trip. He spent years collecting evidence to support his theory and reworking his writings while also undertaking several other projects. Darwin wrestled with making his theory public since he knew it would upset the bedrock upon which science and society was based. Since returning from his voyage, Darwin had married, and his wife, Emma, was an extremely religious person. He truly feared that if he published his theory of evolution, he would not go to heaven since it would mean turning his back on God, and he would be separated for all of eternity from his wife.

In June 1858, a colleague of Darwin's, Alfred Russel Wallace, sent him an essay for Darwin to look over and critique. When Darwin read it, he was astounded. It was nearly exactly the same as the theory of evolution that he himself had been working on. It was decided that a joint paper introducing the theory of evolution would be presented to the Linnean Society, which was done with little fanfare or reaction from the general public.

In 1859, Darwin published his book *On the Origin of Species by Means of Natural Selection,* which is a more detailed outline of his theory of evolution. It attracted great attention, with all of the 1,250 copies of the first edition selling out in just a few hours. Since its publication more than 150 years ago, it has never been out of print.

In the book, Darwin outlines two major points. First, he demonstrates how all life forms that exist on Earth today are descendants of ancestral species. Life on Earth can be compared to a tree, with all life coming from a single ancestor and then evolving over millions of years into different species, which form the different branches on this tree. Some branches are dead ends, and others might have pieces missing, with certain animals that have gone extinct. Scientists can use the fossil record, however, to show those links and demonstrate evolution.

The other major point Darwin made is that the mechanism of this evolutionary process is known as natural selection. Natural selection basically means that those organisms that have traits that are best suited for a particular environment will have greater success at producing offspring, and therefore will be more likely to pass on those traits to their offspring. Over millions of years, these traits can cause the species to change and evolve, and eventually, there are enough changes that they give rise to a new species.

The following resources have more information on Darwin and the theory of evolution:

The Complete Works of Darwin Online. http://darwin-online.org.uk.

Fleisher, Paul. *Evolution.* Minneapolis, MN: Lerner Publications, 2006.

Heiligman, Deborah. *Charles and Emma: The Darwins' Leap of Faith.* New York: Henry Holt, 2009.

King, David C. *Charles Darwin.* New York: DK Publishing, 2007.

University of California Museum of Paleontology. "Understanding Evolution." http://evolution.berkeley.edu.

Discussion Questions

- At one point in the book, Mena says, "Everything happens for a reason, right?" Do you agree or disagree with this? Why?
- What do you think about Mena's approach to dealing with Theresa's and Adam's bullying of her?
- What is science? What does it mean to be scientific?
- What is the definition of *theory* in science?
- Can you be both scientific and religious?
- Where do you think the author stands on whether you can be both scientific and religious?
- Should you always do what you think is right even if it means you might lose friends or make others mad?
- Do you think Mena was right to write the letter to Denny Pierce?
- Would you recommend this book to a friend? To your parents? Who would you not recommend it to? Why?

Extension Activities

- As a group, visit a natural history museum that has an exhibit focused on evolution.
- Watch and discuss the program *Judgement Day: Intelligent Design on Trial*. The program originally aired on the PBS show *NOVA*, and it portrays the conflict that arose when a school board in Dover, Pennsylvania, tried to introduce intelligent design into the high school's biology curriculum.

FURTHER READING

Bryant, Jennifer. *Ringside, 1925: Views from the Scopes Trial.* New York: Alfred A. Knopf, 2008.

Heiligman, Deborah. *Charles and Emma: The Darwins' Leap of Faith.* New York: Henry Holt, 2009.

Kidd, Ronald. *Monkey Town: A Story of the Scopes Trial.* New York: Simon and Schuster Books for Young Readers, 2006.

Exodus by Julie Bertagna (Walker)

Type of Book Club: Teen, Service Oriented

Book Type: Fiction

Book Description: The ice caps and glaciers have melted, flooding new water into the world's oceans. In this futuristic novel, the northern island of Wing is quickly losing land to the ocean. The residents make the hard decision to set out to search for a new place to live, spurred on by fifteen-year-old Mara, who has learned about sky cities. These technologically advanced cities, high above the rising seas, might just be the salvation for the people of Wing. The residents set out in simple boats and arrive at the walls of a sky city, New Mungo, only to realize that getting in is not so easy. Mara must set out on a quest to try to save her community, no matter the risks.

Icebreaker

In the book, the Treenesters each have a name based on where they were originally from. If you could choose anywhere in the world to be from, where would that be? What would be your place-name? Have each participant say his or her real name and then his or her place-name. After everyone has shared this, you can get into a discussion about how it would feel to have to leave the place you live in because the ocean is swallowing it up.

Author Information

Julie Bertagna grew up just outside of Glasgow in Scotland. She studied English literature in university and has worked as an editor of a magazine, a teacher, and a journalist. She has written several other books for children and teens. *Exodus* is the first in a trilogy of books, which includes *Zenith* and *Aurora*. According to her website, Bertagna was inspired to write *Exodus* after reading an article in 1999 that "should have stopped the world in its tracks."[9] The story related how two South Pacific islands had simply disappeared—had flooded and been taken over completely by the sea. Many more islands in the area were at risk, and islanders needed to evacuate, but no one knew exactly where they would go. Bertagna was shocked at the apathy of most of the world in reaction to this news. She started doing research on climate change and decided to write her novel. For more information on Bertagna, you can visit her website, which includes a brief biography, information on her books, and an environmental blog titled *Earthspace*, which she created in response to the many questions she received from readers of the Exodus trilogy (www.juliebertagna.com/start.html).

Background Information:

The first thing to keep in mind when talking about climate change is the difference between climate and weather. Climate is the pattern of weather in a certain area over a long period of time. Climate looks at averages of different factors of weather over a long period of time. Weather is the changes in the atmosphere over a short period of time—the day-to-day changes we experience. It includes rain, sunshine, wind, cold temperatures or hot temperatures, humidity, and so on. For a detailed description of the difference between weather and climate, see NASA's "What's the Difference between Weather and Climate?" (www.nasa.gov/mission_pages/noaa-n/climate/climate_weather.html).

Although many members of the scientific community and the general American public accept global climate change as a very real phenomenon that has largely been caused by human activities, there are still many skeptics that exist. The website How to Talk to a Climate Skeptic: Responses to the Most Common Skeptical Arguments on Global Warming, maintained by *Grist* magazine, provides answers to many questions or comments postulated by climate change skeptics (www.grist.org/article/series/skeptics). This is a useful website to turn to if there are questions that come up in your discussion of the book.

Global climate change poses a very real threat to humans and other life on Earth. *Exodus* presents some possible results of global climate change—the melting of glaciers, ice caps, and sea ice, as well as rising sea levels. At both poles, changes are occurring. Scientists have discovered that since the 1970s, the water in the southern ocean has gotten warmer, causing the Antarctic ice mass to melt on the edges and recede. A similar fate is occurring in Greenland. Like Antarctica, Greenland is a mass of land covered by a dome of ice, which on average is about five thousand feet thick. Scientists have found that there, too, the ice sheet is melting in areas, creating pools of meltwater. These pools are and have been a normal phenomenon, but the difference in the trend in recent years is the increase in number and frequency of them. This causes overall instability of the ice sheet, and more melting.

Mountain glaciers have also receded dramatically over time. Looking at historical photography from the turn of the twentieth century and comparing it with pictures of mountain glaciers today, many of them have shrunk a great deal or even disappeared nearly completely. Rising temperatures and changes in precipitation patterns due to climate change have affected mountain glaciers' ability to replenish ice as it melts. Scientists from Ohio State University who study the glaciers on Mt. Kilimanjaro in Africa have reported that looking at data collected starting in 1912 and analyzing them with other data collected up to the year 2000 (including data collected by their team), about 82 percent of the ice fields have been lost.[10]

As this new water from melting land ice (glaciers and the ice sheets of Antarctica and Greenland) enters the ocean, it causes a rise in overall sea level. Melting of ice that is already in the ocean, however, does not directly cause a rise in sea level because of the properties of water. Water, unlike other liquids, expands when it freezes. Most liquids become denser and contract when they cool. Water follows this same pattern, but only up to a point, because of its molecular structure. Just before freezing (at about 4 degrees Celsius), water molecules arrange themselves into a crystal lattice structure, becoming less dense than the liquid form. Because of this, ice always floats on water. Because ice floats, it is not completely submerged in the water and displaces only the amount of water equal to its mass. When it melts, it will return the same amount of water as it was displacing, thus not altering the overall amount of water in the ocean.

Melting sea ice can indirectly affect sea-level rise, however, because of a reduction in albedo, which is the amount of solar energy a surface reflects. Ice, which is lighter in color, reflects most sunlight, but the open ocean, which is darker in color, absorbs most of the heat from sunlight. This causes the water to warm up, which then leads to further melting of ice sheets in Antarctica and Greenland.

The following resources provide further information on melting glaciers and ice sheets and sea-level rise due to climate change, as well as other effects of climate change and some of the science behind it:

Cherry, Lynne and Gary Braasch. *How We Know What We Know about Our Changing Climate: Scientists and Kids Explore Global Warming.* Nevada City, CA: Dawn Publications, 2008.

Climate Institute. "Oceans & Sea Level Rise." www.climate.org/topics/sea-level/index.html.

CSIRO Marine and Atmospheric Research. "Sea Level Rise." www.cmar.csiro.au/sealevel/index.html.

Dow, Kirstin, and Thomas E. Downing. *The Atlas of Climate Change: Mapping the World's Greatest Challenge.* Rev. ed. Berkeley: University of California Press, 2007.

Gore, Al. *An Inconvenient Truth: The Planetary Emergency of Global Warming and What We Can Do About It.* Emmaus, PA: Rodale Press, 2006.

Intergovernmental Panel on Climate Change. "IPCC Fourth Assessment Report: Climate Change 2007." www.ipcc.ch/publications _and_data/publications_and_data_reports.shtml#1.

Discussion Questions

- What do you think about the decision to leave the "old ones" on the island when everyone else goes to search for New Mungo?
- How would you survive in a world like the one in *Exodus*?
- What exactly are the "ratbashers"?
- Why do you think Wing doesn't eat his sparrow?
- What do you think about the Treenesters putting all of their faith in the "Face in the Stone" to save them? Are there any similarities in this to how people are reacting to climate change today?
- What characteristics does Mara have that help her in her quest?
- Would you follow Mara's advice: "When in doubt, always take the most curious route?" Why or why not?

- What do you think about life in New Mungo? Would you want to live there?
- At one point, Gorbals and Mara are talking about the achievements of humans. Gorbals says, "A human being is the greatest creation of all. Each of us is a new living dream." To which Mara replies, "Except we've become a living nightmare." With which of these statements do you agree and why?
- New Mungo depends on new technologies and science. Can science be both a blessing and a curse?

Extension Activities

- Have participants investigate ways that they could mitigate the effects of climate change in their own community and then implement a project. See chapter 8, on environmental action clubs, for more advice and/or the following resources:

    - David, Laurie and Cambria Gordon. *The Down-to-Earth Guide to Global Warming.* New York: Orchard Books, 2007.
    - Environmental Protection Agency. "A Student's Guide to Global Climate Change." www.epa.gov/climatechange/kids/index.html.
    - Green Schools Initiative. www.greenschools.net.
    - National Geographic. "The Green Guide." http://environment.nationalgeographic.com/environment/green-guide.
    - National Resources Defense Council. "The Green Squad: Kid's Taking Action for Greener, Healthier Schools." www.nrdc.org/greensquad/intro/intro_1.asp.
    - US Conference of Mayors. "Climate Protection Center." www.usmayors.org/climateprotection/revised.

- Have participants calculate their carbon footprint and then write a pledge of ways they can change their lifestyles to reduce the amount of carbon they are adding to the atmosphere. The following websites have carbon calculators:

- Environmental Protection Agency. "Household Emissions Calculator." www.epa.gov/climatechange/emissions/ ind_calculator.html.
- Nature Conservancy. "Carbon Footprint Calculator: What's My Carbon Footprint?" www.nature.org/ greenliving/carboncalculator/index.htm.

FURTHER READING

Bertagna, Julie. *Aurora*. New York: Macmillan Children's, 2011.

Bertagna, Julie. *Zenith*. New York: Walker, 2009.

Flannery, Tim F. *We Are the Weather Makers: The History of Climate Change*. Somerville, MA: Candlewick Press, 2009.

Lloyd, Saci. *Carbon Diaries, 2015*. New York: Holiday House, 2009.

Nausicaä of the Valley of the Wind, Volumes 1 and 2
by Hayao Miyazaki (VIZ Media)

Type of Book Club: Teen, Book-to-Movie

Book Type: Fiction

Book Description: *Nausicaä of the Valley of the Wind* is actually a seven-volume series. For the book club, I recommend reading volumes 1 and 2, since these are the two volumes that correlate most closely to the movie. The book is set in a time thousands of years after the Seven Days of Fire, a great war that destroyed most of human civilization and wreaked ecological devastation. Enclaves of humans live in settlements scattered around the globe, the last remnants of humanity that haven't been engulfed by the Sea of Corruption—a forest full of fungi, which exude poisonous spores, and hoards of deadly insects.

One of these small enclaves is the Valley of the Wind, where Princess Nausicaä will soon become the chieftain of the community since her father is dying, having succumbed to the poisonous spores of the Sea of Corruption. The Valley of the Wind, similar to other outlying communities, has signed treaties aligning it with the Torumekian Empire, which has declared war on the Dorok principalities. All of the outlying communities are called to go to battle, and Princess Nausicaä sets out on her first battle, but she soon learns that all is not as it seems in war. With her strong connection to the natural world and her gentle heart, Nausicaä soon struggles with whether the war itself will end up destroying all of humanity and whether there is a better way to save her people.

Icebreaker

Divide the participants into groups of four or five. Assign each group a chair. If you have four groups, set up the chairs in a cross formation, with space in between all four chairs. If you have two groups, set the chairs facing each other but with a large space in between the two. Everyone should take off their shoes and put them in the space in the middle of the chairs. Tell the participants that the shoes represent the chiko nuts from the story. The participants are citizens of the Valley of the Wind, and they have to try to collect as many chiko nuts as they can. They are collecting them in the forest, though, so there is the miasma all around, and it is hard to see. One representative at a time will have to try to collect the chiko nuts, but he or she will be blindfolded. They also have to collect the chiko nuts on their hands and knees and place them underneath their assigned chair. The other members of the team should stand on the edges between the chairs, partially to help keep the blindfolded members from straying too far. They can also shout directions to their teammate who is collecting the nuts. Give each team two minutes to collect as many nuts as it can. Count up the nuts after the first round and record this. Play a few rounds and see which team collects the most. After the game, talk about how the different participants felt in the activity. Was it easier to find the nuts with the help of their teammates? This could also lead into a discussion of depending on others when completing a task, or whether they think Nausicaä did this in the book or if she tended to go it alone too often.

Author Information

Hayao Miyazaki was born in 1941 in Tokyo, Japan. His father was an aeronautical engineer, and Miyazaki was fascinated with his father's work in his youth and into adulthood. He transferred this fascination into his artwork, with his detailed depictions of aircraft in his books and films.

He studied economics and political science at Gakushuin University with the intention of going into a career that would help rebuild the economy of his country after the devastation of World War II. After graduating, however, he went to work for the animation studio Toei Doga. He created the background scenery in several animated films and fell in love with this type of work.

Miyazaki is considered by many to be one of the most influential animators worldwide. He has written numerous manga and created various well-known anime films, such as *Princess Mononoke, Spirited Away,* and *Ponyo.* His stories often interweave environmental themes and have strong female characters. The following online resources have more information about Miyazaki and his work:

Brooks, Xan. "A God among Animators." *The Guardian.* September 14, 2005. www.guardian.co.uk/film/2005/sep/14/japan.awards andprizes.

"Hayao Miyazaki." www.notablebiographies.com/newsmakers2/ 2006-Le-Ra/Miyazaki-Hayao.html.

The Hayao Miyazaki Web. www.nausicaa.net/miyazaki.

Background Information

The VIZ Media version of *Nausicaä of the Valley of the Wind,* volume 1, has an article at the end that talks about the Nausicaä of Greek mythology, a character in Homer's Odyssey. Miyazaki discusses how this character, as well as another heroine from Japanese literature who was known as the "princess that loved insects," influenced his creation of Nausicaä in his book.

Discussion Questions

- Both volumes are set in the future, but do you see any parallels between the reality in the book and what is happening today?
- What connection does Nausicaä have to the ohmu?

- What connection does Nausicaä have with nature?
- In volume 2, Nausicaä says to the Dorok priest, "Forgive my violence holy one, but I have to stop the fighting at any cost." Is violence ever justified?
- Nausicaä's father advises her on how to act in the face of a crisis to be a good leader. He says, "The greater the crisis, the calmer you must be, like a pinnacle of rock in the whirlwind." What do you think about this advice? How do you react in a crisis?
- Nausicaä has her secret garden where she shows the beauty of the forest. How do most people react to the forest in the book? How do people view forests or other habitats today?
- What do you think the ohmu meant when it said, "Our race is as one. Each of us in the whole, the whole in each of us"?
- What do you think about Nausicaä and Asbel's plan to convince the periphery armies to join forces with the Dorok to fight the Vai Emperor? Can war stop war?
- The Doroks torture a baby ohmu to lure the other ohmus into fighting for them in a battle. In what ways do humans use animals today that are beneficial to humans but harmful to animals?
- What is the daikaisho?

Extension Activities

- As a group watch the movie version of *Nausicaä of the Valley of the Wind* and have a discussion comparing the two.
- The insects and fungi in the book play a role in purifying Earth. Have the book club members research what roles different insects or fungi play in the ecosystems where they live and then share their findings with the rest of the group.

FURTHER READING

Miyazaki, Hayao. *Nausicaä of the Valley of the Wind*. Vols. 4–7. San Francisco: VIZ Media, 2004.
Shitou, Kyoko. *Blue Inferior*. Vol. 1. Houston, TX: ADV Manga, 2004.

Seedfolks by Paul Fleischman (HarperCollins)

Type of Book Club: Teen, Service Oriented
Book Type: Fiction
Book Description: Kim, a young Vietnamese American girl, decides to plant some lima bean seeds in a vacant lot near her apartment building in inner-city Cleveland, as a way to honor her father, whom she never knew. This small act triggers a chain reaction, and soon several other neighbors decide to plant their own things as well. Eventually, the abandoned and trash-filled lot becomes a vibrant community garden. The book consists of thirteen vignettes, each narrated by a different person recalling his or her connection to the garden. Readers witness what it means to be part of a community—both the barriers that keep people apart, such as prejudices and different attitudes, and the strengths that can join people together.

Icebreaker

Have each participant say his or her name and then what he or she would plant in a community garden and why. This could then lead into a discussion of how the different characters in the book decided what to plant in the garden.

Author Information

Paul Fleischman grew up in Santa Monica, California, in a house filled with words. His father is Sid Fleischman, who is also an author, and while he was growing up, his father would often read his books to Sid and his siblings as they were being written. Both father and son have won the Newbery Medal, Paul for *A Joyful Noise: Poems for Two Voices* in 1989 and Sid for *The Whipping Boy* in 1987.

Music also filled the Fleischman household. Paul and his mother both played the piano, his father played the guitar, and his sisters played the flute. When he was in college, he played the recorder and joined a recorder group that toured. On his website, Fleischman shares, "In the past twenty years I've been drawn to America's most-loathed quartet of instruments—the accordion, banjo, bagpipes, and bassoon."[11] His writing reflects his fascination with music not only in his poetry but also in the musicality of his prose.

He has written several novels for young adults, picture books, poetry and plays. Besides, the Newbery, he has won numerous other awards and honors for his writing. On his website, he has an informative article titled "From Seed to Seedfolks" that describes how the idea for *Seedfolks* first came to him and the process he went through in writing it. To read this article and find out more information about Fleischman, visit the following websites:

Houghton Mifflin Reading. "Meet the Author Paul Fleischman."
www.eduplace.com/kids/hmr/mtai/fleischman.html.
"Paul Fleischman." www.paulfleischman.net/index.htm.
"Paul Fleischman." www.charlottezolotow.com/paul_fleischman.htm.

Background Information:

Community, school, and home gardens have long been places that grow more than flowers or vegetables. In preparing for this book club meeting, you might want to research whether there are any community or school gardens in your area and have information on that to share with the group. The following are some general websites on community and school gardens:

American Community Gardening Association—www.community
garden.org.
Community Gardening Toolkit—http://extension.missouri.edu/p/
MP906.
Life Lab—www.lifelab.org.
Real School Gardens—www.realschoolgardens.org.
San Francisco Green Schoolyard Alliance—http://sfgreenschools.org.

Discussion Questions

- In Ana's chapter she talks about how her neighborhood has changed over time. What have those changes been? What's your neighborhood like? Do you know its history?
- What does Gonzalo mean when he says, "The older you are, the younger you get when you move to the United States"?

- What's growing in the vacant lot besides plants?
- Often writers are told, "Write what you know." In addition, there are those who believe that only someone from a particular racial or ethnic background can give a true and accurate depiction of a character from that same racial or ethnic background. Fleischman is a white male, yet the characters in his book come from a variety of backgrounds. How successful was he in depicting those characters?
- Which gardener do you most relate to or have a connection with and in what way?
- What do you think of Sam's contest?
- Gardens are a place of growth and change. What changes does the garden bring to the neighborhood?
- What type of experience, if any, have you had with gardening?
- How is gardening "a soap opera growing out of the ground," as Nora says?
- Does Fleischman perpetuate any stereotypes in the book?
- In what ways did the garden benefit those who didn't grow anything?
- If you could visit Gibb Street today, do you think the garden would still be there? Why or why not?

Extension Activities

- As a group, visit a local school or community garden and learn about who is involved, what they plant and why.
- Start a garden with the group at their school, public library, or elsewhere in the community.

FURTHER READING

Dziedzic, Nancy, and Lynn M. Zott, eds. *Urban Agriculture. Opposing Viewpoints Series*. Farmington Hills, MI: Greenhaven Press, 2012.

Havill, Juanita. *Grow: A Novel in Verse*. Atlanta: Peachtree Publishers, 2008.

Kirby, Ellen, and Elizabeth Peters, eds. *Community Gardening.* Brooklyn, NY: Brooklyn Botanic Garden, 2008.

NOTES

1. Harvey Daniels, *Literature Circles: Voice and Choice in Book Clubs and Reading Groups* (Portland, ME: Stenhouse Publishers, 2002).

2. National Endowment for the Arts, *To Read or Not to Read: A Question of National Consequence* (Washington, DC: Office of Research and Analysis, 2007).

3. Cathy Collins Block and John N. Mangieri, "Recreational Reading: 20 Years Later," *Reading Teacher* 55, no. 6 (March 2002): 572–580.

4. Bonnie Kunzel and Constance Hardesty, *The Teen-Centered Book Club: Readers into Leaders* (Westport, CT: Libraries Unlimited, 2006).

5. Ibid., 104.

6. Donna M. Jackson, "Biography," 2011, www.donnamjackson.net/biography.html.

7. Teens Turning Green, "The Dirty Thirty," 2011, www.teensturninggreen.org/get-educated/dirty-thirty.html.

8. Campaign for Safe Cosmetics, "The Safe Cosmetics Act," http://safecosmetics.live2.radicaldesigns.org/article.php?list=type&type=74.

9. Julie Bertagna, "The Story behind the Story," www.juliebertagna.com/start.html.

10. Michael Seufer, "Snows of Kilimanjaro Disappearing, Glacial Loss Increasing," 2006, www.geology.ohio-state.edu/news_detail.php?newsId=1.

11. Paul Fleischman, "Biography," www.paulfleischman.net/events.htm.

SCIENCE SPROUTS: PRESCHOOL AND KINDERGARTEN PROGRAMS

WHY SCIENCE FOR THE VERY YOUNG?

When I was about four years old, I remember watching my mom ironing some clothes. She warned me not to get near the iron and not to touch it since it was very hot. How hot could it be, I wondered. The iron tempted me to investigate its exact temperature. I stuck out a finger, only to quickly realize that my mom had been right. Never again did I purposely put my finger on a hot iron.

Anyone who has spent time around young children knows that, like me, they are naturally curious, although maybe not in the same injury-inducing way I was. The tendency for young children to put things in their mouths can be a way of exploring their surroundings and making sense of them. The wonder at watching a butterfly flit from flower to flower or at splashing in a pond introduces children to the natural world around them and begins to instill an appreciation for nature. These early explorations often lead to questions. The inevitable and repeated "But why?" is a common query of young children.

Parents and caretakers can tap into this natural curiosity, helping foster the early seeds of scientific skills and future environmental stewardship. Contrary to traditional stage-development theories, such as those
developed by Jean Piaget, that state that young children cannot think
abstractly and cannot engage in scientific reasoning until they are about ten
or twelve years old, research that has emerged more recently shows that
young children, even infants, do engage in certain types of abstract thinking
and embody some of the same characteristics as a scientist.[1] Preschoolers
observe the world around them, they test things out, they make comparisons and ask questions—all things scientists do. In addition, they are able to
distinguish between animate and inanimate objects, a key foundation to scientific thinking. When presented with pictures of novel inanimate objects
that might have animal-like features, such as a statue, they know that the
inanimate objects cannot move on their own because they are not alive.
Animals can move, but statues, even those that look like animals, can't. They
know that the insides of a toy doll are different from their own insides. They
have basic understandings of cause and effect and will continue to seek out
an explanation for a phenomenon if presented with ambiguous evidence.
For example, preschoolers playing with a jack-in-the-box toy will stop playing with it when a new toy is presented if the mechanism that makes the
doll pop out is obvious. If this mechanism is not obvious, they will continue playing with the toy, even if a new toy is presented.[2] These examples
demonstrate that preschoolers are capable of undertaking a certain amount
of abstract thinking related to science and can begin to build the foundation
for more sophisticated reasoning they will undertake later in life.

At the same time, however, it is important to recognize the limitations
to preschoolers' knowledge and experiences, which will shape the type of
reasoning they employ. This makes adult involvement all the more important in these early scientific explorations. Young children possess a naive
understanding of the natural world and often develop conceptual frameworks based on their own experiences and information they have gleaned
from adults. At times, though, these frameworks might be contradictory to
actual scientific theories, and they can be difficult to unlearn in the future.
This is why having opportunities to engage with science at a young age,

with the guidance of parents, caretakers, or educators, is key to dispelling these misunderstandings and fomenting accurate scientific reasoning.

In addition to building on the skills and knowledge that many young children display, there are many other benefits associated with introducing science to young children. It helps make them feel comfortable with science. They begin to see science as something that is all around them and not something that only adults, usually in white lab coats, undertake in a lab. Along these same lines, it can also help level the playing field. Non-Asian minorities and women tend to be underrepresented in science and engineering fields in the United States. Many members of these groups do not go into science because they do not see others like themselves in these fields and/or they see it as something that inherently they are not able to do. Early foundations in science, however, help them to see that it is something that they can do. In addition, early science experiences can lay a foundation for later development of scientific concepts. They will be more likely to transfer prior skills and knowledge to more abstract or complex concepts.

Science activities can also allow preschoolers to develop skills in other areas, as well. When preschoolers partake in authentic science investigations, they often work in groups with their peers, which fosters cooperative learning and the development of social skills. They also need to make predictions, experiment, and record their observations. Making predictions, collecting data, and drawing conclusions are all key critical thinking skills that will serve them in other aspects of their lives, as well. Math is an integral tool of many scientific endeavors, whether it is measuring the length of something or looking for and predicting patterns. In this way, young children build a foundation not only in science but also in math. Finally, they can develop early literacy skills by recording their observations. Even if they cannot write themselves, they can draw pictures and have their adults write notes for them about their observations in a journal or on a data sheet. This allows them to begin to make connections between oral communication and the printed word. They can also develop new vocabulary through the use of scientific terms. In certain activities, they might want to find out more information and can turn to books to find the information they need, which helps develop their early library research skills.

PARALLELS BETWEEN EARLY LANGUAGE SKILLS AND EARLY SCIENCE SKILLS

Libraries might not be the first place one would expect to find science programs for preschoolers. A science museum might appear to be a more likely locale for this, but many libraries across the country have implemented a successful early literacy program, Every Child Ready to Read @ your library, which can serve as a model for implementing early science learning in libraries. In the 1990s, research and reports emerged that outlined the challenges many students face in terms of literacy learning. According to "Ready to Learn," a report published by the Carnegie Foundation in 1991, 35 percent of children enter public schools with such low skill levels and motivation to learn that they are at an extreme risk of having academic difficulties throughout their school careers. Much research has also shown that those students who are poor readers at the end of first grade will continue to be poor readers at the end of fourth grade. It soon became clear that early interventions were needed to correct those problems.

In 1997, Congress instructed the National Institute of Child Health and Human Development (NICHD) to convene a national reading panel that would assess the status of research-based knowledge and strategies for teaching children to read. The panel would then write a report and disseminate its findings in the most effective way possible. The release of the report "Teaching Children to Read," led to the formation of a partnership among NICHD, the Public Library Association (PLA), and the Association for Library Service to Children (ALSC), and to the development of Every Child Ready to Read @ your library.[3] The report contained many research-based techniques for fostering early literacy development in children from birth to five years old. Libraries have had a long history of involvement with and the promotion of early literacy skills, but often their programs had focused more on the children than their parents or caretakers. Through their partnership, NICHD, PLA, and ALSC realized that they could reach a broader audience by developing a tool kit for educating parents and caretakers to play a key role in their children's early literacy development. The Every Child Ready to Read @ your library program provides simple activities and ideas that can have a major impact on a child's future.

An evaluation of the program found that parents of the youngest children were the least likely to read to their children and use the library because they thought their children were too young. After participating in Every Child Ready to Read @ your library programs, their library usage and interactions with their children around books increased tremendously.[4]

Many parallels exist between this program and possible science literacy programs in museums and libraries. Both address a deficiency in early learning experiences for the very young. In both, often parents and caregivers believe that their children are too young for these types of experiences, but the research shows that they can benefit from having this early support. The second edition of Every Child Ready to Read @ your library also includes additional information about promoting science and math activities through the use of informational books, which tie well into a science program for toddlers at the library. In addition, science is often overlooked in preschool and kindergarten programs because of a focus on other areas and the lack of support to teachers to teach science. Many are not required to take science classes to be certified, and professional development opportunities in the sciences tend to be limited to nonexistent. Many preschool teachers may lack the confidence to implement science in their classrooms. Therefore, museums and libraries can become an important source for early science experiences for the very young.

Similar to Every Child Ready to Read @ your Library, libraries and museums can implement programs directed specifically toward parents and caregivers of young children. These programs can focus on simple ways to incorporate science and math in their interactions with their children. They do not necessarily have to be special experiments, but they can be incorporated into everyday activities. Encouraging children to use all of their senses when walking in their neighborhood or playing at the park—listening for birds, comparing and contrasting the shapes of leaves, looking for different textures—is easy to do, and these things are the basis of what scientists do. Simple activities like cooking, caring for pets, and playing with blocks all can incorporate science. Welcoming their children's questions and searching for the answers together is another way to instill scientific behavior. It is all right if they don't have all of the answers, since often scientists don't either. Museums and libraries can develop programs, handouts, websites, and the like, that outline and model some of these simple techniques. If librarians do not feel confident themselves that they can lead these types of programs, this can be an opportunity to partner with museum educators that have more expertise in science learning. It might also expand the reach of their audiences.

Museums can also provide orientations or tours specifically for parents and caregivers. These types of programs can demonstrate strategies they can use when interacting with the exhibits at museums with their children. These can be extremely beneficial to recent immigrants or communities who might not normally visit museums and might not feel fully comfortable in this type of environment. By coming on their own, they can feel more confident about their own knowledge of the exhibits and resources at the museum and can better maximize their time when they come with their children. Research has also shown that with adult mediation in play activities, such as those children might experience at a museum, children are more likely to pay attention to the science concepts incorporated into the activity.[5] Parents or caregivers can help guide and enrich experiences children may have during their museum visit.

PROGRAMMING TIPS FOR PRESCHOOL PROGRAMS

Besides doing parent- and caretaker-focused programs, libraries and museums can deliver programs directed toward toddlers. The following are things to incorporate into your programs to make them more successful:

- **Build on what preschoolers already know.** Use resources that are familiar to them—things they encounter in their everyday lives. Also, prompt them to tap into knowledge they already have from prior experiences at the library or museum or that they might have learned at home.
- **Work in groups.** Encourage participants, including parents and caretakers, to work together on the activities.
- **Repetition is a good thing.** Scientists often test out a hypothesis several times to ensure that they are getting an accurate result. In

the same way, you can incorporate similar concepts in your program, but perhaps presented in new ways, to encourage reinforcement. For those young children who might have already mastered the concept, it can give them a chance to apply that knowledge in a new situation.

- **Use real scientific tools.** Incorporate magnifying lenses, beakers, goggles, scales, and rulers into your program. Model their usage for the participants so that they feel comfortable using them and know how to use them in the correct manner.

- **Use scientific terms.** Pick key scientific terms that you use repeatedly in all of your programs, such as predict, observe, measure, results, and record. In addition, anyone who has been around young children who are fascinated by dinosaurs knows that they can easily rattle off long and complex names of various kinds. In the same way, you can use a term that might seem too complicated in your programs as long as you provide an explanation of it, present it in context, and repeat its usage throughout the activity.

- **Be flexible.** Let the children's questions that arise guide the direction of the activity as much as possible. In some cases, their questions might lead you to develop a new or different program for the next encounter you have with them.

- **Incorporate math.** Math is often an integral part of science experiments, but as in science, preschoolers often do not receive exposure to developing their math skills other than with counting. Use math as a tool for your activities whenever possible.

- **Record observations, results, and conclusions.** Provide a worksheet or notebook for participants to record their observations, results, and conclusions just like scientists do. Even if they cannot write, they can draw pictures to represent their findings and conclusions, or they can share their thoughts verbally and have adults write them down for them.

- **Create a display of further resources.** The activity might spark an interest to learn more or might lead to further questions. Have a display of books and DVDs related to the main concept of the activity for those that want to find out more.

- **Form partnerships.** As mentioned previously, librarians might not feel confident about their science education skills, so partnering with science museum educators can be a great way to develop them and become more confident. Likewise, museum educators might not have as extensive knowledge of quality books and DVDs on science topics specifically for children as librarians do. Again, partnering with a library will open up that world to them.

LITTLE LEARNERS' LAB

At the California Academy of Sciences, the Early Childhood and Family Programs Department delivers the Little Learners' Lab program every other week for children age three to five and their parents and caregivers. Two educators lead each program, and parents or caretakers also participate in the activity with their children. The space for the experiment is set up at two separate tables, with one educator at each table. There are four to five kids and their adults at each table. Since the activity itself only takes about fifteen minutes, often the groups are rotated over an hour so that you can have up to forty kids participating in that hour.

As much as possible, the children act like real scientists. The California Academy of Sciences provides small lab coats and goggles for them to wear during the program. Scientific terms, such as hypothesis, predict, observe, and record are used in context. When appropriate, real scientific equipment such as hand lenses, test tubes (plastic), and tweezers are employed. Safety is stressed throughout the activity, and the educators also demonstrate how to properly use each of the types of equipment so that the children are comfortable using them but also to avoid accidents. Also, they treat the children like scientists so that the children and parents begin to see that science is something we all can do.

Each program starts with the leader asking the participants what a scientist does. Following a brief discussion of this and after letting them know that today they will be scientists, the topic of the experiment that day is introduced, usually with a question, such as, "Who knows what sharks eat?" This generally leads into the group coming up with a hypothesis to test out, such as sharks with sharp teeth probably eat small fish that they can grab

Little Learners' Lab Handout

My Observations

Write about or draw a picture of something you observed in the lab.

Name _____

Date _____

Age _____

CALIFORNIA
ACADEMY OF
SCIENCES

Figure 4.1 Little Learners' Lab Handout

by stabbing them. The children do an experiment to test out their hypothesis, and as a group they talk about the results. Sometimes the children will come up with ideas to modify the experiment or want to test something else out, and if it is feasible and they can do it in a short amount of time, then the leader, with the children, will try that out, too.

With each program, the participants get a sheet to record their observations and conclusions, just like scientists do (see figure 4.1). They can either write or draw these or have an adult write down what they dictate. The program leader, parents, or caretakers can also discuss drawings the children have made with them, which can help children deepen their understanding of the concept by sharing their ideas in another way. Having to pick what to record also allows them to reflect on the experience and decide what is most important to record—what their key learning from the activity was. Recording their findings can also reinforce the use of new scientific terms. Finally, scientists always date their work, so there is a space for them to record the date.

On the other side of the sheet is further information about the activity. It includes the related state content standards for the activity. The educators have used the California standards for kindergarten since that is where the museum is located.[6] Most state standards are listed online, however, and you could incorporate those standards that align with the activities for your own state. Using the state standards reinforces for parents and caregivers the importance of this program in the educational development of their children. In addition, it provides an easy way for school librarians to connect with what the students are doing in their regular classes. The back side of the sheet also includes a list of related resources that adults and children can consult if they want to learn more about the topic or have follow-up questions.

The following are examples of programs that have been delivered or will be delivered in the future at the academy. They can be adapted to meet the needs of your community. At the end of this chapter is a list of other resources that have simple experiments and activities that could be incorporated into a program such as this one.

Ants' Smells

Learning Outcomes
- Properties of materials can be observed, measured, and predicted. (Kindergarten—Physical Sciences)
- Scientific progress is made by asking meaningful questions and conducting careful investigations. (Kindergarten—Investigation and Experimentation)
- Observations are communicated orally and through drawings. (Kindergarten—Investigation and Experimentation)

SCIENCE BEHIND THE TOPIC

Ants, like many other insects, some mammals, and some plants, use pheromones to communicate with other members of their species. Pheromones are chemicals that are released by the organism and have a particular odor. Foraging species of ants often scout out a trail to food. Once an ant has found a good source of food, it leaves a scent trail, using pheromones, so that others from its colony can also find the food. The other ants that come to the food also lay down pheromones, reinforcing the trail. When the food supply runs out, the ants stop secreting pheromones, and the scent quickly dissipates. Some species release a different type of pheromone on the trail that tells their colony mates that food is no longer available that way.

Materials

- squeeze bottles
- cotton balls
- lemon juice
- orange juice
- peppermint extract
- vanilla extract
- string
- observation and conclusion sheets (for ideas on creating these, see figure 4.1)
- pencils

PROCEDURE

Prior to the start of the program, soak each cotton ball with one of the liquids. Place each one in a squeeze bottle and attach a string to the bottle, creating a long loop. Make sure that there are two of each type of liquid for each group of participants.

Ask the group, "If you want to show someone else something you've found, how do you do it?" Let the group know that ants often use pheromones, which are chemicals that have a smell, to let other ants know where there is food. Ants also use pheromones to help them find their way back to the nest when they are looking for food.

Give each participant a bottle to wear around his or her neck. Have the participants go around smelling each other's bottles until they find their partner. Come back as a group once everyone has found each other and ask the following questions:

- How long did it take for you to find your scent partner?
- Were some scents easier to smell than others?
- What makes a scent "strong" or "weak"?
- Can you think of any other animals that use their sense of smell to find each other?

To wrap up, have the children record an observation or conclusion on their sheets.

FURTHER RESOURCES

Books

Allen, Judy. *Are You an Ant?* Backyard Books. Boston: Kingfisher, 2002.

Dorros, Arthur. Translated by Daniel Santacruz. *Ciudades de hormigas. Aprende y Descubre la Ciencia*. New York: Harper Arco Iris, 1995.

Nelson, Kristin L. *Busy Ants*. Pull Ahead Books. Minneapolis: Lerner Publications, 2004.

Stewart, Melissa. *Ants*. National Geographic Readers. Washington, DC: National Geographic, 2010.

DVDs

Ants: Little Creatures That Run the World. DVD. Directed by Nick Upton. 1995; Boston: WGBH Boston Video, 2007.

The Cat in the Hat Knows a Lot about That! Wings and Things. DVD. Directed by Tony Collingwood. Dallas, TX: NCircle Entertainment, 2010.

Filter Feeders

Learning Outcomes

- Properties of materials can be observed, measured, and predicted. (Kindergarten—Physical Sciences)
- Scientific progress is made by asking meaningful questions and conducting careful investigations. (Kindergarten—Investigation and Experimentation)

- Observations are communicated orally and through drawings. (Kindergarten—Investigation and Experimentation)

Materials

- wide-mouthed jars
- coffee grounds
- peas
- water
- measuring cups and spoons
- stop watch
- strainer
- cheese cloth
- coffee filters
- plastic container with a lid
- pictures of sharks and/or shark teeth or jaws
- observation and conclusions sheets (see figure 4.1 for ideas on creating these)
- pencils

PROCEDURE

Prior to the start of the program, pour half a cup of water, a half teaspoon of peas, and one teaspoon of coffee grounds into each of the jars. Cover one jar with the cheesecloth, one jar with the coffee filter, and one jar with the strainer.

Ask the participants what they think sharks eat. Show them the pictures of different types of sharks and the teeth or jaws if you have them. Talk about how some sharks are actually filter feeders, which means that water passes over their gills, and a structure on their body, known as gill rakes, causes the food to stay in their body as the water flows out. Let them know that you're going to do an activity to see how this works.

Show them the different jars and explain that they are going to pour the water out of the jars into another container. Ask them which they think

SCIENCE BEHIND THE TOPIC

Sharks catch their food in many different ways. One of the ways is called filter feeding. Filter-feeding sharks strain food from water using the gill rakes located at the gill slits on their bodies. There are only three kinds of filter-feeding sharks: whale sharks, megamouth sharks, and basking sharks. The basking shark is the only shark that relies exclusively on the passive flow of water through its throat (pharynx) while swimming for food.

will be the best at keeping the peas and coffee grounds in the jar, which will be their hypothesis. Slowly pour the mixture of water, coffee grounds, and peas into separate empty jars. Record the time it takes for all the water to strain out of each jar using the stopwatch.

Ask the group the following questions:

- How long did it take for the water to strain using a cheesecloth? A strainer? A coffee filter?
- Why did it take longer for the water to strain using a cheesecloth than a strainer?
- Was your hypothesis correct? Which straining material kept the most peas and coffee grounds in?

Have the participants record their observations or conclusions on their sheets.

FURTHER RESOURCES

Books

Arnosky, Jim. *All about Sharks*. New York: Scholastic Press, 2003.
Davies, Nicola. *Surprising Sharks*. Cambridge, MA: Candlewick Press, 2003.
Pfeffer, Wendy. *The World of Sharks*. American Museum of Natural History Easy Readers. New York: Sterling Children's Books, 2011.
Rockwell, Anne. *Little Shark*. New York: Walker, 2005.
Simon, Seymour. *Tiburones fabulosos*. SeeMore Readers. San Francisco: Chronicle Books, 2006.
Troll, Ray. *Sharkabet: A Sea of Sharks from A to Z*. Portland, OR: Westwinds Press, 2002.

DVD

Life, Disc 2: Fish, Birds. DVD. Produced by Martha Holmes. 2009; Burbank, CA: Warner Home Video, 2010.

Hunting by Ear

Learning Outcomes

- Properties of materials can be observed, measured, and predicted. (Kindergarten—Physical Sciences)
- Scientific progress is made by asking meaningful questions and conducting careful investigations. (Kindergarten—Investigation and Experimentation)
- Observations are communicated orally and through drawings. (Kindergarten—Investigation and Experimentation)

Materials

- paper-towel rolls
- masking tape
- books
- 8½″ × 11″ cardboard pieces covered in aluminum foil
- 8½″ × 11″ cardboard pieces covered by felt
- 8½″ × 11″ plywood pieces
- 8½″ × 11″ Styrofoam pieces
- observation and conclusions sheets (see figure 4.1 for ideas on creating these)
- pencils

PROCEDURE

Prior to the start of the lab, set up various stations using the paper-towel rolls. Place two of the rolls near the edge of the table, angled toward each other but not touching (creating a V shape with the wide part of the V shape closest to the edge of the table) and tape them down. Place a stack of books about twelve inches away from the paper-towel rolls facing the openings of the tubes. The books will be used to prop up the different pieces of cardboard and plywood, with the longer side facing horizontally in front of the paper-towel rolls.

Ask the participants if they have ever gone swimming in a lake or the ocean. Ask if it is easy to see underwater. Explain that for many animals that

SCIENCE BEHIND THE TOPIC

Dolphins are predators that use echolocation to help them locate their prey, often in dark and murky water. Dolphins make clicking sounds by pushing air between air sacs in the nasal cavity and through the melon, a fatty area in the front of their head. The melon helps focus the clicks so that the sound waves are sent out like a beam, similar to the beam of light from a flashlight focusing on an object. Water is a good conductor of sound, and the sound waves hit the object the dolphin is focusing on. Once they hit the object, the sound waves bounce back and travel through the dolphin's lower jar and to the middle ear, and eventually to the brain, where an audio picture is created. Dolphins are able to distinguish the distance, size, and shape of the object through echolocation.

In addition to traveling through water, sound waves can also travel through the air and through the ground. When sound waves hit different types of surfaces, they react in different ways. Sound waves that hit smooth surfaces bounce off them easily and are echoed back fairly clearly. When sound waves hit a soft surface, the surface absorbs much of the sound. Architects and designers take this into consideration when deciding which types of materials to use in certain buildings. If they want a quieter room, they will line the walls with a soft fabric or add bumpy surfaces to deaden the noise.

live in the ocean, it can often be hard to see, so they depend more on their sense of hearing, particularly when they are looking for food. Talk about how dolphins use echolocation when hunting.

Let the participants know that they are going to do an experiment using echolocation. Show them the different pieces of cardboard and the plywood. Explain that they should put each of the items against the books in turn, and then one participant should whisper something through one of the paper-towel rolls while another participant puts his or her ear up to the other paper-towel roll to listen to what the person says. Ask them which type of material they think will be the best at echoing back what their partner says. This will be their hypothesis.

Have them test out the different materials, taking turns whispering and listening. When they have tried out each of the four types of materials, ask the group the following questions:

- Was it easy or hard to hear what your partner said?
- Which material worked the best?
- Do you know of any other animals that use echolocation?

Have the children record their observations or conclusions on their sheets.

FURTHER RESOURCES

Books

Parsons, Alexandra. *Sound. Make It Work!* Chicago: World Book, 2008.

Pfeffer, Wendy. *Dolphin Talk: Whistles, Clicks, and Clapping Jaws. Let's-Read-and-Find-Out-Science.* New York: HarperCollins Publishers, 2003.

Pfeffer, Wendy. *Sounds All Around. Let's-Read-and-Find-Out-Science.* New York: HarperCollins Publishers, 1999.

Stewart, Melissa. *How Do Bats Fly in the Dark?* New York: Marshall Cavendish Benchmark, 2009.

Is Soil Alive?

Note: This activity might take longer than some of the other ones and might be better to do as a large group at once rather than repeating it several times over the course of an hour.

Learning Outcomes
- Properties of materials can be observed, measured, and predicted. (Kindergarten—Physical Sciences)
- Scientific progress is made by asking meaningful questions and conducting careful investigations. (Kindergarten—Investigation and Experimentation)
- Observations are communicated orally and through drawings. (Kindergarten—Investigation and Experimentation)

Materials

- small basins or lab trays with higher sides
- 2–3 buckets of soil from a forest, prairie, or garden (soil with plenty of organic matter that isn't all decomposed)
- spoons
- tongue depressors
- petri dishes (empty)
- hand lenses
- observation and conclusions sheets (see figure 4.1 for ideas on creating these)
- pencils

PROCEDURE

Prior to the start of the program, distribute the soil to the different basins or trays and set out spoons, tongue depressors, hand lenses, and petri dishes next to each basin.

Introduce the activity by asking the participants what soil or dirt is, and whether all soil is the same. Also ask who or what needs soil. Finally, ask them if they think soil is alive. Their answer will be their hypothesis. Show them the soil in the basins, and tell them where you got it from. Have the participants explore the soil to determine whether or not it is alive. They can use the spoons and tongue depressors to dig around. They can also put things in the petri dishes, such as worms or insects they might find, if they want to look more closely at them either with their naked eye or with the hand lens. For this lab you can suggest that the children record their observations while they are exploring the soil.

After the children and their adults have explored the soil for at least five to ten minutes, bring the group back together and have them share what they discovered. Ask the following questions:

- What did you find in the soil?
- Were things you found alive? Did you find things that weren't alive?
- Is soil alive?

SCIENCE BEHIND THE TOPIC

All around us, soil is often an overlooked yet vital resource. Most soils come from rock that has been eroded, creating sediments. There are many different types of soils, but all contain a mixture of three different types of sediments: sand, clay, and silt. The relative amounts that a soil has of each of these types of sediments affect its ability to hold water. Sand particles are the largest of the three, and water tends to run right through sand. The tiniest particles, clay particles, retain water well, sometimes too well, and puddles can form on top of soils with high clay content.

In addition to these inorganic aspects, soil also contains organic material. This includes decaying matter, such as dead leaves and animals. As this material decomposes, it adds nutrients to the soil, which are essential to plants. Microscopic organisms, as well as larger animals such as earthworms, help break down this organic matter. Many other live animals also call soil their home, from ants to moles.

Without soil, other life on Earth wouldn't exist. Plants depend on soil as a place to put their roots to gather water and nutrients. Humans and other animals depend on plants for food, shelter, and clothing. Predators also eat many animals that depend on plants for their food source. Many people take soil for granted since it is everywhere, but every year large amounts of valuable topsoil is lost to soil erosion, a result of the clearing of vegetation. It can take hundreds of years to create one inch of soil, but much of that topsoil can be lost in a day of heavy rains. Soil is a dynamic ecosystem that like other ecosystems also needs to be protected.

- If we looked at soil from a beach, do you think it would be the same or different? In what ways?

Conclude the activity by pointing out that soil is an ecosystem with both living and nonliving things.

FURTHER RESOURCES

Books

Bial, Raymond. *A Handful of Dirt.* New York: Walker and Company, 2000.

Chase, Ashley, and Marco Bravo. *Without Soil.* Nashua, NH: Delta Education, 2007.

Hall, Pamela. *Dig In! Learn about Dirt.* Mankato, MN: Child's World, 2010.

Stewart, Melissa. *Down to Earth. Investigate Science.* Minneapolis, MN: Compass Point Books, 2004.

Tomecek, Steve. *Dirt.* Washington, DC: National Geographic Society, 2002.

Scattering Seeds

Learning Outcomes

- Students know how to observe and describe similarities and differences in the appearance and behavior of plants. (Kindergarten—Life Sciences)
- Scientific progress is made by asking meaningful questions and conducting careful investigations. (Kindergarten—Investigation and Experimentation)
- Observations are communicated orally and through drawings. (Kindergarten—Investigation and Experimentation)

SCIENCE BEHIND THE TOPIC

Plants don't have feet, so how can each little seed go out and find its own patch of land in which to grow? They do it by different methods of dispersal. Seeds are carried away from the parent plant to a new area so that they will not compete with their parent for space, light, and water. The parts of the plant that travel are called the disseminules. Often the disseminules are the seed and the fruits themselves. However, sometimes parts of the flower form a special structure to help in the dispersal of seeds.

Plants have evolved all sorts of ways to help their seeds disperse, and sometimes they use water, wind, and animals to assist them. The following are examples of different methods of dispersal:

- **Water.** Some seeds, such as coconuts and sea beans, have waterproof shells and enough air inside of them to help them float on water for great distances. Others, such as pussy willow and sea lavender, are light enough that they drift along the water until they find new ground to grow in.

- **Wind.** Seeds that are dispersed by wind tend to be very light so that even the slightest breeze will carry them away. Some seeds have

Materials

- a variety of different kinds of seeds, including several that are dispersed by animals.
- observation and conclusions sheets (see figure 4.1 for ideas on creating these)
- pencils

PROCEDURE

To introduce the activity, ask the participants if plants can move from one place to another on their own. Then ask them if they know where new plants come from. If they don't, explain that most new plants come from seeds. However, since plants can't move from one place to another, they need to have help moving around their seeds. Go over the different ways that seeds are dispersed with the participants.

papery wings that are part of the fruit, such as those from maples, ashes, and lindens. These are usually high up in a tree or vine so that there's a good chance of the disseminule catching the wind when it falls from the tree. The wings can help it glide or twirl like a helicopter's blade away from the parent. Other seeds have tufts of hair that catch the wind and are like a parachute for the seed, such as those from dandelions, clematises, and cattails. Other plants, such as poppies, have seedpods that become dry and split open. When the wind blows them, they sprinkle out their seeds like a saltshaker.

- **Animals.** Plants use animals in all sorts of ways to help move their seeds. Some seeds have burrs or sticky substances that cling to animal fur or people's clothing and hitch a ride to new ground. Examples of this include cockleburs, forget-me-nots, and foxtail barley. Nuts and cones are gathered and stored by squirrels, jays, and other animals. Sometimes the animal will forget about them and the seeds may sprout (such as with acorns and hazelnuts). Animals also eat fruits, and the seed passes whole through the animal's digestive system (such as blackberry and apple).

Give each participant several different kinds of seeds. Ask them to decide which ones they think animals would spread to new places. When all the participants have had time to examine their different seeds, bring the group back together and ask the following questions:

- What did you notice about the different seeds? What were they like? Are they all the same shape, or are they different shapes?
- Which seeds did you think animals would help disperse? Why? What about those seeds do you think would make it more likely that an animal would move them to another place?
- How do you think the other seeds get to another place?

Have the children record their observations or conclusions on their sheets.

FURTHER RESOURCES

Books

Aston, Dianna Hutts. *A Seed Is Sleepy.* San Francisco: Chronicle Books, 2007.

Carle, Eric. *The Tiny Seed.* New York: Simon and Schuster Books for Young Readers, 1987.

Galbraith, Kathryn O. *Planting the Wild Garden.* Atlanta: Peachtree Publishers, 2011.

Macken, JoAnn Early. *Flip, Float, Fly! Seeds on the Move.* New York: Holiday House, 2008.

Schaefer, Lola M. *This Is the Sunflower.* New York: Greenwillow Books, 2000.

DVD

Plant. DVD. Directed by Brian Cummins. 1994; New York: DK, 2006.

Resources for Preschool Science Experiments and Activities

Garrett, Linda and Hannah Thomas. *Small Wonders: Nature Education for Young Children.* Woodstock: Vermont Institute of Natural Science, 2005.

Gelman, Rochel, Kimberly Brenneman, Gay Macdonald, and Moisés Román. *Preschool Pathways to Science (PrePS): Facilitating Scientific Ways of Thinking, Talking, Doing, and Understanding.* Baltimore: Paul H. Brookes Publishing, 2010.

Moomaw, Sally, and Brenda Hieronymus. *More Than Magnets: Exploring the Wonders of Science in Preschool and Kindergarten.* St. Paul, MN: Redleaf Press, 1997.

Sheehan, Kathryn, and Mary Waidner. *Earth Child 2000: Earth Science for Young Children.* Rev. ed. Tulsa, OK: Council Oak Books, 1994.

"Sid the Science Kid" Website for Parents and Teachers—Activities. www.pbs.org/parents/sid/activitiesIndex.html.

VanCleave, Janice Pratt. *Janice VanCleave's Big Book of Play and Find Out Science.* New York: Jossey-Bass, 2007.

NOTES

1. Barbara T. Bowman, M. Suzanne Donovan, and M. Susan Burns, eds., *Eager to Learn: Educating Our Preschoolers* (Washington, DC: National Academies Press, 2000); Richard A. Duschl, Heidi A. Shweingruber, and Andrew W. Shouse, eds., *Taking Science to School: Learning and Teaching Science in Grades K–8* (Washington, DC: National Academies Press, 2007); Rochel Gelman, Kimberly Brenneman, Gay Macdonald, and Moisés Román, *Preschool Pathways to Science (PrePS): Facilitating Scientific Ways of Thinking, Talking, Doing, and Understanding* (Baltimore: Paul H. Brookes Publishing, 2010).

2. Laura E. Schulz and Elizabeth Baraff Bonawitz, "Serious Fun: Preschoolers Engage in More Exploratory Play When Evidence Is Confounded," *Developmental Psychology* 43, no. 4 (2007): 1045–1050.

3. National Institute of Child Health and Human Development, *Teaching Children to Read: An Evidence-Based Assessment of the Scientific Research Literature on Reading and Its Implications for Reading Instruction* (Washington, DC: US Government Printing Office, 2000).

4. Nancy Everhart, "Every Child Ready to Read @ your library," *Knowledge Quest* 33, no. 2 (2004): 77–79.

5. Marilyn Fleer, "Supporting Scientific Conceptual Consciousness or Learning in 'a Roundabout Way' in Play-Based Contexts," *International Journal of Science Education* 31, no. 8 (2009): 1069–89.

6. California State Board of Education, "Content Standards," www.cde.ca.gov/be/st/ss.

DELVING DEEPER:
SELF-GUIDED ACTIVITIES

All Ages

This chapter explores various self-guided environmental activities that can be implemented in libraries and museums. Although they might require more effort and time up front, once established, they can reach a broader audience than facilitated programs and require much less staff time. They also serve as an efficient use of resources, since you need to buy only one set of manipulatives for many of the activities rather than multiple objects for a workshop presentation. The following describes three different types of activities: Naturalist Bingo, Mystery Boxes, and Naturalist Backpacks. Through these activities children (and adults) direct their own learning and follow their interests, which makes the learning more meaningful to them. Hopefully, this will lead them to carry this new knowledge and development of skills to other parts of their lives.

NATURALIST BINGO

Two main skills that scientists use are observation and description. Scientists need to study closely all aspects of their subject. Taxonomists, scientists who study the relationships between living things, particularly need to be able to observe and describe the specimens they are investigating. Description seems like a deceptively easy task, but if you have ever had to fully describe something to another person, you begin to see some of the difficulties that can arise with doing this—finding the exact word and maneuvering differing perspectives (one person's red might be another's magenta), to name just two.

The Naturalist Bingo activity used at the Naturalist Center at the California Academy of Sciences (a natural history museum, aquarium, and planetarium) helps children develop observation and description skills. Figure 5.1 shows the front of one of the laminated bingo boards used for this activity. The back of the board has the instructions for the activity. Children look around the Naturalist Center, which has natural history specimen and library collections, for something that fits each of the categories on the board. They then write or draw the item they found in the space, using a wet-erase marker. Since the boards are laminated, using wet-erase markers allows the cards to be reused many times. When they have filled in all of their spaces on the board, they "win." The Naturalist Center usually has a small prize for them, such as a sticker or a pencil. The boards are left sitting out on one of the tables in the Naturalist Center, with a tabletop sign that lets visitors know they can ask for a marker at the information desk to do the activity. This also gives Naturalist Center staff a chance to make sure that children know what they are doing and to let them know they can get a prize if they complete it. It also prevents markers from walking away or being used for writing on other things.

While doing the activity, children become familiar with different ways of describing things found in the natural world. They are also forced to slow down and really examine the area around them, something that we tend to do less and less of in our fast-paced world. This is a vital skill for scientists, though, who often need to slow down and reflect on what they are observing—to look for anomalies, to look for something new or unique, or to simply look for an explanation of something.

At first glance, librarians and science center educators might wonder how they can do this in their space, since they often do not have specimen collections, like many natural history museums. Various materials used to

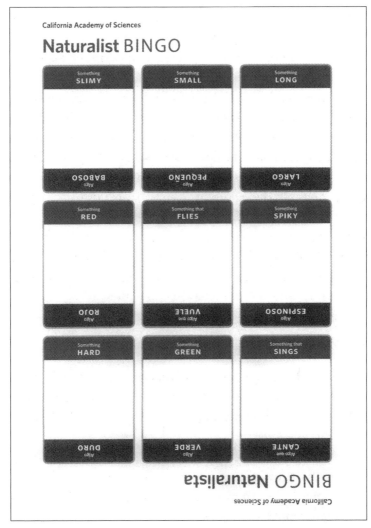

Figure 5.1 Naturalist Bingo Board

create objects, furniture, or displays in libraries and science centers, however, could fit into the different categories, and it is useful for children to begin to think about different types of materials things are made of. Also, the instructions for the academy's version of Naturalist Bingo say that children can look for drawings or photos in books to fit the different categories, something that libraries can also do. I have done this activity at a public library that had a garden just outside its building and was next to a park.

The children could take the boards outside to do the activity and then bring them back into the library when they had finished.

In addition to honing their observation and description skills, the Naturalist Bingo activity can reinforce certain concepts for students. Choosing certain categories for the board can help build children's science vocabulary. Naturalist Center staff have also adapted the activity to fit different themes that were part of museum-wide programming or around certain times of the year, such as a springtime theme or a creepy-crawly theme for Halloween. The following are the categories used for these different versions of the activity at the Naturalist Center. I also translated our boards into Spanish to reach a broader audience when I worked at the Naturalist Center, so the categories are listed in English and are immediately followed by the Spanish equivalent.

Naturalist Bingo (Bingo Naturalista) Categories

Something black—*Algo negro*
Something blue—*Algo azul*
Something brown—*Algo café*
Something with feathers—*Algo con plumas*
Something that flies—*Algo que vuele*
Something furry—*Algo peludo*
Something gray—*Algo gris*
Something green—*Algo verde*
Something that growls—*Algo que gruña*
Something hard—*Algo duro*
Something without legs—*Algo sin patas*
Something long—*Algo largo*
Something with many legs—*Algo con muchas patas*
Something orange—*Algo anaranjado*
Something red—*Algo rojo*
Something rough—*Algo áspero*
Something shiny—*Algo brillante*
Something that sings—*Algo que cante*
Something slimy—*Algo baboso*

Something small—*Algo pequeño*
Something smooth—*Algo liso*
Something soft—*Algo suave*
Something spiky—*Algo espinoso*
Something with spots—*Algo con manchas*
Something yellow—*Algo amarillo*

Creepy-Crawly Bingo (Bingo Escalofriante) Categories

Something that bites—*Algo que muerda*
Something bony—*Algo huesudo*
Something with claws—*Algo con garras*
Something with fangs—*Algo con colmillos*
Something that growls—*Algo que gruña*
Something hairy—*Algo peludo*
Something that howls—*Algo que aúlle*
Something with many legs—*Algo con muchas patas*
Something with many teeth—*Algo con muchos dientes*
Something nocturnal—*Algo nocturno*
Something scary—*Algo que dé miedo*
Something slimy—*Algo baboso*
Something spiky—*Algo espinoso*
Something that squirms—*Algo que se retuerza*

Springtime Bingo (Bingo de Primavera) Categories

Something that is brightly colored—*Algo que tenga colores brillantes*
Something that buds—*Algo que brote*
Something that cares for its young—*Algo que cuide a su cría*
Something that eats its mates—*Algo que se coma a su pareja*
Something that emerges from a burrow—*Algo que salga de una madriguera*
Something that emerges from hibernation—*Algo que salga de la hibernación*
Something that fights for mates—*Algo que pelee por su pareja*
Something that grows flowers—*Algo que produzca flores*

Something that has a pouch—*Algo que tenga una bolsa*

Something that hatches from an egg—*Algo que salga de un huevo*

Something that lays eggs—*Algo que ponga huevos*

Something that makes a nest—*Algo que haga un nido*

Something that makes seeds—*Algo que produzca semillas*

Something that metamorphoses—*Algo que se metamorfosee*

Something that migrates north—*Algo que migre al norte*

Something that releases pollen—*Algo que libere polen*

Something that sings—*Algo que cante*

Something that thaws—*Algo que se descongele*

MYSTERY BOXES

For the past few decades, discovery centers have become more common in classrooms, particularly at the preschool and kindergarten levels, but also in some primary grades. Discovery centers are areas in the classroom that are set up for more self-directed, small-group learning. They usually have objects for the children to interact with and a task to undertake. Many museum exhibits, especially those found in children's museums, share several of the same characteristics as discovery centers. They also include objects that children can explore, examine, and use as a way to learn and make new discoveries, and that also tap into their sense of play. This approach could also be transferred to a public or school library with the establishment of discovery centers in their spaces.

Various benefits can arise from the use of discovery centers in libraries and museums. Many children solidify their learning through hands-on experiences, which are central to discovery centers. They also provide autonomy to children, allowing them to direct their own learning and to take greater responsibility for it. They encourage creative thinking and the development of problem-solving skills. Discovery centers are often multi-disciplinary, which can appeal to a variety of learning styles. They also provide an opportunity for shared learning, either with children's peers or with family members. In some cases, this can help build children's confidence, particularly when one student might know more about a topic and can help guide peers through the activity. Finally, discovery centers can allow children to make connections to prior knowledge or experiences, thus building upon and reinforcing it.

The characteristics of a successful discovery center include the following:

- Clear objectives: in planning and developing the discovery centers it is important to decide on the main ideas or concepts that you want users to walk away with.
- Clear and concise instructions or directives for interacting with the objects.
- Various choices or ways of interacting with the objects are available.
- Promote critical-thinking skills.
- The text included with the discovery center and the activities are appropriate for a range of ages and learning styles.
- Several participants can interact with the materials in the discovery center at once.
- Participants can easily make connections between the ideas and concepts presented and their own prior knowledge or experiences.
- The activities presented are self-corrective. Children can find answers to the challenges presented in the discovery center via the materials and objects themselves.
- The themes presented in the discovery center connect with larger themes of the institution to complement learning. In museums, this might mean having the activities connect with other exhibits or larger institution-wide programming themes. In public libraries, the discovery center might connect to summer reading themes or themes around certain seasons or holidays. In school libraries, they can connect to what the students are studying in their classrooms.
- They include a display of books, DVDs, or other resources to delve deeper into the topic or help answer questions that might arise.
- They provide opportunities for parents, caretakers, or museum or library staff to encourage scaffolding in children. Although discovery centers are self-guided activities, parents or caretakers

accompanying the child can assist in his or her learning by encouraging the child to take his or her thinking to another level. They can do this by asking open-ended questions or helping guide children when they get stuck on a certain aspect of the activity.

Incorporating these characteristics into a discovery center will help make it more effective.

The Naturalist Center at the California Academy of Sciences offers the self-guided activity known as Mystery Boxes, which are very similar to discovery centers. Each box is centered on different themes, such as seeds, corals, chocolate, or skulls. These started out as plastic bins containing natural history specimens, models, photographs, and books, as well as a series of laminated cards with more information on the topic and self-guided activities to do using the objects in the box. The boxes have since morphed into drawers that are part of a large specimen cabinet. Visitors can pull out the drawers, take them to a table, and explore them in depth. The laminated cards have been replaced with small binders that have further information and activities, as well as a bibliography of resources related to the topic. Since the boxes are for all ages, the books listed in the bibliography are a mixture of books for children and adults. There are also labels in the drawers with the objects that have open-ended questions for visitors to begin exploring the objects. Figure 5.2 has a photograph of some of the Naturalist Center's Mystery Boxes in their new incarnation.

Mystery Boxes could be created in school or public libraries, as well as in museums. They can be created as boxes or tabletop displays using signs or laminated cards. Many online stores sell natural history educational materials and scientific models, such as the following:

- Acorn Naturalists (www.acornnaturalists.com)
- Bone Clones (www.boneclones.com)
- Carolina Biological Supply (www.carolina.com)
- Nasco (www.enasco.com/science/)
- Skulls Unlimited (www.skullsunlimited.com)

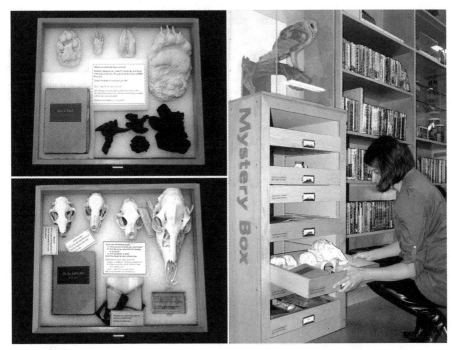

Figure 5.2 Mystery Boxes at the Naturalist Center

You also might be able to find and collect some of the objects for your box or discovery center, such as various seeds or rocks. It also might be possible to make the objects or use laminated photographs.

The following section lists the different Mystery Boxes at the Naturalist Center. It includes a list of the objects in each box, the topics covered in the activities and accompanying binder, and the further resources lists found in each binder.

Becoming Human

Materials in the Box

- *Homo sapiens* skull replica (half scale)
- chimpanzee skull replica (half scale)
- *Homo erectus* skull replica (half scale)

- *Australopithecus afarensis* skull replica (half scale)
- laminated diagram of the human family tree
- replicas of stone tools most likely made by *Homo habilis* and early humans
- replica of the Venus of Willendorf sculpture

Topics Covered in Activities and Binder Information
- characteristics that make humans different from other animals
- overview of the human evolutionary tree
- comparison between humans and chimpanzees (one of our closest living relatives), including morphological comparisons using the skull replicas
- Overview of two early human ancestors (*Australopithecus afarensis* and *Homo habilis*) and how paleoanthropologists use skulls and other bones from these species to explore how humans evolved; opportunity to compare skulls from these early humans to skulls of a human and a chimpanzee
- the development of tool making, art, and culture in humans

FURTHER RESOURCES

Books

Johanson, Donald C. *From Lucy to Language.* New York: Simon and Schuster, 2006.

Rubalcaba, Jill. *Every Bone Tells a Story: Hominin Discoveries, Deductions, and Debates.* Watertown, MA: Charlesbridge, 2010.

Stefoff, Rebecca. *First Humans.* New York: Marshall Cavendish Benchmark, 2010.

Stefoff, Rebecca. *Origins.* New York: Marshall Cavendish Benchmark, 2010.

Thimmesh, Catherine. *Lucy Long Ago: Uncovering the Mystery of Where We Came From.* Boston: Houghton Mifflin Harcourt, 2009.

Zihlman, Adrienne L. *The Human Evolution Coloring Book.* New York: Harper Resource, 2000.

Zimmer, Carl. *Smithsonian Intimate Guide to Human Origins.* New York: HarperCollins, 2005.

DVDs

Becoming Human: Unearthing Our Earliest Ancestors. DVD. Directed by
Graham Townsley. 2009; Alexandria, VA: PBS Distribution, 2010.

Human Family Tree. DVD. Directed by Chad Cohen. Washington, DC:
National Geographic, 2009.

The Incredible Human Journey. DVD. Directed by David Stewart. 2009;
London: BBC Worldwide, 2010.

Journey of Man. DVD. Directed by Clive Maltby. 2002; Alexandria, VA:
PBS Home Video, 2004.

Websites

American Museum of Natural History Hall of Human Origins: www.amnh
.org/exhibitions/permanent/humanorigins/

Fossil Hominids: The Evidence for Human Evolution: www.talkorigins.org/
faqs/homs/

Fundación Atapuerca: www.atapuerca.org

NOVA *Becoming Human* Series: www.pbs.org/wgbh/nova/beta/evolution/
becoming-human-part-1.html

Palomar College Biological Anthropology Tutorials: http://anthro.palomar
.edu/tutorials/biological.htm

Smithsonian National Museum of Natural History: What Does It Mean to
Be Human? http://humanorigins.si.edu

Butterflies and Moths

Materials in the Box
- plastic models of the different stages of a painted lady butterfly's
  life cycle
- Plastomount with specimens from the different stages of a cabbage
  white butterfly's life cycle
- Plastomount with different insect specimens, including a butterfly
- pinned butterfly and moth specimen in a shadow box

Topics Covered in Activities and Binder Information
- physical characteristics of butterflies and moths
- comparison of similarities and differences between butterflies, moths, and skippers
- butterfly and moth life cycles
- butterfly and moth adaptations used for survival
- suggestions of where to observe butterflies and moths in the wild

FURTHER RESOURCES

Books

Bishop, Nic. *Butterflies and Moths*. New York: Scholastic, 2009.

Carter, David J. *Butterflies and Moths*. New York: Dorling Kindersley, 1992.

Fischer-Nagel, Heiderose. *Life of the Butterfly*. Minneapolis, MN: Carolrhoda Books, 1987

Hunt, Joni Phelps. *A Shimmer of Butterflies*. San Luis Obispo, CA: Blake Publishing, 1992.

Opler, Paul A. *A Field Guide to Western Butterflies*. Boston: Houghton Mifflin, 1999.

DVDs

Butterflies. DVD. Directed by George Wrenn. N.p.: Naritas, 2005.

Butterfly & Moth. DVD. Directed by Derek Hall. Originally released in 1994 and 1996; New York: DK Publishing, 2007.

The Incredible Journey of the Butterflies. DVD. Directed by Nick de Pencier. Boston: PBS Video, 2009.

Websites

American Museum of Natural History Butterfly Conservatory: www.amnh.org/exhibitions/current-exhibitions/the-butterfly-conservatory

Butterflies and Moths of North America: www.butterfliesandmoths.org

The Butterfly WebSite: http://butterflywebsite.com

The Children's Butterfly Site: www.kidsbutterfly.org

Chocolate

Materials in the Box

- cocoa beans from the different strains of chocolate—trinitario, criollo, and forastero
- cacao pod
- spice jar with a mixture of cocoa powder, corn meal, cinnamon, and crushed chili peppers. The top has tiny holes and a cheese-cloth covering to be able to smell the mixture but also keep it from spilling out. (This represents the way that Mayans and Aztecs prepared chocolate.)
- laminated wrappers from different bars of chocolate (including some fair-trade bars)

Topics Covered in Activities and Binder Information

- where and how chocolate grows
- the process of making chocolate
- a history of how chocolate was first used by the Olmecs, Mayans, and Aztecs from Mexico and Central America
- importance of the cacao plant in the rain-forest ecosystem
- sustainable ways to cultivate cacao
- introduction of fair trade and an activity to determine how you can tell whether or not a bar of chocolate is fair trade

FURTHER RESOURCES

Books

Burleigh, Robert. *Chocolate.* New York: Harry N. Abrams, 2002.

Coe, Sophie D. *The True History of Chocolate.* New York: Thames and Hudson, 2007.

Gilbert, Trinitat. *Hoy toca chocolate.* Barcelona: La Galera, 2006.

Morganelli, Adrianna. *The Biography of Chocolate.* New York: Crabtree Publishing, 2006.

Nelson, Robin. *From Cocoa Bean to Chocolate.* Minneapolis, MN: Lerner Publications, 2003.

DVD

Elisha and the Cacao Trees / Elisha et les cacaoyers. DVD. Directed by
Rohan Fernando. Montreal: National Film Board of Canada, 2011.

Websites

Catholic Relief Services Fair Trade: www.crsfairtrade.org/chocolate/
Day Chocolate Company: www.papapaa.org
Equal Exchange: www.equalexchange.com
The Field Museum: All about Chocolate: http://archive.fieldmuseum.org/
chocolate/about.html
Global Exchange: www.globalexchange.org/campaigns/fairtrade/cocoa
Manufacturing Chocolate: From Seed to Sweet: http://archive.field
museum.org/chocolate/kids_seedtosweet.html

Corals

Materials in the Box
- specimens of hard and soft coral and photos of what they look like when alive
- map of location of coral reefs around the world

Topics Covered in Activities and Binder Information
- characteristics of corals
- differences between hard and soft corals
- location of coral reefs around the world and description of their importance as an ecosystem
- instructions on making an edible coral polyp at home, which is based on the lesson plan "Build a Coral Polyp," from the California Academy of Sciences website for teachers (www.calacademy.org/teachers/resources/lessons/build-a-coral-polyp)

FURTHER RESOURCES

Books

Albert, Toni. *The Incredible Coral Reef: Another Active-Learning Book for Kids.* Mechanicsburg, PA: Trickle Creek Books, 1996.

Behrens, D. W., Terry Gosliner, and Gary C. Williams. *Coral Reef Animals of the Indo-Pacific: Animal Life from Africa to Hawaii Exclusive of the Vertebrates.* Monterey, CA: Sea Challengers, 1996.

Brown, Ruth, et al. *The Coral Reef Teacher's Guide.* Key West, FL: Reef Relief, 1998

Muzik, Katy. *Dentro del arrecife de coral.* Watertown, MA: Charlesbridge, 1993.

Veron, J. *Corals of the World.* Townsville, Queensland: Australian Institute of Marine Science, 2000.

Walker, Pam, and Elaine Wood. *The Coral Reef.* New York: Facts on File, 2005.

DVDs

The Fragile Reef: Coral in Peril. DVD. Directed by Ron Blythe. Princeton, NJ: Films for the Humanities and Sciences, 2004.

MacGillivray Freeman's Coral Reef Adventure. DVD. Directed by Greg MacGillivray. Chatsworth, CA: Image Entertainment, 2003.

Treasures of the Great Barrier Reef. DVD. Directed by Tina Dalton. 1995; Boston: WGBH Boston Video, 2006.

Websites

Coral Reef Alliance: www.coral.org

Coral Reefs, World Wildlife Fund: wwf.panda.org/about_our_earth/blue_planet/coasts/coral_reefs

Exploring the Environment: Coral Reefs, NASA Educational Modules: www.cotf.edu/ete/modules/coralreef/CRmain.html

National Oceanic and Atmospheric Administration's Coral Reef Conservation Program: www.coralreef.noaa.gov

Ocean World: Coral Reefs, Texas A&M University: http://oceanworld.tamu.edu/students/coral

Reef Base: A Global Information System on Coral Reefs: www.reefbase.org

Rocks and Minerals

Materials in the Box

- streak-test kit (samples of different rocks and a ceramic plate for testing)
- hardness-scale kit (rock specimens with varying levels of hardness)
- examples of items made from various minerals: antacid pill bottle (calcite), paper clip (hematite), drywall (gypsum), and toothpaste (fluorite)
- paper models of different types of crystals
- limestone, marble, and granite specimens

Topics Covered in Activities and Binder Information

- definition of a rock and a mineral, and the difference between the two
- overview of the three different types of rocks (igneous, metamorphic, and sedimentary) and how each is formed
- the rock cycle
- an overview of the physical properties used to identify rocks and minerals and the chance to perform two tests geologists use (hardness and streak tests)
- introduction of a simple dichotomous key to identify different types of rocks
- different uses of minerals in our everyday life
- definition of a crystal and examples of different types of crystals

FURTHER RESOURCES

Books

Brawmwell, Martyn. *Understanding & Collecting Rocks & Fossils.* London: Usborne Publishing, 1983.

Cuff, Kevin. *Stories in Stone: Teacher's Guide.* Berkeley, CA: LHS GEMS, 1995.

Gardner, Robert. *Earth-Shaking Science Projects about Planet Earth.* Berkeley Heights, NJ: Enslow, 2008.

Pellant, Chris. *Rocks and Minerals.* New York: Dorling Kindersley, 1992.

Pough, Frederick H. *A Field Guide to Rocks and Minerals.* Boston: Houghton Mifflin, 1996.

DVDs

Core Geology. DVD. Directed by Ron Meyer. New York: Ambrose Video, 2007.

Eyewitness Rock & Mineral. DVD. Directed by Caius Julyan. 1996; New York: DK Publishing, 2006.

Websites

Geology-General Info: http://geology.com

Kids Geo: www.kidsgeo.com

Mineralogy Database: www.mindat.org

US Geological Survey, "Geology": http://geology.usgs.gov/index.htm

---

Scat and Track

Materials in the Box
- replicas of deer, raccoon, mountain lion, and black bear scat
- resin replicas of deer, raccoon, mountain lion, and black bear tracks

Topics Covered in Activities and Binder Information
- overview of how scientists and naturalists look for signs in nature to help determine which animals have been in an area
- an overview of the different types of mammal feet (plantigrade, digitigrade, and unguligrade)
- a series of clues that describe each of the mammal's tracks and scat; participants try to figure out who left each scat or track

FURTHER RESOURCES

Books

Arnosky, Jim. *Wild Tracks: A Guide to Nature's Footprints.* New York: Sterling Publishing, 2008.

Halfpenny, James C. *A Field Guide to Mammal Tracking in North America.* 2nd ed. Boulder, CO: Johnson Books, 1986.

Johnson, Jinny. *Animal Tracks and Signs.* Washington, DC: National Geographic, 2008.

Murie, Olaus Johan. *A Field Guide to Animal Tracks.* 3rd ed. Boston: Houghton Mifflin, 2005.

Rezendes, Paul. *Tracking and the Art of Seeing: How to Read Animal Tracks & Sign.* 2nd ed. New York: HarperCollins, 1999.

Websites

BioKIDS: Tracks and Sign Guide: www.biokids.umich.edu/guides/tracks_and_sign

New Mexico State University: Identifying and Preserving Wildlife Tracks: http://aces.nmsu.edu/pubs/_circulars/CR561.pdf

Princeton University: Outdoor Action Guide to Tracking: www.princeton.edu/~oa/nature/tracking.shtml

Wisconsin Department of Natural Resources: Track Quiz: dnr.wi.gov/org/caer/ce/eek/cool/trackquizlvlone.htm

Seeds

Materials in the Box
- specimens of various seeds in a shadow box that fit the following categories of seed dispersal: wind, water, and animals
- Plastomount that shows stages of bean germination
- coconut
- acorns in clear, sealed box
- maple seeds in clear, sealed box
- pictures of coconut tree, oak tree, and maple tree

Topics Covered in Activities and Binder Information
- parts of a seed
- overview of seed variety (e.g., largest, smallest, oldest)
- process of germination

- types of dispersal (wind, water, and animals)
- importance of lemurs for seed dispersal in rain forests of Madagascar (we have an exhibit on rain forests in Madagascar, and many of our staff scientists do fieldwork in this country).

FURTHER RESOURCES

Books

Aston, Dianna H. *A Seed Is Sleepy*. San Francisco: Chronicle Books, 2007.

Galbraith, Kathryn O. *Planting the Wild Garden*. Atlanta: Peachtree Publishers, 2011.

Gibbons, Gail. *From Seed to Plant*. New York: Holiday House, 1991.

Heller, Ruth. *The Reason for a Flower*. New York: Grosset and Dunlap, 1983.

Kesseler, Rob. *Seeds: Time Capsules of Life*. Richmond Hill, ON: Firefly Books, 2006.

Macken, JoAnn Early. *Flip, Float, Fly: Seeds on the Move*. New York: Holiday House, 2008.

Thoreau, Henry D. *The Dispersion of Seeds and Other Late Natural History Writings*. Washington, DC: Island Press and Shearwater Books, 1993.

Websites

Discover Seeds: www.seedimages.com

Dried Botanical ID: http://idtools.org/id/dried_botanical/index.php

Seed Germination Videos: http://plantsinmotion.bio.indiana.edu/plantmotion/earlygrowth/germination/germ.html

The Seed Site: http://theseedsite.co.uk

Seedy Characters: dnr.wi.gov/org/caer/ce/eek/cool/seedy.htm

Skulls

Materials in the Box

- replicas of a deer, raccoon, bobcat, and beaver skull
- goggles that simulate how a prey animal can see things coming up behind it (see figure 5.3)
- Plastomount with different types of teeth specimens

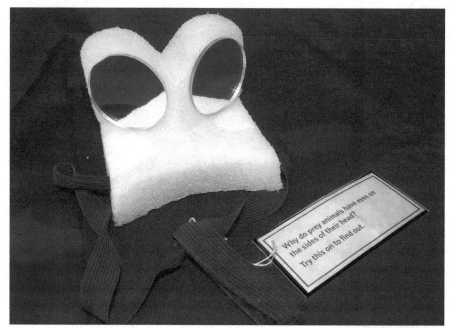

Figure 5.3 Prey Animal Goggles

Topics Covered in Activities and Binder Information

- how an animal skull's teeth can give you clues about whether it is an omnivore, carnivore, or herbivore
- how the location of an animal's eye sockets on its skull can help you determine if it is a predator or prey animal
- clues about each skull's teeth, eye socket placement, and the general shape and size of the skull for participants to try to determine which mammal they are from (with pictures of each animal in the binder)

FURTHER RESOURCES

Books

Collard, Sneed B. *Teeth*. Watertown, MA: Charlesbridge, 2008.

Elbroch, Mark. *Animal Skulls: A Guide to North American Species*. Mechanicsville, PA: Stackpole Books, 2006.

Jenkins, Steve. *Bones: Skeletons and How They Work*. New York: Scholastic Press, 2010.

Pallotta, Jerry. *The Skull Alphabet Book*. Watertown, MA: Charlesbridge, 2002.

Parker, Steve. *Skeleton*. Rev. ed. DK Eyewitness Books. New York: DK, 2004.

Reid, Fiona. *Peterson Field Guide to Mammals of North America*. New York: Houghton Mifflin, 2006.

Roest, Aryan. *Key-Guide to Mammal Skulls and Lower Jaws*. New York: Mad River Press, 1986.

Searfoss, Glenn. *Skulls and Bones: A Guide to the Skeletal Structures and Behavior of North American Mammals*. Mechanicsville, PA: Stackpole Books, 1995.

Websites

eSkeletons Project: www.eskeletons.org

Observing Animals' Teeth: www.brandywinezoo.org/games/teeth_bones.pdf

Skull Terminology and Glossary: www.skullsite.co.uk/glossary.htm

---

Tide Pool Treasures

Materials in the Box

Since many of these specimens are delicate, they are in clear plastic boxes with separate compartments and are taped shut so that the items can survive wear and tear better.

- purple shore crab
- oyster driller shells
- barnacles
- dried brown algae
- whelk egg case
- mussel shells

- sea urchins
- bat sea star
- oyster shells
- turban snails
- chiton

Topics Covered in Activities and Binder Information
- characteristics of tide pools
- adaptations of tide-pool plants and animals to keep from being washed away, to keep from drying out, and to keep from being eaten
- list of places to see tide pools in the area

FURTHER RESOURCES

Books

Coulombe, Deborah A. *The Seaside Naturalist: A Guide to Study at the Seashore.* New York: Simon and Schuster, 1992.

Denny, Mark W. *Encyclopedia of Tidepools and Rocky Shores.* Berkeley: University of California Press, 2007.

Fredericks, Anthony D. *In One Tidepool: Crabs, Snails and Salty Tails.* Nevada City, CA: Dawn Publications, 2002.

Gunzi, Christiane. *Tide Pool.* London: Covent Garden Books, 1998.

Kozloff, Eugene N. *Seashore Life of the Northern Pacific Coast: An Illustrated Guide to Northern California, Oregon, Washington, and British Columbia.* Seattle: University of Washington Press, 1983.

Rosenfeld, Anne W. *The Intertidal Wilderness: A Photographic Journey through Pacific Coast Tidepools.* Berkeley: University of California Press, 2002.

DVDs

The Intertidal Zone. DVD. Directed by David Denning. Oley, PA: Bullfrog Films, 2006.

Life at the Edge of the Sea. DVD. New York: Thirteen/WNET, 1998.

Life on the Edge: A Guide to Pacific Coastal Habitats. DVD. Seattle: Earthwise Media, 2004.

Seashore. DVD. Directed by Bonni Cohen. New York: DK Publishing, 2010.

Seashore Surprises. DVD. Directed by Mark Mannucci. 1992; Lincoln, NE: GPN Educational Media, 2003.

Websites

Cabrillo National Monument: Tidepools: www.nps.gov/cabr/naturescience/tidepools.htm

Marine Science: www.marinebio.net/marinescience/03ecology

National Geographic Magazine: Tide Pools: http://ngm.nationalgeographic.com/2011/06/tide-pools/white-text

NATURALIST BACKPACKS

To extend learning after a museum visit or attending an environmental program at a library, institutions can make Naturalist Backpacks available to their patrons. At libraries patrons can check them out in the same way they borrow other materials in the library collections. Museums can set up systems for checking out the backpacks. Each backpack can contain suggested activities, scientific equipment, educational items, and books related to a particular environmental theme. Similar to the other activities outlined in this chapter, the themes could tie in with museum exhibits, summer reading programs, or other programming themes. The following section outlines the possible contents of some sample Naturalist Backpacks. These are a start to get your juices flowing, but each librarian or museum educator can add or subtract depending on users' needs.

Incredible Insects

- laminated card with a picture of an insect and a spider and highlighting the differences between the two
- laminated card with insect life cycles
- realistic plastic insects or Plastomounts with insect specimens
- plastic insect-collecting containers
- plastic magnifying glasses
- field guides, such as the following, or field guides specific to your area (often nature preserves, entomological societies, or other local environmental groups create their own field guides, which you could include in the backpack):
  - Eaton, Eric R., and Kenn Kaufman. *Kaufman Field Guide to Insects of North America*. With the collaboration of Rick and Nora Bowers. New York: Houghton Mifflin, 2007.
  - Mader, Eric, Matthew Shepherd, Mace Vaughn, and Scott Black. *Attracting Native Pollinators: Protecting North America's Bees and Butterflies*. In collaboration with Gretchen LeBuhn. North Adams, MA: Storey Publishing, 2011.

- Milne, Lorus Johnson, and Margery Joan Greene Milne. *The Audubon Society Field Guide to North American Insects and Spiders*. New York: Knopf, 1980.
- Parker, Steve. *Insects*. Eyewitness Explorer. New York: DK, 1997.
- VanCleave, Janice Pratt. *Janice VanCleave's Play and Find Out about Bugs: Easy Experiments for Young Children*. New York: Wiley, 1999.
- Zim, Herbert S., and Clarence Cottam. *Insects: A Guide to Familiar American Insects*. New York: Golden Press, 1991.

Geology Zone: Rocks and Fossils

- samples of common rocks or minerals found in your area
- samples of each of the different kinds of rocks (igneous, metamorphic, and sedimentary)
- laminated card describing the different types of rocks and the rock cycle
- samples of fossils, some of which you might be able to find in your area
- suggestions of places to go in your area for geology-related field trips
- jewelers' loupes
- field guides, such as the following, or field guides specific to your area (often nature preserves, local parks, geology clubs, or other local environmental groups create their own field guides, which you could include in the backpack):

- National Audubon Society. *Familiar Rocks and Minerals*. New York: Knopf, 1988.
- Parker, Steve. *Rocks and Minerals*. Eyewitness Explorers. New York: DK Publishing, 1997.
- Pough, Frederick H. *Rocks and Minerals*. Peterson First Guide. Boston: Houghton Mifflin, 1991.

- Thompson, Ida. *The Audubon Society Field Guide to North American Fossils.* New York: Knopf, 1982.
- Zim, Herbert S., and Paul R. Shaffer. *Rocks and Minerals: A Guide to Familiar Minerals, Gems, Ores, and Rocks.* New York: St. Martin's Press, 2001.

Look to the Stars!

- planisphere
- night observation light
- sky map or pocket almanac—the California Academy of Sciences publishes a pocket almanac each year that lists moon phases, eclipses, and meteor showers (www.calacademy.org/academy/exhibits/planetarium/pdfs/pocket-almanac-2014.pdf), and Abram's Planetarium also publishes a sky calendar, which is a sky map for all of North America for each month of the year (www.pa.msu.edu/abrams/SkyCalendar/).
- binoculars
- an assortment of books, such as the following:

  - Fredericks, Anthony D. *Exploring the Universe: Science Activities for Kids.* Golden, CO: Fulcrum Publishing, 2000.
  - Horkheimer, Jack, and Stephen James O'Meara. *Stargazing with Jack Horkheimer: Cosmic Comics for the Skywatcher.* Petersborough, NH: Cricket Books, 2006.
  - O'Meara, Stephen James. *Stephen James O'Meara's Observing the Night Sky with Binoculars: A Simple Guide to the Heavens.* New York: Cambridge University Press, 2008.
  - Sneider, Cary I. *Earth, Moon, and Stars: Teacher's Guide.* Berkeley, CA: Lawrence Hall of Science, 2010.
  - Thompson, C. E. *Glow-in-the-Dark Constellations: A Field Guide for Young Stargazers.* New York: Grosset and Dunlap, 1989.
  - Vamplew, Anton. *Simple Stargazing: A First-Time Skywatcher's Guide.* New York: HarperCollins, 2006.

Neighborhood Animals

- laminated card with names and photos or drawings of common animals in your area
- directives on how to carefully observe animals in your area
- tips on creating habitats for wild animals in your yard, such as butterfly gardens, building a bat house or a birdhouse, and so on
- replica tracks and/or scat of common animals found in your area
- binoculars
- an assortment of books that follow these themes (local parks, nature preserves, and/or local offices of the Department of Natural Resources might have pamphlets or handouts with information on local wildlife that you could also include):

  - Amato, Carol A. *Backyard Pets: Activities for Exploring Wildlife Close to Home*. New York: Wiley, 2002.
  - Arnosky, Jim. *Wild Tracks: A Guide to Nature's Footprints*. New York: Sterling Publishing, 2008.
  - Dole, Claire Hagen. *The Butterfly Gardener's Guide*. Brooklyn, NY: Brooklyn Botanic Garden, 2003.
  - Johnson, Catherine J., Susan McDiarmid, and Edward R. Turner. *Welcoming Wildlife to the Garden: Creating Backyard & Balcony Habitats for Wildlife*. Point Roberts, WA: Hartley and Marks, 2004.
  - Landry, Sarah. *Peterson First Guide to Urban Wildlife*. Boston: Houghton Mifflin, 1994.

Our Feathered Friends

- laminated card with a checklist of common birds found in your area
- binoculars
- laminated card with basic birding tips—many field guides have tips you can adapt, or check out the Cornell Lab of Ornithology's Birding Basics website (www.allaboutbirds.org/page.aspx?pid=1200) for ideas or to include as a resource in the backpack

- laminated card with suggestions of local parks or natural areas that are good for bird watching
- National Audubon Society Videoguide to the Birds of North America (DVD, dir. Michael Godfrey [Carrboro, NC: Godfrey-Stadin Productions, 2004]).
- Field guides, such as the following, or field guides specific to your area (often nature preserves, Audubon chapters, or other local environmental groups create their own field guides, which you could include in the backpack):

  - Arnosky, Jim. *Crinkleroot's Guide to Knowing the Birds.* New York: Maxwell Macmillan International, 1992.
  - Boring, Jim. *Birds, Nests, and Eggs.* Milwaukee, WI: Gareth Stevens, 1998.
  - Peterson, Tory Roger. *Peterson Field Guide to Birds of North America.* With contributions from Michael DiGiorgio, Jeffrey A. Gordon, Paul Lehman, Michael O'Brien, Larry Rosche, and Bill Thompson III. Boston: Houghton Mifflin, 2008.
  - Sibley, David. *The Sibley Guide to Birds.* New York: Alfred A. Knopf, 2000.

Plant Party

- examples of pressed plants preserved in between laminated sheets or contact paper found in your area (the National Gardening Association has tips for collecting, pressing, and preserving plants on their Kid's Gardening website, at www.kidsgardening.org/node/11927)
- small plant press and/or instructions on how to make one
- plastic magnifying lenses
- laminated card with basics on different leaf and flower types
- "tree cookies" (small cross sections of tree trunks) from common trees found in your area
- laminated card that shows the different layers of a tree trunk and explains the functions of the layers and how trees grow

- field guides, such as the following, or field guides specific to your area (often nature preserves, local parks, native plant societies, or other local environmental groups create their own field guides, which you could include in the backpack):

  - Arnosky, Jim. *Crinkleroot's Guide to Knowing the Trees.* New York: Bradbury Press, 1992.
  - Brandenburg, David M. *National Wildlife Federation Field Guide to Wildflowers of North America.* New York: Sterling Publishing, 2010.
  - Burnie, David. *Plant.* DK Eyewitness Books. New York: DK Publishing, 2011.
  - Elpel, Thomas J. *Botany in a Day: The Patterns Method of Plant Identification.* 5th ed. Pony, MT: HOPS Press, 2004.
  - Hood, Susan. *Wildflowers.* National Audubon Society First Field Guide. New York: Scholastic, 1998
  - Sibley, David. *The Sibley Guide to Trees.* New York: Alfred A. Knopf, 2009.

Weather Wise

- thermometer
- rain gauge
- laminated card with photos of different types of clouds
- laminated card that describes the difference between weather and climate and has climate information for your area
- laminated card with different weather data that users can collect using instruments in the backpack or by making simple weather instruments (described on the card or in the books included in the backpack)
- an assortment of books, such as the following:

  - Banqueri, Eduardo. *Weather.* Field Guides. New York: Enchanted Lion Books, 2006.
  - Breen, Mark, and Kathleen Friestad. *The Kids' Book of Weather Forecasting: Build a Weather Station, "Read" the*

Sky & Make Predictions! Nashville, TN: Williamson Publishing, 2008.

- Hodgson, Michael. *Basic Illustrated: Weather Forecasting.* Guilford, CT: Falcon Guides, 2008.
- Ludlum, David M. *National Audubon Society Field Guide to North American Weather.* New York: Knopf, 1995.
- Rupp, Rebecca. *Weather!* North Adams, MA: Storey Kids, 2003.
- VanCleave, Janice Pratt. *Janice VanCleave's Weather: Mind-Boggling Experiments You Can Turn into Science Fair Projects.* New York: John Wiley, 1995.

DOING REAL SCIENCE: CITIZEN SCIENCE

Teens and Families with Young Children

At dusk, a man and his son trek out to a pond near their home to listen for and record the various frog calls they hear. On a spring morning, a young girl visiting her grandmother goes into her backyard to watch a mother robin as she feeds her three young hatchlings. A high school student who dreams of going to outer space one day logs onto the Galaxy Zoo website (www.galaxyzoo.org) to help classify images of galaxies taken by the Hubble Space Telescope. A middle school student plays an online game that will help scientists predict the structures of various proteins and develop ways to design proteins, which might help with combating diseases or developing new biotechnologies to help protect our environment and conserve our natural resources.

What do all of these people have in common? They are all citizen scientists—members of the general public who are not professional scientists but who work on actual scientific investigations. Citizen scientists are volunteers, and the amount or level of involvement they have with the research can vary depending on the type of citizen-science project with which they are involved. In many cases, they are simply collecting large amounts of data, but in other projects, they formulate research questions and analyze the results. All citizen-science projects, however, also entail collaboration with professional scientists at some level, and they produce real data that can be used to answer research questions and solve real-world problems.

Citizen-science projects have become popular over the past few decades, but they really are not a new phenomenon. In the late 1800s, the American Ornithologists' Union, concerned about the number of birds hitting lighthouses in the United States, asked lighthouse keepers to keep records of strikes that they observed.[1] In 1900, the Audubon Society started its Christmas Bird Count, which continues to this day and is the longest uninterrupted bird census in the world.[2] Many naturalists and amateur scientists have also long kept phenological records, things such as the arrival of the first migrant birds in spring, the timing of when buds appear on trees, and the first snowfall in winter. Between 1900 and 1923, hundreds of schoolchildren participated in a phenology project in Nova Scotia recording more than two hundred different natural events that took place each year. The Museum of Natural History in Nova Scotia now uses that data and compares it to similar data being collected by citizen scientists today through its Thousand Eyes project (www.thousandeyes.ca). The difference today, though, is in the sheer number of citizen-science projects, which are cropping up all over North America and around the globe. In addition, these projects traditionally started in fields that have had a history of amateur scientists, such as ornithology, astronomy, and geology, but now projects are expanding to other fields, as well. Finally, the scope of the data that citizen scientists collect has also changed, with volunteers often using more sophisticated tools and techniques.

BENEFITS OF CITIZEN-SCIENCE PROJECTS

Citizen-science projects provide myriad benefits. They have helped expand the fields of landscape ecology, population ecology, and natural resource management. Citizen-science projects can gather large amounts of data, over long periods of time, and throughout vast geographic ranges, something that a single scientist or research lab would not be able to do for both logistical and economic reasons. Given the ever-increasing funding cuts to many universities and research institutions, citizen scientists become a valuable resource for helping to advance science. These large-scale data sets can also help scientists to tease out patterns and determine areas or directions to focus their research; perhaps then they can conduct smaller and more focused research projects. They can help conservation managers determine what and where the priority areas are that need their immediate attention. In the realm of invasive species, citizen-science data have been an invaluable tool in several cases to help mitigate their negative effects on certain ecosystems.[3] Having baseline data can make it easier for conservation managers to react to the effects of invasive species and to determine the best course of action to counter those effects. Baseline data can also help inform studies that investigate the effects of climate change on specific species, as well as entire ecosystems.[4] Again, these data are critical for conservation managers and politicians as we all adapt to the changing conditions brought on by our changing climate.

Citizen-science projects can also bring in other viewpoints and perspectives that purely scientific studies might overlook. Often people living in a certain area have intimate knowledge of the natural processes where they live, but traditional scientific research does not always tap into this knowledge. Creating a citizen science program can help ensure that scientists are collecting data relevant to local conservation and management issues. It can also help with buy-in with the introduction of new environmental policies or resource management plans. In a paper by Cooper and colleagues, the authors argue that citizen science can become a key component of the management of urban ecological resources, which are becoming increasingly important as more people live in urban environments and as our natural areas decrease in size. As they state:

> Because citizen science is effective at community engagement, informal education, and research, it can invite stakeholders to express their concerns, consider them along the way, and lead to broader understanding and acceptance of ecology-based management recommendations than if residents were simply presented with recommendations.[5]

Environmental problems and conservation issues are complex and often require complex solutions. Citizen-science programs can help address that complexity, as well as encourage scientists to more pointedly take it into account when conducting research. On a more practical level for scientists, citizen-science projects can also open up new funding sources from organizations that have a science education bent, and they may meet the requirements of many government-funded grants that projects disseminate their results to a broader audience.

Not only scientists receive benefits from these types of projects; so do the citizen scientists. Because these are real scientific investigations, participants have the opportunity to gain a more intimate understanding about the scientific process. For some, these types of experiences are more meaningful and beneficial than a more directed educational activity. Projects are more hands-on, and depending on the type of project, the citizen scientists might have more say in the direction of the research. In addition, participants gain knowledge of specific animals, plants, and/or ecosystems, thus increasing their scientific literacy. An evaluation done on the Cornell Lab of Ornithology's Neighborhood Nestwatch program found that 87 percent of the participants reported increasing their knowledge of bird biology and behavior, and even those who were experienced birders prior to the project reported learning something new about birds.[6] They, like many other citizen scientists, also noted their increase in sense of place and connection to nature in their own backyard, which can often lead to an increased desire to protect it. As people take the time to really delve deeper into their own backyard, into the stream down the street from them, or the natural area where they go hiking on the weekends, they become more invested in those places. They begin to ask questions and want to continue to learn more. It is often said that you protect what you love, and you can only love what you truly know. Citizen-science projects increase scientific literacy, as well as our admiration for the natural world.

CHALLENGES WITH CITIZEN-SCIENCE PROJECTS

Although citizen-science projects offer many benefits, challenges can also crop up with them. Being aware of these potential challenges, however, can assist librarians, museum educators, and scientists in overcoming them or mitigating their effects on the overall project. One criticism of citizen-science projects is whether the data can actually be used for real scientific research, since the projects use people who are not trained scientists, which leads to questions about the quality of the data. Several options exist to address this criticism and to ensure that the data are useful. From the start, designing simple protocols for the citizen scientists to follow in collecting data will make it less likely to introduce errors. Testing out protocols with focus groups before implementing the actual project and holding trainings for citizen scientists will also help ensure accurate data collection. For example, in a study conducted on invasive crabs using one thousand citizen scientists at fifty-two sites along the Atlantic coast, after receiving training and working with a set protocol, third graders accurately identified native versus invasive crabs 80 percent of the time and seventh-grade students showed 95 percent accuracy.[7] In addition, there are many ways, particularly with the use of technology, to build in quality control checks when people enter their data. Scientists can also simply throw out questionable data when analyzing it. Also, in statistics, the larger your sample size, the more accurate your results will be. You are less likely to have anomalies skew your overall data. Most citizen-science projects entail collecting large data sets, which makes them more useful for statistical analysis.

Many citizen scientists might not be professional scientists, but it is very likely that they have some personal experience with the field of interest or basic science knowledge. Many of them are grade school or high school science teachers, avid birders, or amateur astronomers. They are also often extremely dedicated and passionate about the environment. For many of these types of research projects, if citizen scientists are not involved, then the labs rely on graduate students or science technicians to collect the data. Graduate students eventually finish their degrees and move on, so you might have quite a bit of turnover on projects, which can affect long-term monitoring. Dedicated citizen scientists likely will stay with a project much longer than a graduate student will. Also, as the title of a talk given at a citizen-science conference states, "Just because you pay them doesn't mean their data are better."[8]

Time also poses a challenge. Scientists might feel like they do not have the time to work with the general public. Fears of having to constantly answer questions or facing interruptions to other projects they have under way can prohibit scientists from getting involved in projects like these. As mentioned in the previous section, however, many scientists have found that they can gain new insights or perspectives from working with the public. Citizen-science projects can also save them the time of having to gather large amounts of data themselves. Finally, if the projects are well designed from the start, educators, rather than the scientists themselves, take care of much of the interaction with the public.

Another common critique of citizen-science projects is that they don't really allow participants to learn about the scientific process as a whole since they only undertake data collection. One simple way to counter this is to create smaller projects in which citizen scientists engage in all steps of the research process, from formulating research questions to collecting data, analyzing it, and drawing conclusions. Alternatively, you could design projects in which subsets of volunteers might become involved in the different aspects of the work, depending on their skill sets and educational qualifications. Some citizen-science projects, such as Bird Sleuth (www.birds .cornell.edu/birdsleuth), offer a curriculum along with the project that can be implemented in classrooms to more overtly outline the scientific process and provide complementary activities that might entail designing their own research projects. Incorporating ways for citizen scientists to see the data they are collecting and providing a space for them to do their own analysis are other ways to involve them in other parts of the scientific process. Technology can help make this easier. Many citizen-science programs also include enrichments, such as talks by the scientists who are using their data and/or talks by other experts in the field on related topics. All of these types of activities expand participants' learning and make them feel like a valuable part of these scientific endeavors.

Sustaining citizen-science projects can also prove difficult. Recruiting, training, and retaining volunteers are no simple feats. It is imperative that you have staff dedicated to doing these tasks. Incorporating many of the ideas outlined in the previous paragraph will help with the retention of volunteers. Having institutional buy-in and aligning the projects with your overall mission and goals are also key. Many funders readily support novel projects or new undertakings, but they are less likely to provide operational funds. Thus, having institutional support becomes paramount, including providing for these types of projects in your organization's overall budget. Some organizations do charge membership fees or fees for the trainings to help cover costs, too.

TIPS FOR DESIGNING AND IMPLEMENTING A CITIZEN-SCIENCE PROJECT

For many school and public libraries, and some science centers, creating and implementing a new citizen-science project might not be feasible without partnering with a university, environmental organization, or research institute. It isn't impossible, though, and this type of project could be a fruitful way for libraries to partner with other organizations.

Many natural history museums do have scientists on staff, so creating a program might be easier for them. They might also serve as another option for a partner with a library or science center. The following outlines different components that you should consider when designing and implementing a citizen-science project. Several online and print resources exist that outline best practices for establishing a citizen science project; these are listed at the end of this section. The following tips were gleaned from these different resources.

Define Goals, Objectives, and Action Plans

Citizen-science projects combine education and scientific research, so it is important to define goals, objectives, and action plans for each of these areas. Finding a balance between the two and putting equal weight on the importance of each one will also help with the success of your program.

Part of this step involves defining the project's research questions. Obviously, scientists should be involved in this process, but the level of their involvement can vary depending on how you want to design the project. You can have the scientists develop the questions on their own. Alternatively, the questions could come from the citizen scientists themselves but be presented to scientists to get feedback on whether they seem reasonable for a research project. Another approach could entail scientists and citizen scientists working together from the start to formulate the research questions.

The end use and the users of the results of the study should also be considered during this stage. Is this a project that is looking at the spread of a disease among a particular population of wildlife? Is it designed to provide information to conservation managers? Are you collecting data to help change behaviors or implement a new conservation policy? Will only scientists use the data collected, or will politicians, students, or community members also use the data? The answers to these different questions will help direct the kinds of data you collect and in which ways.

This stage also involves determining the scope of your project. How many participants do you envision working on the project? What is your geographic range? How complex or simple will the project be? How long will the project be? Is this an ongoing monitoring project, or is it only for a certain period of time? The answers to these questions will help inform your goals and objectives. This in turn will help you to define the actual activities and steps you will take to implement the project, as well as serving as a guide for evaluation.

Create a Team

Citizen-science projects involve a variety of constituencies, which, therefore, require collaboration among various people with different areas of expertise to ensure the project's success. A scientist needs to be involved to help with designing protocols, in order to ensure scientific accuracy and to assist with and/or undertake the analysis of the data collected.

An educator needs to be involved to communicate the importance of the project to members of the general public—both those directly involved in the project and possible funders or supporters of the project. This person's role will also entail recruiting, training, and retaining volunteers. Some of this person's tasks will likely include communicating how the data volunteers have collected have been used or even working with them to analyze the data themselves. In terms of retaining volunteers, the educator will need to develop support materials and programs for the project, as well as establish systems for participant feedback.

Two other critical roles include a statistician or information scientist and an evaluator. These might be skills that the educator or scientist have and can undertake themselves, but it might also be useful to bring someone else in, at the very least as an adviser. Citizen-science projects often entail large data sets, so it becomes necessary to have a clear plan of how to enter, archive, analyze, and present the data. Information scientists and statisticians are experts at this. An evaluator can ensure that clearly defined goals and objectives get laid out from the start of the project, and assess how well these are met both during and after completion of the project.

Develop a Data Management Plan

The data management step clearly demonstrates the need for collaboration among the different members of the team you formed in the previous step. Once you have decided which questions you want to try to answer with the project, you need to determine what data to collect to be able to answer those questions. Along with this comes determining how you will store, analyze, display, and disseminate the data. The scientist and statistician or information scientist will play key roles in this stage of project planning.

The scientist, working with the educator, will also want to develop protocols for collecting the data. As discussed in the previous section on some of the challenges with citizen-science projects, quality-control issues exist with data collection, but various techniques can mitigate them. Creating simple, easy-to-follow protocols is one way to do this. Test out the protocols with a pilot group before going live to get out any bugs and help ensure more accurate data collection. Also, educators should set up training programs and support systems to provide feedback or help if problems arise once the volunteers begin gathering data. These can include workshops, online tutorials, and educational materials to help with the identification of species, and Listservs or online forums for discussion between volunteers and the educator.

Technology can also help with data quality. Online forms that don't allow you to submit the data until all boxes are completed help ensure more complete data collection. You can also build in automatic checks by putting limits on what can be entered in a particular data field on the online form. It can also make it easier to flag anomalous data, which scientists can later check and decide to keep or throw out. Overall, having a good data management plan from the start will prevent many possible pitfalls as the project is under way.

Recruit, Train, and Retain Volunteers

The type of citizen-science program you are undertaking will influence how you recruit participants. If it is a large-scale project in which the citizen scientists are simply collecting data, you can use a more broad-based approach, likely utilizing many of the outlets you do for other programming in your library or museum. This might include your website, blog, social media, e-mail lists, or newsletters. With this type of project, it is also important to stress why the work they are doing is important—how it fits into the larger goals of the project.

If your project targets a specific group, such as scouting groups or high school students, be sure to include those groups in your planning from the start. Teachers have packed curriculum requirements that they need to meet, so designing the project to fit in with those goals will lead to higher buy-in. The same could be said for other organizations or groups that might have their own guidelines or goals. Special-interest groups, though, can also be a wonderful ready-made source of volunteers, such as local birding groups, anglers, hikers, or amateur astronomers. Offering different points of entry or different ways to get involved with a citizen-science project can also make recruiting easier. Some volunteers might prefer being in the field collecting data. Others might prefer sorting through and cataloging specimens collected or doing other lab or office work. Volunteers with more expertise in the field might be able to serve as trainers for new recruits or a resource for fielding questions or concerns from the other participants.

Once you have your group of volunteers, they need to be trained. Establish a clear training program. Again, the scope of the project and the volunteers' level of involvement will help shape the training program. In some cases, having online tutorials and information sheets might work fine. In general, though, you are likely going to want to have some sort of face-to-face workshop to ensure that participants clearly understand how to use the protocols and feel comfortable and confident in their data-collecting abilities. The training should include information on the scientific process and the importance of research ethics and scientific integrity so that they clearly understand their role in the process and the importance of collecting accurate data. You should also include ways for participants to follow up after the trainings if they have questions or concerns about the project. This could happen via e-mail, phone, Listservs, or other online forums.

How you are going to retain volunteers is another aspect to consider. Demonstrating to participants how their data is being used provides one key way to maintain their interest in the project. Creating a newsletter, website, blog, or regular e-mail updates on the project can sustain interest. Making the data sets available online will provide access not only to scientists but also to the citizen scientists to do their own analyses, which will make them feel more invested in the project. For example, the Cornell Lab of Ornithology, which has a citizen-science project titled eBird (www.ebird .org), found that when it made modifications to features on the website that allowed participants to track their own observations and compare them to observations made by others, the number of individuals submitting data nearly tripled.[9] Also, if participants' data are used in published scientific articles, letting the participants know about this will highlight the importance of the research and the role they play in it.

Providing enrichment opportunities can also help sustain volunteer interest. This might entail delivering workshops or hosting talks by scientists or other experts on topics related to the project. For example, the California Academy of Sciences had a citizen-science project in which volunteers were gathering baseline data on its Living Roof—which plants were blooming at different times of the year and which birds and insects used the roof as habitat. In conjunction with this project, horticulturists on staff presented a workshop on the importance of native plants (the Living Roof is planted with California natives) and gardening at home with native plants. Other citizen-science projects, such as the Cornell Lab of Ornithology's BirdSleuth (www.birds.cornell.edu/birdsleuth), have developed supporting curriculum that can be used by teachers, homeschoolers, or informal educators who are also part of the citizen-science project.

Conduct Evaluations

Evaluation of your citizen-science project should come directly from the goals and objectives you established at the outset. Having clear and measurable goals and objectives will make it easier to evaluate the project and can also help with developing an evaluation plan from the start. For guidance in developing strong goals and objectives and creating an evaluation plan for your project, you can consult the National Science Foundation's *Framework for Evaluating Impacts of Informal Science Education*.[10]

Because citizen-science projects generally have both scientific and educational goals, you will want to evaluate both aspects of the project, which might mean using different methodologies for each aspect. Some questions you might want to consider for ongoing evaluations of your project might include the following:

- Are the protocols working? Do they need to be modified? Are you getting accurate data?
- Are volunteers receiving enough support?
- Is the training program valuable and meeting the needs of the volunteers?
- Is participating in the project valuable for the scientist? Is it worth his or her time? Has the scientist published anything based on the data collected from the project?
- What do the volunteers find most valuable about participating in the project? Why do they continue to volunteer? Why do they leave if they have stopped volunteering?

Again, many of the questions you will want to ask in your evaluations will depend on your goals and objectives for your particular project, but these are some questions you might also want to keep in mind. You might want to consider involving an outside evaluator in your project. In addition, several books and other resources exist on conducting evaluations, and the resources listed in the following section include recommendations for specific sources.

RESOURCES FOR DESIGNING AND ESTABLISHING A CITIZEN-SCIENCE PROJECT

The following is a list of resources with further information about designing and implementing citizen-science projects. Some include step-by-step outlines to follow, and others have examples of already-established projects that you could use as models:

Bonney, Rick, Caren B. Cooper, Janis Dickinson, Steve Kelling, Tina Phillips, Kenneth V. Rosenberg, and Jennifer Shirk. "Citizen Science: A Developing Tool for Expanding Science Knowledge and Scientific Literacy." *BioScience* 59, no. 11 (2009): 977–984.

Citizen Science Academy—National Ecological Observatory Network. www.citizenscienceacademy.org.

Citizen Science Toolkit—The Cornell Lab or Ornithology. www.birds.cornell.edu/citscitoolkit/toolkit.

Citsci.org—Natural Resources Ecology Lab at Colorado State University. www.citsci.org.

Conrad, Catherine T., and Tyson Daoust. "Community-Based Monitoring Frameworks: Increasing the Effectiveness of Environmental Stewardship." *Environmental Management* 41 (2008): 358–366.

Cooper, Caren B., Janis Dickinson, Tina Phillips, and Rick Bonney. "Citizen Science as a Tool for Conservation in Residential Ecosystems." *Ecology and Society* 12, no. 2 (2007): 11. www.ecologyandsociety.org/issues/article.php/2197.

Managers' Monitoring Manual—USGS Patuxent Wildlife Research Center. www.pwrc.usgs.gov/monmanual.

Prysby, Michelle, and Paul Super. *The Director's Guide to Best Practices Programming—Citizen Science.* Logan, UT: Association of Nature Center Administrators, 2007.

EXAMPLES OF CITIZEN-SCIENCE PROJECTS

Citizen Science at the California Academy of Sciences

In 2011, the California Academy of Sciences embarked on a journey to define what citizen science means for its institution and to establish a list of best practices to inform all of its future citizen-science projects. As mentioned previously, citizen science can mean different things to different people, and slightly different approaches can be taken when creating new projects. Through discussions with educators, researchers, and citizen scientists, the academy established the following overarching goals to direct all future citizen-science projects:

- Engage the public in real, active scientific research connected to the academy.
- Create projects with direct impact on biodiversity, science literacy, and/or conservation.
- Provide an opportunity for tiered involvement by members of the public with varying expertise and time.
- Provide multiple entry points for participants at different stages of the scientific enterprise: defining the research, planning, data collection, analysis, and sharing outcomes.
- Engage scientists and participants in mutually beneficial work together.
- Innovate in the use of mobile and other digital media.

Examining these goals and applying them to their current citizen-science projects, the academy found some gaps in what it was doing, particularly in the number of possible participants and their involvement in the different stages of the scientific enterprise. Therefore, they decided to discontinue them and put their efforts into developing new projects that better aligned with these goals.

Although it might not immediately jump to mind when thinking of biologically rich areas of the world, California represents one of the richest biodiversity hotspots in the world. Biodiversity hotspots are regions in the world that exhibit high levels of species endemism (organisms found nowhere else in the world), which are also severely threatened because of human activities. As an example, 61 percent of the 3,500 plant species found in California are endemic, but at the same time about 75 percent of the original vegetation has been degraded. The California Academy of Sciences holds the largest and most comprehensive specimen collection of California biodiversity in the world, and its scientists have and are conducting research projects in biodiversity hotspots around the world, including California. Therefore, the academy decided to leverage these resources and knowledge to develop new projects that focus on California biodiversity—focusing on monitoring what exists now, how species' ranges have changed or are changing, and helping to inform conservation decisions to preserve California's natural resources for the future.

To launch this new initiative, the academy developed two test cases. The test cases would allow them to test out ways to engage, enlist, and collaborate with citizen scientists to glean information about California biodiversity. They also would provide baseline data about what organisms exist in each of the regions today, and enable comparisons of this to historical data from the academy's collections, which can help inform conservation priorities and be used in modeling for the effects of climate change.

The first test case was terrestrial, focusing on plants in the Mt. Tamalpais watershed. The academy partnered with the Marin Municipal Water District on this project, which manages more than twenty-one thousand acres of land, including a large portion in the Mt. Tamalpais watershed. These lands provide some of the main sources of water for the district, so ensuring the ecological health of the watershed is a high priority. A group of more than sixty citizen scientists were trained and then went out on three different days to do surveys of the plants on Mt. Tamalpais. They took geo-referenced photos, recorded data, and in some cases collected specimens to be incorporated into the academy's collections. Another team of volunteers worked with the academy's Botany Department to mount the specimens that were collected for storage in the herbarium, thus achieving the goal of allowing for multiple-entry points for the project. To date, more than 300 species have been identified in the watershed and 323 specimens have been collected to help fill in the gaps in the academy's botanical collections.

The second test case is focusing on marine species found in the Fitzgerald Marine Reserve in Moss Beach, California, which is one of the richest intertidal areas along the California coast. Tide pools hold a variety of life in small spaces that have constantly changing environmental factors with the movement of the tides. For this test case, the academy partnered with the Fitzgerald Marine Reserve, Gulf of the Farallones National Marine Sanctuary, which administers the Fitzgerald Marine Reserve; the Friends of the Fitzgerald Marine Reserve; and the Farallones Marine Sanctuary Association. The Fitzgerald Marine Reserve already serves as a Long-Term Monitoring Program and Experiential Training for Students (LIMPETS) monitoring site (www.limpetsmonitoring.org). This citizen-science program developed by the Farallones Marine Sanctuary Association brings high school and college students to the Fitzgerald Marine Reserve to monitor intertidal invertebrates and algae as part of larger studies that look at the effects of climate change on these organisms and ecosystems. The LIMPETS program also conducts monitoring in tide pools near the reserve in an area known as Pillar Point, which is not a protected area. The current protocols used by LIMPETS do not include specimen collecting or photo documenting of the area. Therefore, the academy sought to expand its protocols to include these two components. Using data from the two areas could also allow scientists to look at differences in the effects of climate change in protected and unprotected areas. More than fifty volunteers were trained to do surveys of intertidal invertebrates. As of the end of 2012, more than four hundred observations had been made of about two hundred different species, and twenty-two specimens had been collected to be incorporated into the academy's research collections.

Future steps for the academy's citizen-science initiative include continuing and expanding the current test cases. The academy hopes to more directly incorporate the overall goals that were not a focus of the test cases—creating tiered involvement in the scientific process, creating more types of entry points, and developing innovative uses of mobile and other digital media in the projects. For future developments, check out its citizen-science website: www.calacademy.org/science/citizen_science.

LARGE-SCALE CITIZEN-SCIENCE PROJECTS

Some libraries and museums might not have the capability to create their own citizen-science project, but they could serve as participants, promoters, or disseminators of information about already-existing citizen-science projects. Many projects will likely fit into already-existing programs at your institution or match the interests of your visitors or users of library resources. The following are examples of large-scale and well-established citizen-science projects that cover a range of areas, including birding, astronomy, and earth sciences.

Foldit (fold.it/portal)

Rather than rescuing princesses, finding a lost treasure, or ridding the streets of criminals, why not help find treatments for human diseases or design more efficient biofuels? Gamers can do just that by participating in Foldit. In 2008, researchers from the Center for Game Science and the Department of Biochemistry at the University of Washington rolled out their online game Foldit to help solve biological riddles related to how proteins fold.

Each human contains thousands of different kinds of proteins, which help us function, including by moving our muscles, breaking down food, and fighting diseases. These proteins are made up of long chains of amino acids, but rather than staying in a long straight line, the proteins tend to fold into different configurations. Understanding how a protein folds tells us how it functions, and for many proteins we do not fully understand or know how they fold. Foldit attempts to draw on humans' spatial and puzzle-solving skills (something we still do better than computers) to predict the structure of various proteins.

Several human diseases also involve proteins. Learning more about the different ways proteins fold can aid scientists in designing new proteins to combat various diseases. In 2011, in just ten days, gamers determined the structure of a protein that plays a vital role in the reproduction of the HIV virus, something that biochemists had been working on for decades. Knowing the structure will enable scientists to develop drugs to target this protein. The results of this study were published in the journal *Nature*

Structural and Molecular Biology, with the scientists and gamers listed as coauthors.[11]

Anyone around the world can participate in Foldit by going to the website and downloading the game. There is information about protein folding on the website, which it is good to look over before starting the game. New players also go through a series of introductory puzzles that familiarize them with the basic tools and concepts they'll need to move on to the more complex puzzles. There is also a FAQ section on the website and forums in case people run into snags. The website also lists "community rules" to avoid any problems, and moderators can step in if necessary. Players can also keep up-to-date on new game features, challenges, and how their work is being used in research on the website's blog. For those looking to mix gaming and science, this is the citizen-science project for them.

FrogWatch USA (www.aza.org/frogwatch)

Many frog and toad populations in the United States and worldwide have been experiencing dramatic declines. Their permeable skin and the fact that they spend part of their lives in water and part on land make frogs and toads more susceptible to pollution or other disturbances to their habitats. Many populations have also fallen victim to the infectious disease chytridiomycosis. To confront these widespread challenges and to set conservation priorities, scientists and conservation planners need to have information about frog and toad populations, including their current status, how well they can and are adapting to changes in their environments, and more about basic biology for certain species.

In 1998, the US Geological Survey (USGS) initiated the FrogWatch USA program to gather concrete data to prove that amphibian populations were in decline and to help educate the public about this crisis, as well as providing tools to reverse these trends. In 2002, the National Wildlife Federation took over administration of the program, and in 2009, this responsibility passed to the Association of Zoos and Aquariums, which continues to manage the program today. Throughout all these changes in leadership, the methods used to gather data have remained the same. Volunteers, who do not need to have any background in the sciences or expertise in amphibians, go through a training workshop with a local FrogWatch USA chapter. The training covers how to accurately collect and record data, including learning the different mating calls of frogs and toads in your area. The volunteers then agree to monitor a wetland for at least three minutes throughout the breeding season. This entails listening and recording all of the different frog or toad calls they hear during those three minutes. These data are entered in a nationwide database, which wildlife managers, zoologists, and ecologists use throughout the country.

Given that the Association of Zoos and Aquariums now manages this program, most FrogWatch USA chapters, which recruit and train volunteers, reside in zoos and aquariums. Some chapters, however, have been established in nature preserves and museums. FrogWatch provides training for establishing a chapter, as well as ongoing support materials for maintaining one. With its ready-made materials and support system, this project can be a way to more easily incorporate conservation programs in your museum or library. The FrogWatch USA website includes more information about establishing a chapter (www.aza.org/host-a-frogwatch-chapter). Libraries, museums, and schools—whether as a chapter hub or simply as promoters of the project—can join in the froggy fun while assisting with important conservation work.

Galaxy Zoo (www.galaxyzoo.org)

Imagine sitting in the comfort of your own home and peering into a part of the far reaches of the universe that no other human has seen before. Participating in Galaxy Zoo allows you to do just that. A pair of researchers, Kevin Schawinski from Yale University and Chris Lintott from Oxford University, launched Galaxy Zoo in 2007. Schawinski was in the midst of a project looking at star formation that entailed examining millions of images captured by the telescope used in the Sloan Digital Sky Survey. The task of picking out and analyzing features of galaxies was one that humans could do more accurately than a computer, meaning hours upon hours of work. Schawinski had spent a week working twelve hours a day and got through fifty thousand galaxies. Exhausted from the monotony of the work, he and Lintott devised a plan to harness the power of the Internet to achieve the goals of the project more rapidly and with less strain on Schawinski. They set up a website where registered participants could classify different images of galaxies on the basis of their features. With hopes that maybe the work would get done in two years, they quickly realized the full power of our modern connected world: within twenty-four hours of launching the site, they were receiving seventy thousand classifications an hour.

Given the success of this first iteration of the project, the two organized a larger team and formalized the project. They launched Galaxy Zoo 2, which asked participants more detailed questions about the characteristics of a subset of the galaxies analyzed in the first phase of the project. They have now moved on to having citizen scientists evaluate images from the Hubble Space Telescope. These projects are all part of a larger umbrella of citizen-science projects, known as Zooniverse (www.zooniverse.org), which use a similar approach to harnessing public help with large data sets. In addition to inspiring and informing the creation of these other citizen-science projects, Galaxy Zoo has led to the publication of many scientific papers and has enabled researchers to gain valuable time on telescopes around the world to further their investigations, thus leading to new discoveries. Specific examples of this can be found on the Galaxy Zoo website.

Participating in Galaxy Zoo does not require background knowledge in astronomy. All you need to do is read over the brief online tutorial about how the project works: the classification system used and the types of further questions you will be asked when looking at the images of the galaxies. Once you have read this over, you can begin classifying galaxies. The project has a blog and forum to help with any questions or concerns participants might have and to keep them updated on the results of their work, as well as information and news on related topics. For those interested in the depths of the universe, this is the project for them.

The Great Sunflower Project (www.greatsunflower.org)

Over the past few years, many beekeepers, farmers, and scientists have noticed a dramatic decline in honeybee populations across the United States due to colony collapse disorder. What most people do not realize is that many native bee populations (honeybees were introduced from Europe) have suffered reductions in their populations, too. Gretchen LeBuhn, a biology professor at San Francisco State University, found that although much research has been done into how the decline in honeybees is affecting agriculture on a large scale, not much is known about native bee populations and the effect of their declines on our gardens, crops, and wild plants. In 2008, she started the Great Sunflower Project to gather information about bee populations in urban, suburban, and rural areas.

To partake in the project, participants must plant flowers and then observe the number and types of bees that visit a particular flower in fifteen minutes. The citizen scientists make these observations twice a month during the blooming season, and then record their data and other information about their location and submit it to the project. Originally, the project required that participants plant a specific type of sunflower, Lemon Queen, to standardize the quality and amount of nectar and pollen the bees were receiving and to ensure that the flower would provide food to bees. Some varieties of sunflower do not actually produce pollen. Since the start of the project, the flower choices have expanded to include bee balm, cosmos, rosemary, tickseed, and purple coneflower. All of these plants do not have many varieties, so the level of rewards for bees that visit them will be fairly standardized from garden to garden.

In 2012, the project hit one hundred thousand people who had signed up. According to the project website, it has created the "largest single body of information about bee pollinator service in North America." The researchers involved in the project have created a map of pollinator service across the United States based on data received, and they provide information on how the amount of development, garden size, and the habitat around a garden affect pollinator service, all of which can be viewed on the website. To join in the buzz about bees, plant some flowers, grab a stopwatch, and start taking note of these industrious insects that are vital to the survival of many of our crops and other wild plants.

NestWatch—The Cornell Lab of Ornithology (www.nestwatch.org)

The Cornell Lab of Ornithology has been one of the pioneers and leaders in the field of citizen science. NestWatch is just one of several bird-related citizen-science projects it oversees. This nationwide project entails recruiting people of any age (it is recommended that kids be accompanied by an adult) or background to monitor the reproductive behaviors of songbirds. To become a volunteer, you must read over the online materials and pass an online quiz. Once you pass the quiz, you look for a nest to monitor by visiting it every three or four days throughout the breeding season and recording your observations. The website includes materials to help you locate nests and identify bird species. NestWatch also has a "Focal Species Guide," which lists species that are of particular interest to scientists and can be searched by region so you can become familiar with what birds might be in your area.

Scientists and members of the public use the data collected through the NestWatch program to monitor the status and trends of the reproductive biology of North American birds. By combining these data with historical data, scientists can explore how populations might be changing over time due to climate change, habitat loss or degradation, and the introduction of invasive or nonnative animals and plants. One key advantage of NestWatch is that many of the nests observed are on private land (in people's backyards), which normally would not be easily accessible to scientists. Given the urbanization of much of the United States, this proves vital to looking at how different bird species are adapting to these changes. Several scholarly articles on bird reproduction and citizen science have been published as a result of the project, and they are listed on the NestWatch website. This is an excellent project for people to get up close and personal with our feathered friends in our neighborhoods.

Project BudBurst (www.budburst.org)

Many scientists and members of the general public agree that our world's climate is changing. We have entered a period of unusual warming, which is affecting all forms of life on our planet, although in different ways. Plants, in particular, are affected by changes in climate. With changes in the timing of the arrival of warmer spring temperatures and cooler fall temperatures and variations in rainfall patterns due to climate change, the phenophases (timing of different life cycle stages of plants) are also shifting. Given the dependence of many animals on plants for nourishment and the important interplay of flowers and pollinators, it becomes vital to record and understand the changes in plant phenophases to be able to make predictions about future conditions in our environments.

Project BudBurst began in 2007 as a way for members of the general public to make a meaningful contribution to investigating and understanding the changes to our environment due to climate change. Comanaged by the National Ecological Observatory Network and the Chicago Botanical Garden, the project's mission summarizes its goals and activities: "Engage people from all walks of life in ecological research by asking them to share their observations of changes in plants through the seasons." Participants can be of any age and ability, and their involvement can entail either engaging in regular observations or making onetime reports. Regular observations involve choosing a plant to monitor over an entire growing season; recording important phenological events (e.g., the emergence of the first leaves, the first flowers, and fruiting); and recording other information about the plant, which is then added to a nationwide database. Alternatively, participants can make single reports about specific plant species chosen by the project coordinators as species of particular interest for scientists. This option works well for those who cannot commit to regular monitoring over an entire year or for those who might be going on vacation to a particular area and want to add to the project's database. The website has links to the forms participants need to fill out and background information on plants to help them with making their observations.

Since its inception, Project BudBurst has gathered nearly fifteen thousand observations from all fifty states in the United States. All of the data collected are uploaded to a public database, making it available for use by anyone, including scientists, educators, and project participants. Phenology has a long history in the United States and around the world, which means that scientists can use current data and compare them with historical data to detect longer-term impacts of climate change. Current data can also help scientists to examine the impacts of climate change on specific plant species and how they are responding to those changes locally as well as nationally. It's a growing movement that will likely lead to many fruitful results.

The Quake-Catcher Network (http://qcn.stanford.edu)

Earthquakes strike suddenly, violently, and often without warning. Scientists and engineers, however, are working to better understand the science behind earthquakes to create early-warning systems and to improve the design of human-made structures to withstand these natural disasters. Legions of people, or rather, their computers, can assist with this process through the Quake-Catcher Network (QCN). Elizabeth Cochoran, a US Geological Survey (USGS) scientist, and Jesse Lawrence, a geophysicist at Stanford University, initiated the project while they were postgraduate researchers at the Scripps Institute of Oceanography as a way to create a large-scale, low-cost, strong-motion seismic monitoring network. Today, several research institutions and the USGS collaboratively manage the project.

The project entails having volunteers utilize motion sensors, known as micro electromechanical systems (MEMS) accelerometers, either within or attached to Internet-connected computers. Many newer models of laptops, cell phones, and other electronic devices already have MEMS sensors in them for hardware protection purposes. For those computers that do not already have an internal MEMS sensor, you can attach one externally through a USB cable. These sensors are available from QCN at a low cost or in some cases for free, such as for teachers and volunteers in high-risk areas. Once you join the network, the sensors run in the background, sending signals to QCN's servers when strong motions are observed. Receiving signals from a variety of computers in an area can help scientists to better understand ground motion around faults during an earthquake and aid in the design of early-warning systems, which could save lives and mitigate the effects of a disaster. For example, on March 5, 2012, a network of two thousand QCN computers detected a 4.0 earthquake in El Cerrito, California, sending signals to the network's servers in Palo Alto (forty-five miles away) ten seconds before the ground motions actually reached Palo Alto.[12] Ten seconds might not seem like much, but it could be enough time to warn people to find a safe spot or to leave more vulnerable structures.

In addition to the monitoring goals, the project also seeks to raise awareness about the science behind earthquakes and to promote earthquake preparedness. The researchers have developed software, QCNLive, which can be used with the sensors to teach about earthquakes, and they provide a variety of other curriculum resources on their website related to earthquakes. School librarians could partner with teachers in promoting this project and implementing the curricular resources. This is also an ideal project for museums that have earth sciences exhibits to promote. Public libraries can promote the network with their patrons and even set up a sensor at one of their public computers, particularly in earthquake-prone areas.

NOTES

1. Sam Droge, "Just Because You Paid Them Doesn't Mean Their Data Are Better," in *Citizen Science Toolkit Conference*, ed. Catherine McEver, Rick Bonney, Janis Dickinson, Steve Kelling, Ken Rosenberg, and Jennifer Shirk (Ithaca, NY: Cornell Lab of Ornithology, 2007), 13–26.

2. National Audubon Society, "Christmas Bird Count," http://birds.audubon.org/christmas-bird-count.

3. Alycia W. Crall, Gregory J. Newman, Catherine S. Jarnevich, Thomas J. Stohlgren, Donald M. Waller, and Jim Graham, "Improving and Integrating Data on Invasive Species Collected by Citizen Scientists," *Biological Invasions* 12, no. 10 (2010): 3419–3428; David G. Delany, Corinne D. Sperling, Christiaan S. Adams, and Brian Leung, "Marine Invasive Species: Validation of Citizen Science and Implications for National Monitoring Networks," *Biological Invasions* 10, no. 1 (2008): 117–128.

4. Theresa Crimmins and Michael Crimmins, "The Critical Role That Citizen Scientists Can Play in Identifying Adaptation Strategies to Climate Change," *Arid Lands Newsletter* 60 (2008): 25–28; Janis L. Dickinson, Benjamin Zuckerberg, and David N. Bonter, "Citizen Science as an Ecological Research Tool: Challenges and Benefits," *Annual Review of Ecology, Evolution, and Systematics* 41 (December 2010): 149–172.

5. Caren B. Cooper, Janis Dickinson, Tina Phillips, and Rick Bonney, "Citizen Science as a Tool for Conservation in Residential Ecosystems," *Ecology and Society* 12, no. 2 (2007): 6, www.ecologyandsociety.org/issues/article.php/2197.

6. Celia Evans, Eleanor Abrams, Robert Reitsma, Karin Roux, Laura Salmonsen, and Peter P. Marra, "The Neighborhood Nestwatch Program: Participant Outcomes of a Citizen-Science Ecological Research Project," *Conservation Biology* 19, no. 3 (June 2005): 589–594.

7. See Delaney et al., "Marine Invasive Species," 117–128.

8. Droge, "Just Because You Paid Them," 13–26.

9. Rick Bonney, Caren B. Cooper, Janis Dickinson, Steve Kelling, Tina Phillips, Kenneth V. Rosenberg, and Jennifer Shirk, "Citizen Science: A Developing Tool for Expanding Science Knowledge and Scientific Literacy," *BioScience* 59, no. 11 (2009): 977–984.

10. Alan J. Friedman, ed., *Framework for Evaluating Impacts of Informal Science Education* (Washington, DC: National Science Foundation, 2008).

11. Firas Khatib, Frank DiMaio, Foldit Contenders Group, Foldit Void Crushers Group, Seth Cooper, Maciej Kazmierczyk, Miroslaw Gilski, Szymon Krzywda, Helena Zábranská, Iva Pichová, James Thompson, Zoran Popović, Mariusz Jaskolski, and David Baker, "Crystal Structure of a Monomeric Retroviral Protease Solved by Protein Folding Game Players," *Nature Structural and Molecular Biology*, no. 18 (2011): 1175–1177.

12. Steve Tung, "Stanford's Quake-Catcher Network Detects a Tremor 10 Seconds Before the Tremor Reaches Campus," *Stanford Report,* March 6, 2012, http://news.stanford.edu/news/2012/march/quake-catcher-warning-030612.html.

COMING TOGETHER FOR SCIENCE FUN: FAMILY SCIENCE PROGRAMS

A refrigerator door can give you insights into a family, according to science education expert James A. Shymansky and his colleagues.[1] It often acts as a showcase of the activities and accomplishments of the children in the family. Works of art tend to abound—finger-painting masterpieces or a carefully crafted pencil sketch. You might also find a successful spelling test or a poem about winter, a holiday celebration, or a family pet. Examples of work done related to science almost never appear, though.

In many ways this survey of refrigerator doors reflects the state of science learning in the United States today. As highlighted in other sections of this book, just as science gets short shrift on the refrigerator, it also often loses out in terms of class time in schools, particularly during the elementary years. With more and more emphasis on standardized testing and many elementary teachers not feeling adequately prepared to teach science, the focus tends toward language arts and math. A large-scale study on third-grade classrooms across the country found that on average, 48 percent of instructional time is spent on literacy and language arts activities, 24 percent on math, and 5 percent on science.[2] In many cases, much early science learning falls on parents and caretakers to undertake at home.

As our refrigerators show, however, science at home does not always happen either. Many parents likely have bad memories of school science if they encountered a more rote approach to learning it. Science to them was just a series of facts that they needed to memorize rather than a process and means of inquiry to help explain phenomenon in the world around them. It is likely that they did not experience a hands-on approach to doing science, and in many cases, particularly for women, they might have been made to feel that they couldn't do science or be a scientist. Since our understanding of certain aspects of science is also constantly changing as new discoveries are made, many parents might feel like they do not know enough about scientific principles to be able to help their children to learn about them. Parents often pass on these fears and negative attitudes toward science to their children, sometimes in a more overt way and sometimes subconsciously. Gender can also play a factor in how much science parents do with their children. A study that analyzed parent-child conversations during science-related tasks found that "fathers of sons used more cognitively demanding talk than fathers of daughters" during a physics-related task.[3] This same study also explored parents' views on their children's attitudes and ability in relation to science. The authors found that fathers tended to think that science is less interesting and more difficult for girls than boys. Given these findings, not only might there be a lack of science talk and/or science activities in certain homes, but also gender roles might subconsciously or consciously play into how much science children are exposed to in the home.

Facing this context, libraries and museums can play an important role in getting more families involved in science through family science programming. Whether it is a single, focused workshop or more of a family science fair with several different stations, family science programs reap many benefits. These type of programs present science in a hands-on and nonthreatening way so that both parents and children can begin to see that they do have the skills necessary to be scientists and that science can be fun.

Parents can then continue the learning at home, too, since they can begin to shed some of the fears or negative attitudes they might harbor toward science. It also gives children the chance to see their parents doing science, acting as role models. Studies have shown that regardless of ethnic or racial background or socioeconomic status, increased parental involvement in children's learning leads to increased academic success.[4] Attending family science programming increases parents' involvement in their children's science learning. In some cases, too, the kids themselves might act as a teacher to their parents, which can greatly boost their confidence. Finally, many parents might view math and reading as more important skills than science for their young children to learn, and they might not immediately see the relevance to their everyday lives of sciences. Family science programming can help make them aware that science is all around us, and that many of the skills used in science are important and useful in other areas. Also, many of the higher-paying jobs of the future are predicted to be within the sciences, particularly engineering. Building early science skills will better prepare children to go into these fields in the future.

TIPS FOR DEVELOPING AND DELIVERING FAMILY SCIENCE PROGRAMS

Family science programs can encompass a variety of approaches. One way to implement them can be as a workshop focused on one particular topic, such as birding or ways to make your house more eco-friendly. The California Academy of Sciences, for example, has offered Naturalist 101 workshops for families with children age ten and older. Each workshop lasts two hours and focuses on a different topic, such as birding, insect identification, and native plants. Generally, the program starts in the lab so that the participants get some background information, such as identifying the parts of an insect, some of the main families of insects you might find in the San Francisco area, an overview of the different tools scientists use to collect insects, and the importance of insects in different ecosystems. Then, participants apply their new knowledge and skills by going outside (for the academy, this means Golden Gate Park) to collect and identify insects. The parents and children learn together in these programs, and everyone is directly involved in the activities. These workshops are for smaller groups of up to about twenty people, with two instructors.

A family science night or family science fair is another approach to family programming. Generally, these types of programs reach a much larger number of people, even up to a hundred or more. Usually, they are centered on a theme. When deciding on the theme, look to your community. Is there a predominant cultural group that you would like to target by incorporating cultural connections to science, such as Mayan astronomy or the physics of kite making or kite fighting, which is popular in several Asian countries? You can look at some of the environmental resources and issues in your community, too, and maybe focus on those. For example, are you in a watershed? What is significant about watersheds? How can you help care for your watershed? Looking at the community might also help you find volunteers to participate in the event—as guest speakers, facilitators of activity stations, or hosts of community organization tables that you might want to include. It also will help ensure that the topics covered are relevant to the participants so that they make connections to how science fits into their everyday lives.

The main portion of family science fairs or science nights entails a series of different stations at which families can partake in short, simple science activities. The stations should consist of stand-alone activities, and it should not matter what order families do them in or if they do not complete them all. This allows families to go at their own pace and focus on the stations that interest them most. As an added incentive to visit a variety of stations, you could create a sort of passport that families get stamped at each station, and if they get a certain number of stamps, they can get a small prize or be entered into a raffle for larger prizes. In some cases, though, you might want to have an introductory speaker to launch the event, which could be a community member who works in a scientific field.

The number of stations can vary depending on how many people you want to attract to the event and the number of staff members or volunteers you have to run it. There are various sources you could tap into for volunteers to lead each of the stations. High school students often need to complete service hours, so with a little bit of training, you could have them staff the stations. In this way, they just might learn some new science, too, and often, younger children get more out of near-peer interactions than if an adult were leading the activity. Another option is to work with student teachers. A study by Harlow that involved preservice teachers who facilitated stations at a family science night found that not only the families and children benefited from the experiences, but the student teachers did, as well.[5] The event provided them with the opportunity to test out more hands-on and collaborative approaches to teaching science, which would help them be more confident when implementing them in the classroom. They also were able to develop their skills around interacting with parents and learned techniques for quickly assessing what students already know about science, which they could later apply in the classroom. Finally, a family science fair could be an opportunity for libraries to partner with local science museums, such as by inviting their staff to facilitate some of the stations.

Activities at the stations should be simple and easy to complete in a short amount of time. They should use inexpensive and easy-to-find materials so that parents can see that the activity is something they could also do easily at home with their kids. You could connect the activities to the school standards, particularly if you decide to limit the program to a particular age range. In this way, you can help build on what the children are already studying in school. The following are some sources for activity ideas:

Books

Heil, David, Gayle Amorose, Anne Gurnee, and Amy Harrison, eds. *Family Science*. Portland, OR: Portland State University, 1999.

Markle, Sandra. *Family Science: Activities, Projects, and Games That Get Everyone Excited about Science!* Hoboken, NJ: John Wiley & Sons, 2005.

Sarquis, Mickey, and Lynn Hogue. *Science Night Family Fun from A to Z: 26 Activities for School or Community Family Science Nights*. Middletown, OH: Terrific Science Press, 2000.

Websites

How to Smile: All the Best Science & Math Activities: http://howto
smile.org

TryScience Experiments: www.tryscience.com/experiments/
experiments_home.html

Zoom—Activities from the Show: http://pbskids.org/zoom/
activities/sci

Whether you implement a stand-alone workshop or a family science night or science fair, you should include some sort of takeaway for families. For a stand-alone workshop, it could include the school standards the activity aligns with, extension activities to do at home related to the theme of the workshop, and general tips on helping parents see how they can encourage their kids to think and act like scientists (for more on this, see chapters 2 and 4). For a family science night or science fair, you could incorporate this into the passport you give the families for the different stations. You could also create a website or blog that could include this information.

EXAMPLES OF FAMILY SCIENCE PROGRAMS

In February 2012, the California Academy of Sciences hosted the Celebrate Engineering family day as part of National Engineers Week, an annual event (www.discovere.org/our-programs/engineers-week). In planning the event, my colleague and I searched for four simple activities to do at four stations:

- Building a boat out of a square piece of aluminum foil and then testing how many seashells it can hold before sinking (adapted from the APEX Science curriculum developed by the Miami Museum of Science, at www.miamisci.org/apex/#).
- Building a structure out of coffee stirrers and marshmallows and then testing it on a model shake table to see how well it can withstand an earthquake (adapted from the APEX Science curriculum developed by the Miami Museum of Science, www.miamisci.org/apex/#)

- Making and flying a Borneo glider (adapted from www.cal academy.org/teachers/resources/lessons/build-a-borneo-glider)
- Testing the building strength of squares versus triangles (adapted from www.pbs.org/wgbh/buildingbig/educator/act_straw _ei.html)

Once we chose the activities, I trained a group of high school interns who are part of the academy's Careers in Science youth program to lead the activities on the day of the event. We also invited another staff person who works in our audiovisual and electronics department to sit at a table to talk about his work and demonstrate some of the things that he had created for use in our exhibits. The program lasted from 11 a.m. to 3 p.m. on a Saturday. It was a drop-in program, and visitors could visit any or all of the stations, in any order. We had nearly 250 people come to the event to share in the wonder of engineering as a family.

The following are two family science workshops that we have delivered at the California Academy of Sciences and that could be adapted and used at libraries, science museums, or nature centers. In both of these activities, similar to the Naturalist 101 workshops, the parents or caretakers are active participants in the workshops along with the children. In this way, they have an opportunity to learn together.

WSI: Wildlife Scene Investigation

Age Level: Families with children age 8 and older
Time: 45–60 minutes

Science behind the Topic

Wildlife biologists often use clues to determine which animals have been in a certain area and how they interact with their environment and other animals. An important clue is animal tracks. Different types of animals can leave different types of tracks. Scientists often divide animals into three main walking styles, which can affect the types of tracks they leave:

- **Plantigrade:** walking with the entire sole of the foot on the ground. Often tend to be slower walkers. Examples include bears, raccoons, skunks, and humans.
- **Digitigrade:** walking on your toes with the heel completely raised. Tend to be faster than plantigrade walkers. Examples include bobcats, mountain lions, wolves, coyotes, foxes, rabbits, squirrels, and mice.
- **Unguligrade:** walking on the tips of your toes, usually hooves. This group tends to include some of the fastest-moving animals. Examples include deer, pronghorn antelopes, and wild boars.

Different surfaces, mud versus snow, for example might affect the impression left of a foot and can cause slight variations in tracks from the same type of animal. The gait, or distance between tracks, can also give you clues about whether the animal was walking or running.

Scat, or animal feces, is another important clue for wildlife biologists. Different kinds of animals have different kinds of scat. Learning how to tell them apart can help you figure out which animals have gone through the area. Scientists also often use scat to learn what different animals have been eating by analyzing it. In addition, herbivores tend to eat more frequently than carnivores to ensure they get enough calories, and because of this, they tend to leave more scat behind. This is why you often see piles of small pellets left behind by deer or rabbits. If you encounter scat in the wild, however, you should not pick it up with your bare hands since there are diseases that wild animals can transfer through their feces to humans. Instead, take a picture or draw a sketch with detailed descriptions of the scat if you want to try to identify it later.

Animals' skulls can also give you clues about an animal's behaviors. For example, looking at an animal's teeth helps you figure out whether it is an herbivore, carnivore, or omnivore:

- **Herbivores** are animals that eat only plants. They have broad, flat molar teeth located in the back of the mouth. These teeth are good at grinding and mashing plants. They may also have larger, well-developed incisors, or front teeth, useful for cutting and gnawing on plants.

- **Carnivores** are animals that eat only meat. They have large, pointed canine teeth found on either side of the incisors. These are used for piercing and holding prey. They also have sharp and pointy molars good for cutting and tearing flesh.
- **Omnivores** are animals that eat both plants and meat. They have both herbivore and carnivore teeth characteristics. They can have well-developed incisors for tearing plant material and long pointy canines for capturing and holding prey. An omnivore's molars are both flat and pointy so that they can crush and grind plant material, as well as cut and tear flesh.

Eye placement on the skull can tell you whether an animal is a prey species (hunted) or a predator species (hunter). There are, however, some species that are both predators and prey animals in some cases, such as wolves, which can be predators of deer or elk, but also the prey of humans. In general, when we look at the eye sockets on skulls, a herbivore skull's eyes point out to the side of the head. This allows herbivores to have a field of vision that is much wider than that of predators so that they can see something creeping up behind them. Carnivores have eyes that face forward, which allows them to have binocular vision, improving their abilities to zero in on their prey. Omnivores usually have eyes that are in a sort of intermediate position.

Finally, animals might leave other general clues as to what they were doing or what they were eating. For example, you might find tall grass matted down in large areas where deer slept the night before. Nibbled-on branches or small tree trunks might be a clue that there are beavers nearby. Feathers or pieces of fur can also let you know that a bird or a mammal might have passed by recently. Several kinds of birds—particularly owls—leave pellets, which consist of the bones and fur of the small creatures, which they cannot digest. They regurgitate these as compact pellets. By looking at all of these different clues, you can begin to gain an understanding of the complex lives of the animals in your area.

Materials

- variety of animal skull replicas (at least one of each type of animal—carnivore, omnivore, and herbivore)
- variety of fake scat from different animals
- 2 owl pellets
- at least 4 pieces of white butcher paper or poster paper
- scat and track field guides (enough for four groups to have at least 2 books)
- markers
- variety of animal-track stamps
- stamp pads
- pencils
- cardboard cut into rectangles about 6″ × 5″
- white paper cut into rectangles that are slightly smaller than the cardboard
- yarn cut into pieces about 7–8″ long
- hole punches
- colored pencils or crayons
- small trash can
- examples of trash (clean)
- ping-pong balls or golf balls
- oyster, clam, and mussel shells
- small sticks that look like they have been gnawed on the ends
- fish bones (real or replicas)
- goose scat (replica)
- snakeskin shed (optional)
- deer scat (replica)
- deer skull (real, replica, or photo)
- acorns
- woodland bird feather—photo or real (optional)
- soda-can six-pack rings (optional)
- 2 sheets of 8½″ × 11″ white paper
- Scotch tape

Note: Acorn Naturalists (www.acornnaturalists.com), Bone Clones (www
.boneclones.com), Skulls Unlimited (www.skullsunlimited.com), and Nasco
(www.enasco.com/science) are good sources for fake scat, skull replicas,
animal-track stamps, and owl pellets.

PROCEDURE

Prior to the start of the program, prepare the four wildlife scenes on the
pieces of butcher paper. Lay the papers on different tables (separated from
each other) and place the other items on top of them. The participants will
interpret the scenes in groups of about four or five, so if you have a larger
group, you might want to repeat one or more of the scenes (i.e., have two
groups working on the same type of scene), or you can make up your own
additional scenes. At the end of this section you can find illustrations and
explanations of each of the wildlife scenes.

At the start of the program, use the information found in the "Science
behind the Topic" section to introduce the activity and give the participants
some background information. Tell the group that when you go exploring
outdoors, you won't always see animals because they are usually shy and
afraid of people. Then ask them, "How do you know if animals are close
by or have been in an area recently?" Use their answers to guide your discussion about the different clues that wildlife biologists use to tell whether
animals have been in an area. When going over each of the clues (skulls,
tracks, scat, and pellets), you can use the skull replicas, pictures of tracks or
track stamps, scat replicas, and one of the owl pellets to help explain them.

Next, divide the participants into groups of four or five. Give each group
a skull, based on what you just talked about, and have the groups decide
whether their animal is a carnivore, herbivore, or omnivore, and whether it
is a prey animal or a predator. Give each group about five minutes to look at
their skull and discuss this. If they want to, they can also try to guess what
kind of animal their skull might be from. After the five minutes, have each
group share their answers and the evidence they used to support them.

Now, tell the group that they are going to continue to act like wildlife
biologists, but this time by looking at an entire wildlife scene. They will
imagine they have been transported to a different habitat—a river, an urban

environment, a forest, or a seashore (you should let each group know which environment they have been assigned to). Tell the participants that they need to investigate this mysterious scene and try to determine what happened on the basis of the clues they find there. Encourage them to think about the following: What animal might have made this track? What does it eat? What was it doing? Give each group at least two scat and track field guides that they can use to help them with their investigations. Give the groups about eight to ten minutes to investigate their scenes. Then, have each group present their scene and their explanation of what happened to the other groups while all participants are standing in front of the scene.

As a final activity, have the participants make their own track field guide. To do this, they should use the precut pieces of white paper (which could be paper that has writing on one side that you are reusing) and cardboard (which could also be from cracker boxes or cereal boxes that you are reusing). You can either preassemble the books or have the participants do it. They should decide how many pages they want (about fifteen to twenty is usually a good amount). Then have them punch two holes through the pieces of paper along the long side of the paper, making sure to line up the holes if they don't punch all of the sheets in their book at once. Do the same with two pieces of cardboard for the front and back of the book. Then string the paper and cardboard together with the yarn.

Now they can stamp different tracks on each sheet, writing the name of the animal above or beside the stamp. They can leave some of the pages blank so that they can take notes or draw pictures of things they see the next time they go out exploring in nature. They can also decorate the cover using the crayons or colored pencils. They are now set to explore their own wildlife scenes in the wild.

Wildlife Scenes

Forest

Use figure 7.1 as a guide to set up the forest scene. Draw or stamp the deer and wolf tracks as shown in the picture. Place the deer-scat replica anywhere you like in the scene. Place a deer skull near where the tracks end. You can also draw some blood splatters near the skull. In the other section

Figure 7.1 Forest Scene

of the scene, draw or stamp the squirrel tracks. Using one of the 8½″ × 11″ sheets of paper, tape the two short sides down to the butcher paper, creating a small arch, and put the acorns underneath it. If you are using a bird feather, place it wherever you would like in the scene.

In this scene, a wolf pursues a deer and is successful in its hunt. This deer or another deer seems to have left some scat behind, which the wolf might have seen and knew to look for deer in the area. A squirrel or squirrels have been busily gathering acorns, storing them up for the winter. From the feather, we know that a bird might have flown over or might have a nest nearby.

Figure 7.2 River Scene

River

Use figure 7.2 and the following instructions as a guide to set up the river scene. Draw part of the river and the shoreline. Draw or stamp the beaver tracks. Place some sticks that look like they have been nibbled on near the beaver tracks. In another part of the scene, draw or stamp the bear tracks. Place the fish bones near the bear tracks. Finally, draw or stamp goose prints near the water, and place the goose scat near the prints.

In this scene, a beaver has been busy gathering sticks for its lodge or to create a dam, or maybe just to eat. Some geese stopped by the river, maybe on their way migrating south or north. A hungry bear stopped by. It caught and ate some fish from the river.

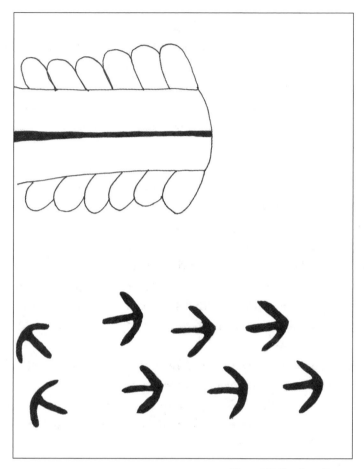

Figure 7.3 Seashore Scene

Seashore

To set up this scene, draw the sea turtle tracks as depicted in figure 7.3. At the end of the tracks, make an arch with the other piece of 8½″ × 11″ paper, similar to the one you made for the acorns. Place the ping-pong or golf balls under this arch. In another part of the scene, draw or stamp the oyster-catcher prints. Place the oyster, clam, and mussel shells near the prints. If you are including the soda-can six-pack rings, you can place them anywhere in the scene.

In this scene, a female sea turtle has left tracks on the beach as she came ashore to lay eggs, which are represented by the ping-pong or golf balls. Some oystercatchers have come ashore to feast on oysters, clams, and mussels. If you are using the six-pack rings, they were likely left by a human who visited the beach. You can then talk about the dangers of plastics to marine wildlife. Six-pack rings can get caught around the necks of animals, leading to suffocation. Many shorebirds eat pieces of plastic, which can clog up their intestinal systems. Sea turtles often eat plastic bags, mistaking them for jellyfish, also leading to intestinal blockage and often death.

Urban

To set up this scene, draw or stamp the raccoon tracks as depicted in the scene. The small trash can should be at the end of the tracks, flipped over with trash spilling out. Coming from a different direction toward the trash can, draw the house cat tracks as depicted in figure 7.4. Also, draw another set of raccoon tracks going away from the trash can. In another section of the scene, draw or stamp house mouse tracks with blood splatters at the end of them. A little ways after the tracks, place an owl pellet. Finally, if you are using the snakeskin shed, you can put that anywhere you would like in the scene.

In this scene, a raccoon has raided a trash can but was interrupted by an approaching house cat. The raccoon wasn't sure how big or exactly what kind of animal was coming, so it decided to leave the trash can. In another area, a house mouse became a meal for an owl, which later left a pellet behind. Finally, there appears to be a snake in the area as well, as shown by the snakeskin shed

FURTHER RESOURCES

Arnosky, Jim. *Crinkleroot's Book of Animal Tracks & Wildlife Signs.* New York: Putnam, 1979.

Arnosky, Jim. *Wild Tracks: A Guide to Nature's Footprints.* New York: Sterling Publishing, 2008.

Collard, Sneed B. *Teeth.* Watertown, MA: Charlesbridge, 2008.

Elbroch, Mark. *Animal Skulls: A Guide to North American Species.* Mechanicsville, PA: Stackpole Books, 2006.

Johnson, Jinny. *Animal Tracks & Signs.* Washington, DC: National Geographic, 2008.

Figure 7.4 Urban Scene

Levine, Lynn. *Mammals Tracks & Scat: Life-Size Tracking Guide.* East Dummerston, VT: Heartwood Press, 2008.

Morlock, Lisa. *Track That Scat!* Ann Arbor, MI: Sleeping Bear Press, 2012.

Olaus, Murie J., and Mark Elbroch. *Peterson Field Guide to Animal Tracks.* 3rd ed. Boston: Houghton Mifflin, 2005.

Selsam, Millicent E., and Marlene Hill Donnelly. *Big Tracks, Little Tracks: Following Animal Prints.* Let's-Read-and-Find-Out Science. New York: HarperCollins Publishers, 1999.

Design Your Own Eco-House

Age Level: Families with children age 10 and older
Time: 45–60 minutes

Science behind the Topic

According to the US Green Building Council, building-related activities are responsible for the following:

- 38 percent of the nation's carbon dioxide emissions
- 73 percent of the nation's electricity consumption
- 40 percent of the use of raw materials globally
- 13.6 percent of the nation's potable water use, or fifteen trillion gallons per year[6]

In addition, according to an estimate by the Environmental Protection Agency, the United States generated 170 million tons of construction and demolition waste, with 39 percent coming from residential sources.[7]

Given these statistics and the rise of the sustainability movement, many are looking at ways to make our buildings more eco-friendly. By incorporating green features into our homes, we can reduce the impact that they have on the environment by

- improving natural surroundings
- reducing consumption of resources and raw materials
- reducing energy consumption
- reducing water consumption and wastewater output
- improving indoor surroundings and air quality for occupants

Green building design benefits not only the environment but also our own human health.

Some simple and not-too-costly things you can do to start greening your home today include the following:

- **Installing Compact Fluorescent Lightbulbs (CFLs):** Compact fluorescent lightbulbs (CFLs) use about 75 percent less energy, produce the same amount of light, and last up to ten times longer.[8]

- **Replacing Showerheads:** A high-efficiency showerhead disperses less than 2.5 gallons per minute, using up to 60 percent less water than a traditional showerhead.[9]
- **Setting Up Programmable Thermostats:** Programmable thermostats can save $150 in annual electricity costs.[10] By customizing a schedule for heating and cooling, excess use can be greatly reduced.
- **Buying Energy-Efficient Appliances:** Energy Star certifies efficient appliances that use 10–50 percent less energy and water than standard models.
- **Use Eco-Friendly Cleaning Products:** The EPA has a list of products at www.epa.gov/dfe/pubs/projects/formulat/formpart.htm that have been certified as safer for the environment.

With these simple steps you can begin to create your own eco-house.

Materials
- wooden dollhouse
- desk lamps
- compass
- eco-house category sheets (see appendix, page 231)
- eco-house shopping lists (see figures 7.5 and 7.6)
- pencils or pens
- 7 labeled boxes with the samples (enough for 4 houses—one of each sample type) stored in individual zip-top plastic bags:

    - **Insulation Box:** denim (jeans), cellulose (newspaper), sheep's wool, and foam. Write "Insulation Box—Choose 1 material" on the box.
    - **Interior Wall Box:** paint, drywall, wood paneling, and vinyl wallpaper. Write "Interior Wall—Choose 1 material."
    - **Flooring Box:** bamboo, carpet, linoleum, and finished hardwood. Write "Flooring Box—Choose 1 material" on the box.
    - **Window Box:** single pane, double or triple pane, low-emissivity (Low E) glass, plastic blinds, cotton curtains, and orientation of the house. Write "Window Box—Choose 1 material" on the box.

- **Energy Use Box:** solar panels, washer-dryers (non–Energy Star versus Energy Star), clothesline, air conditioner, fan, lightbulb (incandescent and florescent). Write "Energy Box—Feel free to pick and choose" on the box.
- **Water Use Box:** rain barrels, shower heads, toilet, irrigation, washing machine. Write "Water Use Box—Feel free to pick and choose" on the box.
- **Landscaping Box:** green lawn, trees, native plants, nonnative plants, living roof. Write "Landscaping Box—Feel free to pick and choose" on the box.

Notes on the materials: When planning this activity at the California Academy of Sciences, we initially envisioned having four groups and a dollhouse for each group. When we thought more about the costs and storage needs of these, we decided to just purchase one and have the different groups insert their materials and/or orient the house when they presented their information. If you want each group to have its own house, however, you can do that, too. The lamp is meant to represent the sun, and the compass is to help the participants decide how to orient their houses if they want to include passive solar features. Another alternative could be to use building plans rather than a three-dimensional house and have the participants lay the different samples on the paper and orient the lamp next to the paper.

For the samples, you can check with local home-building supply stores or different green-building companies to see whether they might be willing to give you samples to use for the activities. Otherwise, you can find other items to stand in for the objects, such as denim scraps for the jeans insulation and cotton balls for the sheep's wool insulation. Alternatively, you can use photos to represent the different choices.

PROCEDURE

Using the information in the "Science behind the Topic" section, introduce the group to the facts about some of the environmental impacts of construction and homes in the United States, as well as the concept of green building. You can also ask the group if they have any green features in their own homes, or if they know of some strategies for making homes more eco-friendly.

Eco-House Shopping List

Within your group, study the product information for each category. Place a checkmark next to the items that you think you should purchase to construct your eco-house. Be ready to present your selections to the group, listing the reasons for your ultimate decisions.

Insulation
- ☐ Denim
- ☐ Cellulose
- ☐ Sheep's wool
- ☐ Foam
- ☐ Straw bale

Reasons:

Interior Walls
- ☐ Drywall
- ☐ Natural paint
- ☐ Regular wall paint
- ☐ Vinyl wallpaper
- ☐ Wood paneling

Reasons:

Flooring
- ☐ Bamboo
- ☐ Natural carpet
- ☐ Synthetic carpet
- ☐ Linoleum
- ☐ Finished hardwood

Reasons:

Windows
- ☐ Single paned glass
- ☐ Double/triple paned
- ☐ Low-e glass
- ☐ Plastic or wooden blinds
- ☐ Organic cotton curtain
- ☐ House orientation

Reasons:

Eco-House Shopping List (continued)

Energy Efficiency
- ☐ Solar panels
- ☐ Regular washer and dryer
- ☐ Energy Star washer and dryer
- ☐ Clothesline
- ☐ Regular air conditioner
- ☐ Energy Star air conditioner
- ☐ Ceiling fan
- ☐ Incandescent light bulbs
- ☐ Compact fluorescent light bulbs

Reasons:

Water
- ☐ Rain barrel
- ☐ Low-flow shower head
- ☐ Regular shower head
- ☐ Drip irrigation system
- ☐ Sprinklers
- ☐ Low-flow toilet
- ☐ Regular-flow toilet

Reasons:

Landscaping
- ☐ Green lawn
- ☐ Trees
- ☐ Native plants
- ☐ Nonnative plants
- ☐ Living roof

Reasons:

Figure 7.5 Eco-House Shopping List

Next, divide the group into four teams. Tell them that they are part of an architectural firm that has been hired to design an environmentally friendly home. Their goal is to create a home that is energy efficient and water wise and that uses sustainable materials, keeping in mind costs. Give each group copies of the eco-house categories, the eco-house shopping list, and a set of samples for each of the categories. Let the groups know that they will be exploring seven different categories when making decisions about the design of their house: insulation, interior walls, flooring, windows, energy and appliances, water use, and landscaping. For each category, they should look over the information on the categories sheet, and then as a group decide which item or items to include in their house. They should fill out their eco-house shopping list sheet while doing this, writing down their reasons for the choices they made. If you are going to have each group use their own house, then you can let them know that they can change the orientation, using the lamp and compass to help, and they can put their items directly in and around the house. Give the groups about twenty to twenty-five minutes to make their decisions.

When time is up, bring the participants back together as a large group. Have each group present their designs. They should place the items they chose in the dollhouse while they are explaining their choices. Also, let them know that if they chose to include passive solar, they can change the orientation of the house, using the compass, and turn on the lamp to represent the sun to demonstrate their design. Once everyone has presented, have a discussion with the group using the following questions as a guide:

- Which choices involved our own comfort and personal preferences?
- Which choices were the most realistic, given price and convenience?
- Which choices minimized damage to the natural world?
- How might an ideal green building present a challenge for the average family?
- Overall, was it easy or hard to make decisions about what to include or not to include in your group's design?

To wrap up, share some simple, low-cost steps that the participants could take to make their own house greener (using the information from the "Science behind the Topic" section). These could be part of handout that also includes a bibliography of green-building resources.

FURTHER RESOURCES

Books

Baker-Laporte, Paula, Erica Elliott, and John Banta. *Prescriptions for a Healthy House: A Practical Guide for Architects, Builders & Homeowners.* Gabriola Island, BC: New Society Publishers, 2008.

Dunnett, Nigel, Dusty Gedge, John Little, and Edmund C. Snodgrass. *Small Green Roofs: Low-Tech Options for Greener Living.* Portland, OR: Timber Press, 2011.

Dunnett, Nigel, and Noël Kingsbury. *Planting Green Roofs and Living Walls.* Portland, OR: Timber Press, 2008.

Johnston, David, and Kim Master. *Green Remodeling: Changing the World One Room at a Time.* Gabriola, BC: New Society Publishers, 2004.

Owens, Ted. *Building with Awareness: The Construction of a Hybrid Home.* Corrales, NM: Syncronos Design, 2006.

Pahl, Greg. *The Citizen-Powered Energy Handbook: Community Solutions to a Global Crisis.* White River Junction, VT: Chelsea Green Publishing, 2007.

Ramsey, Dan, and David Hughes. *The Complete Idiot's Guide to Solar Power for Your Home.* New York: Alpha Books, 2007.

Snell, Clarke, and Tim Callahan. *Building Green: A Complete How-to Guide to Alternative Building Methods: Earth Plaster, Straw Bale, Cordwood, Cob, Living Roofs.* New York: Lark Books, 2005.

Snodgrass, Edmund C., and Lucie L. Snodgrass. *Green Roof Plants: A Resource and Planting.* Portland, OR: Timber Press, 2006.

DVDs

Building Green. Directed by Tippy Bushkin. Boston: WGBH Boston Video, 2008.

Green Builders: A Green Revolution Takes Root in the Garden State. Written and produced by Bob Szuter. Englewood: New Jersey Network (NJN), 2008.

Websites

Bay Localize—*Use Your Roof!*: www.baylocalize.org/programs/green-your -city/use-your-roof

Build It Green Fact Sheets: www.builditgreen.org/build-it-green-fact-sheets

Energy Star: www.energystar.gov

Green Roofs for Healthy Cities: www.greenroofs.org

Environmental Protection Agency, "An Introduction to Indoor Air Quality": www.epa.gov/iaq/voc.html

National Invasive Species Information Center: www.invasivespeciesinfo.gov

US Green Building Council—Green Building Facts: http://new.usgbc.org/ sites/default/files/Docs18693.pdf

WaterSense: An EPA Partnership Program: www.epa.gov/watersense

NOTES

1. James A. Shymansky, Larry D. Yore, and Brian M. Hand, "Empowering Families in Hands-on Science Programs," *School Science and Mathematics* 100, no. 1 (January 2000): 48–56.

2. National Institute of Child Health and Human Development Early Child Care Research Network, "A Day in Third Grade: A Large-Scale Study of Classroom Quality and Teacher and Student Behavior," *The Elementary School Journal* 105, no. 3 (January 2005): 305–323.

3. Harriet R. Tenenbaum and Campbell Leaper, "Parent-Child Conversations about Science: The Socialization of Gender Inequities," *Developmental Psychology* 39, no. 1 (2003), 44.

4. Sophia Catsamibs, "Expanding Knowledge of Parental Involvement in Children's Secondary Education: Connections with High School Seniors' Academic Success," *Social Psychology of Education* 5, no. 2 (2001): 149–177; Charles Desforges and Alberto Abouchaar, *The Impact of Parental Involvement, Parental Support and Family Education on Pupil Achievements and Adjustment: A Literature Review* (London: Department of Education and Skills, 2003); William H. Jeynes, "A Meta-Analysis of the Relation of Parental Involvement to Urban Elementary School Student Academic Achievement," *Urban Education* 40, no. 3 (2005): 237–269.

5. Danielle B. Harlow, "The Excitement and Wonder of Teaching Science: What Pre-Service Teachers Learn from Facilitating Family Science Night Centers," *Journal of Science Teacher Education* 23 (2012): 199–220.

6. US Green Building Council, "Green Building Facts," https://new.usgbc.org/sites/default/files/Docs18693.pdf.

7. Environmental Protection Agency, "Estimating 2003 Building-Related Construction and Demolition Materials Amounts," 2009, www.epa.gov/osw/conserve/imr/cdm/pubs/cd-meas.pdf.

8. Energy Star, "Light Bulbs for Consumers," www.energystar.gov/certified-products/detail/light_bulbs.

9. Environmental Protection Agency, "Green Building: Bathroom," www.epa.gov/greenhomes/bathroom.htm.

10. Environmental Services Department of the City of San Diego, "Watts Up? Energy Saving Tips," www.sandiego.gov/environmental-services/energy/conservation/wattsup.shtml.

ENVIRONMENTAL ACTION CLUBS

Tweens and Teens

The ice caps are melting. Smog and poor air quality shroud many large cities. Habitat for plants and animals continues to shrink. Every day we are bombarded with messages about environmental problems we face. It can sometimes feel overwhelming and hopeless. Often, environmental education programs have also been criticized for focusing on doom and gloom—as if they could scare people into action. Yes, knowing the facts is important, but young people also need to know that they can do something about it. They can make a change for the better. An environmental action club for tweens or teens is one way to do just that.

Why tweens or teens? What difference can they make? For one thing, young people have enthusiasm, fresh ideas, and creativity. Many of them likely also have time. They have not started a career. They aren't raising their own children, so they can devote time to a cause they feel passionate about. The underestimation of many adults can also work to their advantage. Adults might be more likely to take notice of or listen to a campaign instigated by youth rather than other adults. Also, participating in real-life environmental projects can help young people develop skills and gain knowledge that will serve them well as adults. Environmental issues are often complex—intertwining social, economic, and scientific concepts, as well as involving various stakeholders. By undertaking an environmental project, youth begin to unravel this complexity and learn how to work with others within certain social and economic realities. Finally, they can gain self-confidence and self-efficacy countering the gloom and doom of environmental problems. As Ralph Nader, a well-known environmental and social activist wrote:

> So then, what builds civic motivation? A sense of the heroic progress against great odds achieved by our forebears helps. Think what stamina and inner-strength drove abolitionists against slavery, women seeking the right to vote, workers demanding trade unions to counter callous bosses of industry. . . . These efforts advanced our country immeasurably. They were efforts by ordinary people doing extraordinary things without electricity, motor vehicles, telephones, faxes or e-mail.[1]

Just as young people today might face criticism and obstacles when becoming environmental activists, others, too, have encountered roadblocks to achieving their goals. They overcame them, however, just as youth can. It might not seem like a small group of young people can make a difference, but they can. Many small acts can also add up to immense change.

Public libraries can serve as an ideal space to host an environmental action club. They often have a meeting room or rooms that the club could use. Many public libraries have teen and/or tween advisory boards that give advice on programming, collections, and the teen and tween spaces in the library. Librarians could tap into this type of group when forming an environmental action club, possibly with some of the same teens or tweens or with suggestions they have gathered from other youth. Libraries also have access to a plethora of resources and librarians who can help guide the youth when doing research for their projects. Much as with other programs described in this book, environmental action clubs can also be an ideal way for science museums or nature centers and libraries to partner. The museums and nature centers have the expertise in science-related issues, and the libraries can help with research and conveniently located meeting spaces. Whether or not a museum, nature center, or library (or a partnership among any of these groups) starts the club, it should be youth driven. Adult leaders of the group should act mainly as facilitators. They likely will need to be there for the first meeting, but from then on, they should take a more hands-off approach and become involved only as the youth need them. As McClaren and Hammond, experts on environmental education, point out, "When students are involved in selecting, planning, implementing, and evaluating effective projects, there are opportunities to develop an enhanced sense of personal competence and overcome the syndrome of powerlessness."[2] Youth are more likely to feel ownership and commitment to a project if they, and not adults, are the ones pushing it forward. They will learn that they truly can make a difference.

Several resources are available that outline ways for youth to design, implement, and evaluate environmental or other projects that work to make the world a better place. Many of them are written for youth, with suggestions and tips for them to undertake the project themselves. The following outlines some of the best practices for planning, implementing, and evaluating an environmental project as part of an environmental action club, which have been gleaned from various resources, all of which are listed at the end of this chapter.

FORM A TEAM

The first step is to find youth who are interested in working on environmental projects. As mentioned previously, this group might grow out of a teen or tween advisory board at a public library. School librarians might be able to form an after-school club with students from the school where they work. Museums or nature centers could partner with schools, after-school programs, or libraries to find youths to participate in the project, or it might grow out of a youth program they already offer.

HAVE A FIRST MEETING

For the first meeting of the group, the adult facilitator should attend to get things started. The facilitator can use the meeting as a model for how good meetings are run, and the youth could then emulate that in future meetings, which they will likely have on their own. This includes having an agenda, having someone take notes, and ensuring that those notes (or minutes) are distributed after the meeting to those who attended and those who couldn't attend.

At this meeting, the youth should come up with group norms. As they will quickly learn, working in a group can be both very rewarding and very challenging. Everyone in the group will bring special skills and strengths, which will benefit the group, but pitfalls can arise, particularly when there are differences of opinion. By stepping back at the beginning to establish and agree on group norms, some of these pitfalls might be avoided. This is also a good time to think about how decisions will be made in the case that there isn't consensus. Will it be by open voting or blind voting? Who will have the final say if there is a tie? Having an adult facilitator at the first meeting can help to guide the youth through this process.

PICK THE GROUP'S PASSION

Once group norms have been settled on, the group can begin to brainstorm ideas for their first project. Environmental issues can be complex, so the youth will want to narrow their choices and be as specific as possible. They obviously are not going to reverse climate change on their own, but there might be smaller projects they could do to mitigate its effects. The environment also doesn't recognize political boundaries, so they should think about what level they want to work at—local, national, or international. In most cases, however, it is probably best to start with something smaller that is more concrete and then move onto a more complex project. For example, they could start by having a campaign at their school(s) to reduce the amount of waste created by school lunches. This might then lead to a more complex project of starting a composting program at their school(s), and then eventually campaigning to create a composting system for their town or city.

In some cases, there might be a problem that the youth have noticed in their schools or community that they would like to tackle. Alternatively, they could also do a survey with community members to see which environmental issues or problems the community sees as most pressing.

Several of the resources listed at the end of this section have tips on creating effective surveys. Also, environmental action groups often focus on the negative side of environmental issues or the problems we face. Alternatively, the group could work on a more positive project that celebrates the natural beauty in their area. Maybe they want to do a photography exhibit of nature in their community or a play about the animals and plants in their neighborhood. You could also direct the youth to the websites for various youth environmental awards, such as the Eco-Hero Awards (www.action fornature.org/ecohero_awards.aspx) or the President's Environmental Youth Awards (www.epa.gov/education/peya/index.html). These list past winners and describe the projects they worked on, which might inspire the group about what they want to do. The group doesn't have to decide on an exact project during this step, but they should have a general idea of what aspect of the environment they want to work on.

DO RESEARCH

Once the group has chosen a general area in which to work, they need to do some research. This is an area in which libraries and librarians can help. They could hold a workshop on developing research questions, finding and evaluating resources, and note taking and organizing sources. Encourage the youth to also research opposing viewpoints, since during the project they will likely need to answer to people who don't agree with what they are doing. They might also want to interview people who work for organizations that are also confronting the same issue as the one they have chosen. The youth can learn what approaches they are taking to tackle the problem, and they might find ways to collaborate with the organization. The research phase will also help the group to refine their focus and determine exactly what project they want to undertake.

DEVELOP A PLAN OF ACTION

Now that the group has done their research, they are ready to develop their plan of action. The first thing they need to do is define their overall goal or goals for the project. The goals should clearly and succinctly explain what they hope to achieve and how they will do it. The goals should be things that can be easily measured, that is, that can clearly show whether or not the group achieved their goals.

Once the group has established their goals, then they can devise the other parts of their action plan. This should include all of the steps they need to take to achieve their goal or goals. The four *W* questions can help outline their action plans in the following way:

1. *What* are the exact steps they are going to take to achieve their goal?
2. *Who* is going to carry out each step?
3. *When* are they going to carry out each step? When do they need to have it completed?
4. *Where* are they going to undertake each step?

In assigning the different roles for undertaking the various steps or aspects of the project, they should focus on drawing on the different strengths of the group. They also should ensure that they are as inclusive as possible and that everyone has a role. Finally, it is important to ensure that everyone understands his or her role and that everything the group does relates back to the overall goal or goals.

Depending on the type of project the group decides to undertake, there are different techniques and tools they can draw on to help them achieve their goals. The adult leader can introduce the group to these tools and help guide them in using them. Several of the resources listed at the end of this chapter also discuss these tools, so the youth can turn directly to them, as well. These techniques include the following:

- **Promoting Their Event or Project:** The group will want to get the word out about what they are doing. They could do this by creating flyers or posters, which they distribute at school, at the library, at the museum, and in community centers and local businesses. They can also write up a press release and/or invite the press to their event. Often, local media like to have stories that involve young people. Social media is another free and easy way to get the message out to a large group of people. Finally, encourage the youth to develop an "elevator pitch" about the project, which they can use in a variety of settings to help garner support for their project.

- **Lobbying:** One approach the group might want to take is to contact politicians. Even though group members can't vote, they can still connect with their politicians, since it is their job to represent all constituents. They could contact local politicians via letters or arrange for an interview with the politician or one of his or her staff. Politicians are very busy people and get many requests from their constituents, so it is important to stress with the youth that they need to grab the politician's attention but also be succinct and direct in their request. This is where that elevator pitch can come in handy. Many of the resources at the end of this chapter have sample letters and suggestions for how to prepare for an interview. Depending on the scope of their project, they also might want to contact politicians from other countries, as well.

- **Petitions:** As part of their project, they might find it useful to draw up a petition if they think there is a large number of other people in the community who agree with their cause. Gathering signatures on a petition proves to political leaders that this is an issue of concern to the community and that something needs to be done to address it. When writing a petition, they should make the language clear and to the point. It should state the group's request but in a polite and respectful way. When gathering signatures, the youth need to be sure to get the signer's address. Several of the resources listed at the end of this chapter include sample petitions.

- **Fund-Raising:** Depending on the project they decide to work on, they might need to raise some money to do it. Many approaches to youth fund-raising abound, including bake sales; car washes; and walkathons, runathons, and jump-rope-athons (or any other "athon" they can dream up). If planning a larger, more complex project, the group might look into applying for a grant from a foundation or a local business.

IMPLEMENT THEIR PLAN OF ACTION

Once the planning is done, the group can put their plan into action. They should check in regularly with one another to make sure that all of the steps are getting done and to see whether or not they need to revise or add other steps. Implementing the plan can be hard work, so they should be sure to mix in some fun and make sure to take care of themselves. Be sure to take photos and/or videotape their project. It is also a good idea to keep a journal or take notes as they are implementing the project. This will help with their evaluation of it.

REFLECT ON THE PROJECT

After the project has been completed, the group should come together to reflect on how it went. They can take their action plan and compare it to what really happened. Did they meet their goals? Did things go as they planned? What were some lessons they learned? What would they do differently if they could do it again? This debriefing should be done soon after the project is finished, while things are still fresh in their minds. It is also important to record what is shared during the evaluation so that they can refer to it when undertaking another project. The group might also want to invite outside experts or observers to comment on how the project went.

If the group received outside funding or had outside collaborators, now is the time that they should send thank-you notes to them for their support. For funders, it is likely they will need to write up a report about the project, which they can develop from their evaluation session. They also might consider submitting their project for an award. There are several organizations that offer awards for youth involved in environmental projects, including the following:

Brower Youth Awards from Earth Island Institute: http://brower youthawards.org/article.php?list=type&type=54

Eco-Hero Awards from Action for Nature: www.actionfornature.org/ecohero_awards.aspx

The Gloria Barron Prize for Young Heroes: www.barronprize.org

President's Environmental Youth Award from the EPA: www.epa.gov/ education/peya/index.html

These prizes not only will increase recognition for the group's project; the group might also win money that they could use toward a future project. Once they have finished one project, they will likely have a greater sense of self-efficacy and soon be on their way to dreaming up the next one.

RESOURCES FOR STARTING AN ENVIRONMENTAL ACTION CLUB

Collard, Sneed B. *Acting for Nature: What Young People around the World Have Done to Protect the Environment.* Berkeley, CA: Heyday Books, 2000.

Halpin, Mikki. *It's Your World—If You Don't Like It, Change It: Activism for Teenagers.* New York: Simon Pulse, 2004.

Hoose, Philip M. *It's Our World, Too! Young People Who Are Making a Difference: How They Do It—How You Can, Too!* New York: Farrar, Straus, and Giroux, 2002.

Kielburger, Marc, and Craig Kielburger. *Take Action! A Guide to Active Citizenship.* Hoboken, NJ: John Wiley & Sons, 2002.

Lewis, Barbara A. *The Teen Guide to Global Action: How to Connect with Others (Near & Far) to Create Social Change.* Minneapolis, MN: Free Spirit Publishing, 2008.

Lublin, Nancy, Vanessa Martir, and Julia Steers. *Do Something! A Handbook for Young Activists.* New York: Workman Publishing, 2010.

NOTES

1. Ralph Nader, "Activism Is a Civic Duty," in *Activism*, ed. Jill Hamilton (Farmington Hills, MI: Greenhaven Press, 2010), 17–18.

2. Milton McClaren and Bill Hammond, "Integrating Education and Action in Environmental Education," in *Environmental Education and Advocacy: Changing Perspectives of Ecology and Education*, ed. Michael J. Mappin and Edward A. Johnson (Cambridge: Cambridge University Press, 2005), 278.

APPENDIX

Eco-House Category Sheets

Eco-House Category: Energy Efficiency

A home without the essential appliances is a lifestyle that very few people embrace. There is nothing wrong with having air-conditioning or a large-screen television set. The problem occurs when people buy inefficient models and use polluting, nonrenewable resources to power them. Appliances account for 36 percent of energy consumption in a typical American household. The good news is that appliance manufacturers are actively working to lower the energy requirements of their products, the Energy Star appliances. Smart shoppers should look for the Energy Star logo to ensure energy savings and reduce monthly utility bills.

	Pros	Cons	Did you know?	Cost
Photovoltaic cells (solar panels)	• Saves money after initial investment is recovered; energy from the sun is practically free • The recovery or payback period for the investment can be very short, depending on how much electricity the household uses • Financial incentives are available from the government via tax breaks • Solar energy is clean, renewable, and sustainable • Does not require any fuel • Systems are maintenance free and last for decades	• Installation has high starting cost • Solar panels require quite a large area for installation to achieve a good level of efficiency; some aren't pleasant to look at • They work only when the sun is shining; at night you have to rely on stored energy or have an alternative system • The efficiency of the system depends on the sun's location, the presence of clouds, and air pollution	• Germany is a world leader in solar power despite the fact that on average clouds dominate Germany's sky for 67% of daylight hours	$800–$3,000 per panel or kit, or $37,500–$45,000 to install a larger residential system

continued ››

Eco-House Category: Energy Efficiency *(continued)*

	Pros	Cons	Did you know?	Cost
Energy Star washer and dryer	• Uses 35% less water and 20% less electricity than non-energy-efficient models • Uses less soap • Cuts utility bills by an average of $70 per year • Saves 7,000 gallons of water per year	• More expensive	• Over 11 years, you save enough water to fill up three backyard swimming pools or to provide a lifetime of drinking water for 6 people	~$400–$800 for a washer or dryer
Regular washer and dryer	• Cheaper than energy-efficient models	• Can cost $550 or more to operate over its lifetime compared to an Energy Star washer and dryer	• The average household does almost 400 loads of laundry each year, consuming about 13,500 gallons of water	~$200–$300 for a washer or dryer
Clothesline	• Solar powered • No operating costs • Clothes last longer, smell better, and do not require artificial fragrance sheets	• Weather dependent • Requires outdoor space	• Putting up a clothesline is easy; it can be a great weekend project, and within a week or so you will start saving money and enjoy fresh-smelling laundry	~$20

continued ››

Eco-House Category: Energy Efficiency *(continued)*

	Pros	Cons	Did you know?	Cost
Air Conditioner	• Look for a Energy Star central AC to reduce operating costs by more than 30% • Energy Star window air conditioners use 15% less energy than standard units; more efficient for cooling only a couple rooms	• Central air requires professional installation • Expensive • Consumes a lot of energy • Takes up physical space	• Energy consumption for home air-conditioning accounts for almost 5% of all electricity produced in the United States	~$300–$500
Ceiling fan	• A very effective way of cooling the entire house without central AC (unless you live in a very humid climate) • Easy installation • Uses less energy than an air conditioner	• Can harbor dirt and dust	• Look for Energy Star products, which use 50% less energy than conventional ceiling fans	$60–$200
Compact fluorescent light bulbs	• Last 10 times longer than regular bulbs • Wide color range • Produce less heat (up to 80% cooler than incandescent) • High efficacy (30–110 lumens per watt) • Long life (7,000–24,000 hours) • Low operation and maintenance costs	• More expensive than regular bulbs • Needs special ballast for dimming control • Fewer (but increasing) fixture choices • Consult local waste authority for disposal	• A 15-watt CFL can produce the same amount of light as a 60-watt incandescent bulb	$5–$7 for a 2-pack of 40-watt bulbs
Incandescent bulbs	• Cheaper than CFLs • Easily dimmed	• Produce lots of heat (90% heat, 10% light) • Short life (750–2,500 hours) • High operation and maintenance costs • Disposal: conventional refuse collection	• We owe our thanks to Thomas Edison, who developed this alternative to the kerosene lamp. But with technological advances, it's time to say good-bye to our old but wasteful friend incandescent light	$2.50–$4 per 2-pack of 40-watt bulbs

Eco-House Category: Insulation

Insulation helps save energy and money used to heat or cool a home. Unlike traditional fiberglass (melted glass spun into threads) or mineral wool (melted volcanic rocks or steel spun into threads), none of the below releases particulate chemicals that affect your health.

	Pros	Cons	Did you know?	Cost
Denim (jeans)	• Recycled, reducing landfill waste • Made of cotton, an all-natural, biode-gradable, renewable resource • Takes little energy to manufacture • Good for blocking sound	• Cotton farming requires large volumes of water and pesticides • Absorbs moisture	• Often denim insulation comes from post-industrial recycled denim: the fabric originates from factory scraps, not people's old jeans	~$64.50 per 106 sq. ft., or $1,526 per average home[a]
Cellulose (newspaper)	• Requires up to 30 times less energy to make than fiberglass and mineral wool • At least 75% post-consumer recycled content in the form of newspapers	• Absorbs moisture, which can lead to mold growth • May consume paper pulp usable for other applications • Requires professional installation	• Some people even use old telephone directories!	$1,000–$2,000 per average home

continued ››

Eco-House Category: Insulation *(continued)*

	Pros	Cons	Did you know?	Cost
Sheep's wool	• Biodegradable and recyclable • Uses very little energy to produce into insulation pads, and you can install yourself • Sound absorbent; flame and water resistant • Superb insulation qualities • Able to absorb high humidity, which protects building timbers	• Can attract pests, although is naturally pest repellant • Expensive! • If shipped from afar, the environmental cost of the product increases • Sheep belch methane, which contributes to global warming	• Popular insulation method in New Zealand, where the population of sheep outnumbers that of people!	$2.40 per sq. ft., or $6,019 per average home
Foam (plastic)	• Quick to install • May cut annual energy costs by 35% because it seals surfaces • Good resistance to moisture, rot, compression	• Some contain ozone-depleting chemicals • Some are not recyclable • Takes lots of energy to make: impacts due to extracting, refining, and transporting oil • Releases toxic gas if burned	• So durable that it may last the life of a home	$1.25–$2.25 per sq. ft., or $3,100–$5,600 per average home
Straw bale	• Durable, inexpensive, and resists fire and pests • Avoids damage from air pollution caused when farmers burn straw in the field to clear it for replanting crops • Renewable resource; waste product that is in plentiful supply • Extremely energy efficient and has superior insulating qualities	• During the building process, straw must be kept dry or it will start to rot, causing both structural problems and strong odors	• Straw-bale construction has been around in the United States since the turn of the century. It features bundles of straw from wheat, oats, barley, rye, and/or rice in walls covered by stucco	$2–$4 per bale, or $1,350 per average home (500 bales)

[a] The average home is 2,508 square feet, per the 2008 Western United States Census.

Eco-House Category: Interior Walls

Often people take the walls around them for granted. They don't think about how different paints or materials can have varying environmental impacts.

	Pros	Cons	Did you know?	Cost
Drywall	• Cheap! Gypsum covered by paper on both sides • Can contain up to 75% recycled content (at least 10% post-consumer)	• The mining of raw gypsum creates habitat disruption; need to transport • If not recycled, becomes solid waste in landfill or waterways[a]	• There is a synthetic gypsum, which is a waste product generated by utility companies, so it is reused	Drywall materials (e.g., drywall sheet, screws or nails, joint compound, tape) average $0.25–$0.65 per sq. ft.; ~4,000 sq. ft. of drywall on all the walls and ceilings of a small home
Paint	• Eco-friendly paints include natural paints, which reduce waste and pollution because they don't include petroleum-based solvents; don't cause allergies; and don't smell (water-based), or they smell like citrus or essential oils (oil based)	• Volatile organic compounds (VOCs), which are found in paints, evaporate at room temperature and react in sunlight to form ozone, a key part of smog • VOCs cause respiratory, skin, and eye irritation; headaches; nausea; and muscle weakness	• EPA, state, and local rules limit amount of VOCs based on smog regulations, not indoor air quality • EPA study found that indoor concentrations of several common VOCs can be 2–5 times higher indoors than outdoors[b]	$38–$63 per gallon (e.g., Mythic, Benjamin Moore)
Wood paneling	• Has one of the lowest energy debts, as very little waste is produced in the manufacturing process • Biodegradable • Highly durable	• Old-growth forests can't grow back quickly; destroys special habitats • Requires maintenance of paints and sealants to ensure lasts for a long period of time	• Look for certifications from third parties that show forest where it comes from is managed properly	$30–$300 per panel

continued ››

Eco-House Category: Interior Walls (continued)

	Pros	Cons	Did you know?	Cost
Vinyl wallpaper	• Durable; water resistant, so prevents mold in bathrooms and kitchens • Good insulator • Cheap and easy to use • Excess is recyclable— can be repeatedly ground up, melted, and re-formed	• Producing or burning vinyl releases dioxin, a toxic fume that causes cancer and other health problems • People, wildlife, or rivers near factories are affected • Can't easily recycle post-consumer products	• Also known as polyvinyl chloride, or PVC	$25–$50 per roll; papering a typical 16" × 20" room requires 16–20 rolls, at a total cost of $400–$1,000

[a] Drywall waste can end up in waterways when it is placed in overflowing garbage cans or on the street outside of a garbage can and wind or rain carries it away. This waste can then go into storm drains, which often empty into nearby natural bodies of water.

[b] Lance A. Wallace, *The Total Exposure Methodology (TEAM) Study: Summary and Analysis,* vol. 1 (Washington, DC: Environmental Protection Agency, 1987).

Eco-House Category: Flooring

Often people take the walls around them for granted. They don't think about how different paints or materials can have varying environmental impacts.

	Pros	Cons	Did you know?	Cost
Bamboo	• Sustainably harvested bamboo is a fast-growing, self-replenishing resource • Very hard, durable flooring material • Harder than hardwoods and lasts 30–50 years • Can harvest every 3–5 years	• Bamboo strips are laminated, emitting small amounts of formaldehyde over time • Imported from Southeast Asia (must transport) • Overuse may destroy natural bamboo forests, which provide erosion control in Asia	• Bamboo is not a tree but a grass! • Some species grow up to 3 feet per day (up to 60 feet in 3 months)	$4–$8 per sq. ft., or $10,032–$20,064 per average home
Carpet (synthetic vs natural)	• Comes in natural fibers or recycled synthetic ones • Warm, comfortable, soft • Good sound-absorbing properties	• Synthetic fibers are made from petroleum, a nonrenewable resource • Difficult to clean • Can harbor dirt, dust, and mold	• About 5 billion pounds of carpet end up in US landfills each year	$4+ per sq. ft., or $10,032 per average home
Linoleum	• All-natural: made of wood flour, cork dust, limestone, natural oils and pigments • 30–40 years life span • Easy to clean • Good foot support	• Some people are sensitive to the linseed oil fumes it emits over time • Vulnerable to mold, so can't use in bathrooms • Made in Europe, so must transport	• Invented in 1863, and still uses the same ingredients!	$4 per sq. ft., or $10,032 per average home

continued ››

Eco-House Category: Flooring *(continued)*

	Pros	Cons	Did you know?	Cost
Finished hardwood	• Renewable resource if from a sustainably managed forest • Low embodied energy, particularly if harvested and produced locally[a] • Easy to clean	• Can be harvested only every 40–60 years • Conventional forestry causes overharvesting and habitat destruction • Naturally has formaldehyde • Must be sealed with chemicals	• Old-growth trees can live thousands of years, serve as homes for people and wildlife, make O_2, and absorb CO_2 • Be sure to use certified, salvaged, or recovered hardwood	$3–$6 per sq. ft., or $7,524–$15,048 per average home

[a] Embodied energy is the overall energy required to produce something, including energy required to extract and transport the raw materials and produce and transport the final product. It can also include the energy required for maintaining the product for as long as it is used.

Eco-House Category: Windows

Windows are passive solar collectors. If placed strategically, they can help to save energy and money used to heat or cool a home. Even though infrared radiation doesn't pass easily through windows, they do lose heat. In fact, windows can lose several times as much heat as the same area of the wall. Don't you feel colder when you stand near a window?

	Pros	Cons	Did you know?	Cost
Single-pane glass	• Affordable price • Easy to install	• Have one single piece of glass or plastic • No protection for heat transfer • Higher heating and cooling costs	• Over the past 30 years many advances in window design have happened.	~$200–$300 per window
Double- or triple-pane glass	• Layers of glass increase insulation • Provide a more comfortable environment • Lower heating and cooling costs	• More expensive • Installation requires knowledge	• Have 2 or more layers of glazing separated by layers of air or inert gases (e.g., argon, krypton)	~$600–$800 per window
Low e-glass	• Passive solar design allows sun's rays to enter but doesn't let them pass back out • Prevents heat loss in winter months and provides a more comfortable environment • Lower heating and cooling costs	• More expensive • Installation requires knowledge	• Has a thin metal coating that reflects heat • Gives a metallic look to the window	~$450 extra per window compared to standard glass, or $30–$35 per sq. ft. (before frame and installation costs)

continued ››

Eco-House Category: **Windows** *(continued)*

	Pros	Cons	Did you know?	Cost
Plastic or wooden blinds	• Inexpensive • Wide slat blinds reflect direct sunlight to walls and ceiling, providing soft natural light without bright glare • Adjustable blinds let sunlight in when and where you want it • Slows heat loss through windows, keeping the house warmer • Keeps house cooler in the summer	• Can harbor dirt, dust, and mold • Not biodegradable (plastic) • Hard to clean • Don't use natural dyes	• You can find affordable blinds made of bamboo • Bamboo is sustainably harvested and it is a fast-growing, self-replenishing resource	$15–$50 per window blind
Organic cotton curtains	• Uses sustainable manufacturing practices • Recyclable and/or natural fiber • No toxic dyes or treatments • Thin curtains let some direct light into the room but still reduce heat gain, keeping house cooler in summer • Slows heat loss through windows, keeping the house warmer in winter	• Expensive • Can harbor dirt and dust	• Cotton cultivation is crucial for the economy but also presents a major environmental problem, as cotton requires more pesticides and insecticides than any other crop. These toxins can be a threat to people and wildlife	$50–$400 per curtain panel
House orientation	• For home heating, aim windows directly south • Have the longer side of the building facing south • Put fewer windows on the north side, so a house doesn't lose a lot of heat • On the south, the winter sun should be able to enter windows; use a coating that transmits the most sunlight • On the west and east, more summer sun enters windows. Use a coating that transmits less sunlight	• A lot of homes use fossil fuels to stay warm in the winter and use air conditioners in the summer • Most people give no thought to ensure that a house is oriented to capture as much sun as possible in the winter and to provide appropriate shade in the summer	• In the Northern Hemisphere the sun is in the southern sky • Orientation strategies are different in the country and city. When designing a home in the city, take into account the sun's path and the possibility of shading effects by future buildings	

Eco-House Category: Water

More than 70 percent of Earth's surface is covered in water, but of that water, less than 1 percent is easily available for human use. Water is a central part of our homes, and we take for granted that it will flow freely when we turn on the faucet.

	Pros	Cons	Did you know?	Cost
Rain barrel	• Captures rainwater; catchment water can be used to water plants and lawns	• Requires regular maintenance • Some think they detract from yard's attractiveness	• For every inch of rain that falls on a 1,000 sq. ft. catchment area, you can collect ~600 gallons of rainwater.	$50–$300; cheaper if you make it yourself
Shower heads (low flow vs regular)	• Low-flow showerheads save 500–800 gallons of water per month • Regular shower heads tend to use ~25 gallons of water per shower	• Costs money to change and install	• Showering is a main source of water use in US homes, accounting for about 1.2 trillion gallons of water used per year	$10–$50 for a low-flow shower head
Toilets (low flush vs regular)	• Can convert regular toilet into a low-flush toilet by putting a bottle or plastic bag with pebbles in the tank • A regular toilet uses about 5–7 gallons of water with each flush	• Cost to purchase and install low-flush toilet • Waste disposal for replacing toilet (might be best to purchase low flush when need to replace rather than replacing one that works)	• Toilet with plastic pebble-filled plastic bottle or bag in tank saves 300 gallons of water per month • High-efficiency toilets (HETs) are fairly new to the US market but have long been used overseas; HETs flush at least 20% less than standard models, and many are dual-flush toilets, with two flush-volume options.	~$350 for a low-flush toilet; converter kits are available for ~$30

continued ››

Eco-House Category: Water *(continued)*

	Pros	Cons	Did you know?	Cost
Drip irrigation system vs sprinkler system	• Uses 50% less water than sprinklers • Delivers water directly to root zone • Waters slowly so little is lost to runoff • Reduces insect and leaf fungal problems (insects and disease like wet foliage)	• Cost and logistics of installing • Requires regular maintenance	• Drip irrigation exceeds 90% efficiency, whereas sprinkler systems are 50%–70% efficient.	• A home sprinkler system costs $1–$1.50 per square foot, so ~$1,000s of dollars. A drip system for a home garden area costs $200–$600
Regular washer vs high-efficiency washer	• Clothes washing machines account for more than 20% of indoor water use; conventional washing machines can use more than 50 gallons of water per cycle and more than 16,000 gallons a year for laundry alone • Efficient washers use approximately 35% less water and 20% less energy	• Cost of purchasing and installing new washing machine • Waste disposal for replacing washing machine (might be best to purchase high-efficiency washer when need to replace rather than replacing one that works)	• Some states offer rebates or credits for purchasing high-efficiency washers	• ~$200–$300 for a regular washer or dryer, and ~$400–$800 for a high-efficiency washer or dryer

Eco-House Category: Landscaping and Roof

The type of landscaping around your house can affect the environment in various ways. Often homes include a variety of landscaping types.

	Pros	Cons	Did you know?
Green lawn	• Fairly easy maintenance • Typical landscaping style; for many is aesthetically pleasing	• Might have to use more fertilizers and herbicides, since it is a monoculture environment (one type of plant) and generally nonnative grasses are used	• Using a power mower to mow the lawn emits more exhaust in a half hour than driving a car 187 miles • Typical suburban homeowner uses 6 times more pesticides and synthetic fertilizers per acre than a conventional farmer
Trees	• Help cool house in summer • Can act as windbreaks • Can provide food • Provide food and habitat for animals	• Can be expensive to purchase and plant new trees • Can cause damage to house if they fall in storms • Need to choose proper tree for site	• Carefully positioned trees can cut total household energy consumption by 20%–25% • Through evaporation alone, 1 tree can produce cooling effects equal to about 10 room-size air conditioners working 20 hours per day
Native plants	• Tend not to need as many inputs (e.g., fertilizers, pesticides, water) since they are adapted to the region's growing conditions (e.g., soil, water availability, climate) • Help restore areas to their natural state in a small way, which can also help restore animal species that might have been lost or diminished in certain areas	• Might be more expensive than other types of plants • Might be difficult to find; not always carried at all nurseries or plant centers	• Many states have native plant societies that can give advice on using native plants in your garden

continued ››

Eco-House Category: Landscaping and Roof *(continued)*

	Pros	Cons	Did you know?
Nonnative plants	• Often readily available in nurseries and garden centers • Aesthetically pleasing	• Might require more fertilizers, herbicides, and water if not adapted to region's growing conditions • Some can be invasive and spread to other areas besides your own property; compete with native plants • Often don't have native predators to keep them in check	• Many invasive plants (e.g., purple loosestrife, kudzu) can greatly disrupt natural habitats and require funds to help eradicate them
Living roof	• Acts more like natural terrain, which is often missing in cities. Reduces runoff, absorbs solar radiation rather than reflecting it, and creates habitat • Built-in air conditioner—plant layer creates evaporative cooling through transpiration • Moderates daily temperature fluctuations in most traditional buildings • Beautiful	• Labor intensive, need strong support structure • Require input from architects and builders before undertaking; might require major home renovations, which could be costly	• Urban areas are often 2–8°F warmer in the summer than surrounding areas, known as the urban heat-island effect • Summer utility loads rise 1.5–2% for each 1°F increase • Study in Toronto showed that by greening 6% of city roof spaces for $45.5 million (CDN), as much stormwater was retained as a $60 million storage tank[a]

[a] Steven Peck, "Toward an Integrated Green Roof Infrastructure Evaluation for Toronto," *Green Roof Infrastructure Monitor 5*, no. 1 (2003): 4–5.

INDEX